GREAT
VICTORIAN
DISCOVERIES

GREAT
VICTORIAN
DISCOVERIES

Astounding Revelations and
Misguided Assumptions

Caroline Rochford

AMBERLEY

For my dog, Bruno, who I trust will become a fluent reader once he's had a go at the canine reading lesson in chapter four.

First published 2015

Amberley Publishing
The Hill, Stroud
Gloucestershire, GL5 4EP

www.amberley-books.com

British Library Cataloguing in Publication Data.
A catalogue record for this book is available from the British Library.

ISBN 978 1 4456 4542 1 (paperback)
ISBN 978 1 4456 4550 6 (ebook)

Typeset in 10pt on 12pt Celeste Pro.
Typesetting and Origination by Amberley Publishing.
Printed in the UK.

CONTENTS

Preface   6

1   Time and Space   7

2   Down to Earth   31

3   Botanical Studies   67

4   The Animal Kingdom   89

5   Victorian Anthropology   126

6   Medical Research   156

7   Food and Drink   191

8   Society's Hidden Dangers   210

9   Make Do and Mend   229

10 Bewildering Phenomena   256

Index   284

PREFACE

The Victorians lived in an age when knowledge could be shared faster than ever before. New railways and steamships had made it easier for intrepid explorers to visit regions of the world hitherto unseen by Western eyes, telephones enabled communication across vast distances and speedier printing presses ensured the delivery of the latest news to almost every household in the land. Those with a thirst for knowledge were able to read about the astounding discoveries of natural historians, who published thrilling accounts of the strange new plants and creatures they had encountered during their forages.

Indeed, modern technology had kick-started an information revolution in every field of science. With the aid of photography, microscopes and other new contraptions, researchers were happening upon daily discoveries that promised to change the way the world worked. Leading scientists claimed that the nation's rising fuel demands could be met by converting ordinary sugar into electricity, they professed a telephone call could be made through one's bare hand and it was found that the Indian subcontinent held the secret to a long and happy life. These and many other remarkable discoveries were described in the pages of forgotten Victorian compendia revealing the wondrous experiments and bizarre theories of the great – and not-so-great – minds of science, engineering and natural history.

Drawn from editions of Cassell's *Family Magazine*, this book examines just some of the incredible findings made across the world between 1875 and 1895, inviting the reader to rifle through the secrets in nature's hidden drawer, as seen through the eyes of a Victorian.

HelloFresh

Say hello to the new way to cook!

A special voucher for **Amazon** customers

£40 OFF

CODE: PFRW23BR

"We're very excited about HelloFresh"
COSMOPOLITAN

"Genius!"
GRAZIA

Each week we deliver a box of recipes and fresh ingredients to your door

1 We create step-by-step recipes

2 We source exact fresh ingredients

3 We deliver everything to your door for free

4 You save time & cook great dinners at home

£20 off your 1st and 2nd box

How to claim your voucher

1. Go to **HelloFresh.co.uk/special40**
2. Choose your box
3. Enter **your code** at checkout

Code PFRW23BR

TIME AND SPACE

The Absolute Unit of Time (1887)

What is time? Learned men of every human age have debated the answer to this complex question. Throughout history mankind has measured the passage of time in some form or other, be it by the shadows of a sundial or the trickling of a water clock. The art of timekeeping became more precise in the seventeenth century when the pendulum clock was invented, the swinging of the weight marking the passage of an exact interval of time.

The Victorians, particularly, were fascinated by the concept of the fourth dimension. Science fiction novels by Monsieur Jules Verne (1828–1905) and Mr Mark Twain (1835–1910) fired the imagination of children and adults alike, and new technological machines meant that science was scrutinised more closely than ever before.

Monsieur Jonas Ferdinand Gabriel Lippmann (1845–1921) was a well-known physicist of his day. He put it to the French Académie des Sciences that a second was an indiscriminate and variable unit of time and proposed to scrap the traditional clock in favour of an electric resistance, which would become the 'absolute unit of time'. This, he declared, was because the resistance of mercury was an interval of time, and one that could be measured with a high degree of accuracy. In correspondence to the academy, Monsieur Lippmann described one of several methods by which the interval could be measured. This involved the use of a condenser and a resistance apparatus, which he deemed preferable to the time-honoured clock.

Lippmann's proposal didn't go very much further, although

in recent times the definition of the second has once again been disputed. From the first millennium AD right up until the 1960s it was mathematically defined as one 86,400th of a solar day, before being reclassified in 1967, according to the Bureau International des Poids et Mesures, as 'the duration of 9,192,631,770 periods of the radiation corresponding to the transition between the two hyperfine levels of the ground state of the caesium 133 atom'.

Decimal Time (1885)

To simplify the measurement of time, it was proposed in the 1880s to introduce decimalisation, whereby each day was subdivided into ten hours, each hour into 100 minutes and every minute into 100 seconds. This wasn't an original notion, having first been implemented in France for a brief period during the 1790s by a mathematician named Monsieur Jean-Charles de Borda (1733–1799).

In 1885 a grand fair known as the International Inventions Exhibition was held in South Kensington. Its patron was Queen Victoria, and Prince Albert was appointed president of the organising committee. The latest inventions and breakthroughs from across the globe were put on display, and visitors were permitted to wander freely around the gardens, listen to concerts and savour the technological delights of the day. One of the exhibits featured a collection of new types of dials for clocks and watches, which indicated both local time and universal time. The former was an indication of the sun's transit over the local meridian, while the latter was based on the rotation of the Earth. The dial marked the hours one to twelve in the ordinary way, but inside the circle of these hours was another dial, which revolved once in twenty-four hours in the same direction as the hour hand. This bore the hours of universal time: one to twenty-four. By this arrangement the hour hand indicated both local and universal time, and the dials could be adjusted for any part of the world.

Despite several attempts over the years to introduce decimal time to the Western world, the idea was finally laid to rest at the turn of the twentieth century.

Twenty-Four O'Clock (1884)

In 1840, following the introduction of timetables by Mr George Bradshaw (1801–1853), 'railway time' was adopted in Britain to standardise the many different local time systems, and in 1884 the Americans, too, were keen to update their method of timekeeping. A plan to number the hours consecutively up to twenty-four o'clock, scrapping the a.m. and p.m. system entirely, attracted considerable attention. The Cleveland, Akron & Columbus Railway began printing new timetables based on this plan, and watches and clocks were designed with twenty-four hours marked consecutively in a double circle inside the ordinary figures.

A decade later Italy became the first European country to adopt the twenty-four-hour system of measuring time, but it took British Rail until 1964 to print timetables for the twenty-four-hour clock. The BBC, one of the largest public sector organisations in the world, still uses the twelve-hour system to time its news bulletins, though its weather forecasts strictly employ the Victorian twenty-four-hour method.

Shifting Latitudes (1892)

William Thomson, 1st Baron Kelvin (1824–1907), more commonly known as Lord Kelvin, was one of the greatest physicists of his age. In 1876 he concluded that changes in the sea level brought about by the weather might displace the direction of the earth's axis in space, or, in other words, sway the world from its own balance. This, he warned, could produce an alteration of latitude to such an extent that the solar day would be shortened or lengthened by the extent of half a second.

Scientists were so concerned that they began to monitor the situation closely, and sixteen years later Lord Kelvin's conclusion was verified. It was observed that in that period alone the latitude of Berlin and other continental cities had altered by about a third of a second. A team of researchers was sent to Honolulu, almost directly opposite Berlin on the earth's surface, in order to find out whether it had shifted by a corresponding amount in the opposite direction. The results were startling: it had.

With the aid of computer technology, modern science has been able to show that the earth's axis does indeed shift, and natural geological occurrences, such as earthquakes, have been held responsible for this. The Sendai earthquake, which struck Japan on 11 March 2011 and measured nearly 9.0 on the Richter scale, was so powerful it caused the earth to move as much as 25 cm on its axis. NASA believes that other planetary changes have occurred as a result of the disaster, such as the length of the solar day, which was shortened by nearly 2 microseconds after the earth's spin was accelerated.

The Earth's Tail (1892)

Astronomy was a burgeoning field of science in Victorian times. Though space travel was still decades away, stargazers had their eyes fixed on the heavens. With new telescopes, spectroscopes and hi-tech observatories, Earth-based astronomers were able to glean a better understanding of the universe.

It was already well known that comets had tails of very low density, which could be seen streaming behind as the celestial bodies hurtled their way through space. A Russian physicist who studied this phenomenon believed he had discovered that the earth, too, possessed a tail of cosmic dust, and his findings have since been confirmed.

Space is said to be thick with 'dust' particles, which come from colliding asteroids, meteors and suchlike; as the earth moves around the sun, it sweeps along these particles, dragging them along in its wake by the pull of its gravity. Thanks to this discovery, twenty-first-century scientists have been searching for signs of similar planetary tails in faraway solar systems, in the hope of identifying new worlds and perhaps even alien life.

Photographing Meteorites (1895)

The late nineteenth century was a fruitful era for inventors, whose fertile minds envisaged an array of revolutionary machines and gadgets. The camera was one such example of Victorian technology, and the photographic plate, being more sensitive to light than the retina of the human eye, was instrumental in helping astronomers of the day to discover new stars, asteroids and nearby planets. By 1895 photography had been employed for pinpointing the radiant points and fiery tracks of 'wandering stones' that streamed through space on their way to who knew where.

It was widely accepted that meteorites, which the Victorians dubbed 'the leavings of creation', were attracted by the gravitational pull of the earth if they came too close, but thankfully few of them ever reached the ground. The majority were burned up by the heat of friction as they plummeted through the atmosphere, appearing to the eye as shooting stars. Yet these interstellar missiles weren't merely spectacles of beauty; they were, in fact, of great importance from an astronomical point of view. Scientists held that they were actually essential building blocks for planets, and also a supply of fresh fuel for the sun. It was thought that the impact of a shower of meteorites was transformable into heat in the same way as a blacksmith's hammer heated the anvil it struck, and thus the sun was kept burning by the meteorites that collided with it.

Being so essential to the upkeep of the universe, stargazers

felt it was important to keep an eye on the comings and goings of these capricious bodies, so the observational apparatus shown in the engraving was employed at the Yale Observatory in the United States. It was the design of two astronomers, Messrs Worcester Reed Warner (1846–1929) and Ambrose Swasey (1846–1937). The contraption consisted of a polar axis, A, about 12 feet long, supported on bearings and driven by clockwork, T, which caused it to move with the heavens, so the stars appeared on the photographic plates of the attached cameras, C, as points of light. Were the cameras stationary, the stars would have been traced as lines of light. The radiant points and luminous trails of meteorites were thus easily distinguishable on the photographs, and their paths measured with respect to the stars. The six cameras were so directed as to cover a large portion of the night sky, and the clockwork was controlled by electricity.

The Mont Blanc Observatory (1893)

The accompanying illustration shows the astronomical and meteorological observatory that was erected on the summit of Mont Blanc under the patronage of the eminent astronomer and mountaineer Monsieur Pierre Jules César Janssen (1824–1907). The celebrated architect Monsieur Gustave Eiffel (1832–1923) agreed to raise the construction providing there were suitable foundations at the top of the mountain. Upon examination, it was found that the summit was formed by a narrow edge of rock 100 metres long, which was perpetually covered with snow and ice many feet thick. As the rock was too difficult to reach, Monsieur Eiffel pulled out of the project, but, keen to press on nonetheless, Monsieur Janssen decided to build the observatory on top of the snow.

To avoid the disturbing effect of the furious storms that often raged on the summit of the mountain, the framework of the two-storey building took the form of a truncated cone. The roof was flat, thus serving as a platform for meteorological observations. The walls, doors and windows were doubled in order to protect the scientists from the cold. The floor was also doubled, and traps permitted the observers to reach the surface of the snow to inspect the screw-jacks that were used to adjust the level of the building in the event of the snow sinking. In case of accident, a cottage was erected 300 metres below the summit, serving as a refuge.

For the first few years all seemed to be going well at the observatory, but without proper foundations, the building soon

began to lean, and in 1909 the damage had become so severe that the astronomers were forced to abandon the observatory before it collapsed entirely.

The Green Moon (1884)

Many will be familiar with the old expression 'Once in a blue moon', though few will have heard of the phenomenon once witnessed in the south of England on the evening of Wednesday 5 December 1883. During a remarkably bright red sunset, the crescent moon appeared a distinctly green colour, comparable to the 'green sun' that was witnessed in Ceylon – present-day Sri Lanka – some months earlier, which first emerged from behind a bright green cloud. The light from the sun was so subdued it was possible to look directly at it without hurting the eyes. This strange phenomenon lasted several days, and as the sun traversed across the sky it turned an ethereal blue, almost comparable to

moonlight, even at midday. As it began its descent, it assumed its green hue once more.

From different parts of the world came accounts of similarly strange atmospheric phenomenon. At the Cape of Good Hope, one sunset was said to be so remarkably brilliant it caused the foliage and flowers to deepen in hue. In Madras, India, the perfectly rayless sun was silvery white, which appeared from behind a bright pea-green cloud. As the sun made its way towards the horizon, it too turned green.

Some supposed these unusual occurrences were connected to Krakatoa, which violently erupted on 27 August 1883. Clouds of fine dust polluted the air in such volumes that the whole earth was afflicted for the next five years.

Mars and Its Martians (1893)

Victorian astronomers were sure that Mars, Earth's second closest neighbour in the solar system, possessed polar snow-caps, a cloudy atmosphere and a surface comprised of a mixture of sea and land, meaning it was a similar planet to our own.

The image of Mars, as it appeared through the nineteenth-century telescope, showing one polar icecap, is represented in the first figure, overleaf; the second illustrates a portion of its land surface as intersected by the water channels, or 'canals', identified by Signor Giovanni Schiaparelli (1835–1910). In the early 1880s this Italian astronomer observed doubled waterways, as if they had been formed by intelligent beings for the coming and going of their Martian vessels. However, top astronomers at the Lick Observatory in California, and others in Peru, began scrutinising the existence of double canals, believing nearly all of them to be single courses. The apparent doubling, they explained, occurred during Mars' springtime, when the watercourses would have been overflowing with the melting snows.

Professor Pickering, of the Peru Observatory, discovered two mountain ranges near the south pole of Mars, and asserted that on 5 August 1893 snow fell on the equatorial ranges, covering two summits, which melted after a couple of days. He also observed eleven lakes, connected by dark lines, which he said were probably rivers, and identified two large dark areas, like seas, though they

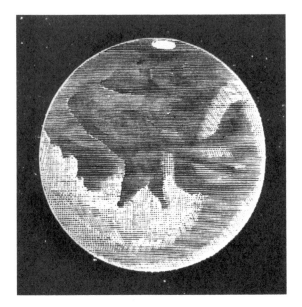

weren't blue. Above the surface were storm clouds, which the professor said were 'yellowish and partially transparent'.

By 1893 the possibility of communicating with the inhabitants of Mars by means of visible signals was hotly debated. It was proposed to use powerful electric lamps to flash a Morse signal to the Martian astronomers, and a French lady even bequeathed a considerable sum of money to see this plan put into action, but sadly the cost of the electricity bill was too great. Another suggestion was to use sunlight flashed from mirrors, though this was dismissed as a ridiculous idea, for a big enough mirror couldn't be sourced.

Towards the end of the year Mars began travelling away from Earth, so unfortunately the Victorians' chance of saluting the dwellers of another planet, which would have been the crowning triumph of nineteenth-century science, diminished into the void of space.

Jupiter and Venus (1893)

Though Mars was receding, its bigger brother Jupiter was approaching, illuminating the earth's evening sky. In former years this gaseous planet was supposed to have only four moons, but in 1892 Professor Edward Emerson Barnard (1857–1923), also of the Lick Observatory, detected a fifth, Amalthea, which he believed to be only about 100 miles in diameter. The satellite revolved around Jupiter in eleven hours and fifty-nine minutes, and was 112,400 miles distant from the centre of the planet.

Professor Pickering also came to the conclusion that Jupiter wasn't self-luminous, as previously believed, but was, nevertheless, very hot. A dense envelope of clouds surrounded the globe, but outside this, the atmosphere of the planet extended to a distance of at least 1,900 miles into space.

The figure below illustrates the appearance of the much smaller planet Venus as drawn by Monsieur Etienne Léopold Trouvelot (1827–1895), a well-known French astronomer. In the sketch the planet is partially illuminated by the sun, and the white areas at the top and bottom are the poles, which were thought to be snowfields and glaciers such as the ones believed to lie on Mars. This, however, was later disproved, owing to the incredibly high temperatures to which the surface of Venus is subjected.

The Rings of Saturn (1895)

It was once thought that the colourful rings of Saturn, which looked spectacular through the most powerful Victorian telescope, were solid masses that were somehow hovering around the centre of the planet like gigantic hula-hoops. This belief held fast until about 1895, when Professor James Clerk Maxwell (1831–1879), the celebrated electrician, proved mathematically that they were in fact composed of myriads of small bodies, or minute satellites, in rapid rotation round their primary.

To test this theory, Professor James Edward Keeler (1857–1900), the director of the Alleghany Observatory of the United States, applied a spectroscopic examination, which showed that the small satellites comprising the rings were moving at different velocities. His method of observation was based on the Doppler effect, according to which scientists could tell whether a heavenly body was moving towards or away from Earth by examining the light coming from it, as observed through the spectroscope. If the object was moving with sufficient rapidity, the light would fracture into the colours of the spectrum, and some estimation of its velocity could be made by measuring the displacement of light.

Gravity and the Hidden Energy of Ether (1892 and 1895)

In the late nineteenth century a band of scientists resolved to further their understanding of gravity, the inexplicable force that held the solar system and all the visible parts of the universe together. In earlier years it was thought that the attraction of gravitation was an 'action at a distance', that is to say, the force acted through an empty space between the two bodies that were held together, without any intervening mechanism. However, Sir Isaac Newton (1642–1727), who discovered the law of gravitation, dismissed this theory, believing there must have been some sort of mechanism involved, though he couldn't explain what it was.

Long before Professor Albert Einstein (1879–1955) came up with his theory of relativity, scientists of a new school of thought were considering the existence of 'luminiferous ether', which was said to pervade the material universe. In the late Victorian era it was 'discovered' that this invisible medium was the vehicle of light, responsible for conveying waves of light from one luminous body to another. After much study, scientists began to believe that luminiferous ether was an illimitable and inexhaustible reservoir of energy, which was ordinarily concealed from human senses. This postulation gave rise to the conviction that gravity must similarly be conveyed by a fine molecular substance, such as an invisible ether, or something else.

It was the Swiss-born scientist Herr Georges-Louis Le Sage (1724–1803) who was first to propose a mechanical explanation of gravity. He theorised that streams of minute atoms, or corpuscles, travelled from beyond the limits of the universe, and in passing through, it pressed the molecules of gross matter together. Two bodies, by sheltering each other from the streams of corpuscles, were inevitably forced towards one another, just as somebody barging their way through a crowded tramcar would push the other passengers closer together.

In the nineteenth century Lord Kelvin modified Herr Le Sage's hypothesis, and his contemporaries could find little fault with it, except that it necessitated a constant supply of corpuscles that came from nobody knew where, and went who knew whither.

By the 1890s a new theory materialised, one that gained credibility as it dispensed with the need for a perpetual influx of particles from the infinite. Its champion, Dr Samuel Tolver Preston (1844–1917), replaced Le Sage's stream of corpuscles with a 'gravity-gas', or, in other words, a cloud of inconceivably minute particles, constantly colliding with each other. This gas, the doctor supposed, infiltrated gross and ordinary matter in every direction, and as its atoms were so small they could travel around the space in between the molecules, pushing them together, like gravity.

If correct, this theory meant that gravity didn't necessarily exist throughout the entire universe, as was popularly supposed, but only through certain spaces where gravity atoms were prevalent. Before the conception of the Big Bang theory, which holds that the universe is continually expanding, scientists pictured a mutual attraction of all the different parts of the universe, but Dr Preston's philosophy seemed to disprove this notion. It followed that the solar system, for example, could have coincidentally fallen within a cloud of gravity-gas, making its position in the universe fixed, or certainly limited. Perhaps even the stars, which were thought to be slowly gravitating towards the pull of the solar system, weren't doing so after all. In other words, Dr Preston had ensured the stability of the universe.

Electromagnetic Photography (1890 and 1892)

In around 1890 Dr Heinrich Hertz (1857–1894), the German physicist, made a number of remarkable experiments tending to support the late Professor Maxwell's theory that light, electricity and magnetism were all caused by a wave-like disturbance through the luminiferous ether, and were therefore formed of the same substance. This challenged an earlier notion proposed in 1704 by Sir Isaac Newton, who believed that light consisted of tiny particles that were released into the atmosphere from luminous bodies, such as the sun. However, Dr Hertz was able to decisively prove that electromagnetic waves existed. In 1886 he developed equipment that could pick up radio waves, and demonstrated that these waves travelled at exactly the same speed of light.

A little later a scientist named Herr von Dobrzynski discovered further confirmation of Maxwell's electromagnetic theory of light. Basing his own research upon Dr Hertz's investigations, Herr von Dobrzynski found that waves of electromagnetism, set up by the discharge of induction coils, were capable of affecting a sensitive plate and producing a photographic action just like waves of light. Dry plates of silver bromide and gelatine, exposed to these electromagnetic disturbances for three hours, were developed and found to be marked with bright and dark bands.

The French physicist Monsieur Marie Alfred Cornu (1841–1902) was also engaged in the study of spectroscopy during the nineteenth century, and found by the most careful experiments that the velocity of light was 300,300 km per second. One of his contemporaries, Monsieur Pellat, by equally careful observations, discovered the ratio of electromagnetic waves to be represented by a velocity of 300,900 km a second. Though these calculations were later proved slightly inaccurate – modern science having since confirmed the speed of light to be exactly 299,792.458

km a second – these measurements afforded further proof that Professor Maxwell was correct in his theory that light and electromagnetic waves were of the same nature.

The experiments of Dr Hertz showed that electric waves and the waves of light differed only in dimensions. The former were much greater than the latter; but he believed if science could one day produce them of the same size, it would be possible to make light. Dobrzynski, too, theorised that if electromagnetic waves could be made small enough, they would, in all probability, become light itself.

It was many more years before scientists were able to prove beyond any doubt that the visible rays of light formed just one part of the vast electromagnetic spectrum, from gamma radiation all the way across to radio waves, arranged in the increasing order of wavelength. The frequencies of the waves are now measured in Hertz (Hz), in honour of the German physicist who first discovered them.

The Velocity of Light (1881)

Over the ages the velocity of light has been measured by many different methods, and although the experiment proved difficult to formulate, Victorian scientists came close to the mark with their estimations. Monsieur Cornu recorded it at 186,700 miles per second, just slightly faster than the modern calculation of precisely 186,282 miles, and Mr Albert Abraham Michelson (1852–1931), an American physicist, obtained a closer result of 186,500 miles. A subsequent determination by Professor George Forbes FRS (1849–1936) and Dr James Young (1811–1883), both of Scotland, placed it at 187,200 miles per second, but this higher number was believed to be due to the quality of the light employed in their experiments. Cornu used an oil lamp, and Michelson sunlight, whereas the Scotch observers used the electric light. It was believed the latter contained a greater proportion of blue rays than the yellower beams of the sun and oil, and thus Professor Forbes concluded that blue light must travel at least 1 per cent faster than red light. For instance, in a given period of time a blue ray would travel 101 miles for every 100 covered by a red ray.

His analysis was found to be erroneous, as modern-day physics has proved that all the colours of the spectrum travel through a vacuum at exactly the same velocity. However, when travelling through a medium, such as air, water or glass, the varying wavelengths of light travel and refract at different speeds. Often the red waves will travel faster than the blue.

Light as a Motive Power (1875)

It seemed to the Victorians as if the world was growing more wonderful by the day, as breath-taking scientific discoveries continued to gain prominence. In 1875 attention was drawn to one particular discovery that promised to rank among the most remarkable of the era. For some years Sir William Crookes FRS (1832–1919), the physicist who discovered the metallic element thallium, had been engaged in investigating the action of light and heat upon bodies suspended in a vacuum. It had hitherto been accepted that light, apart from providing heat, exercised no mechanical action upon an object whatsoever; but this, Crookes discovered, wasn't the case. At a meeting of the Royal Society, he suspended a bar of pith upon a silk fibre, contained within a bulb at the bottom of a tube from which the air had been completely removed. A lighted candle was then placed near the outside of the tube, and the pith immediately began to spin.

Sceptical attendees at the meeting pointed out that the candle was radiating heat as well as light, and it was simply the heat that was producing the motion. In answer to this it was shown that when the heat was sifted away from the light by a screen of alum, the effect produced was the same: it was light, and light alone, that triggered the movement.

This astounding property of light enabled Crookes to construct an instrument he termed a 'radiometer', or light mill, by which the intensity of rays could be measured as accurately as heat could be measured by a thermometer. His device consisted of four pith discs, fixed at their extremities by two crossed arms of straws, balanced upon a pivot at the point where the straws crossed each other, so they could spin round with little resistance. The pith discs were coloured white on one side and black on the other, and the whole arrangement was enclosed within a vacuum inside a glass bulb.

To use the mill, it was exposed to the daylight. The stronger the light, the more merrily the discs would spin on their pivot. So perfectly could the mechanical force of light be measured that Crookes was able to record the rates at which different types of light at different distances would drive the radiometer.

It appeared to the public, who had never before heard of a phenomenon like this, that the accomplished physicist was paving the way for an undreamt-of expansion of human knowledge. It seemed undeniable that when light was poured upon bodies free from atmospheric friction, it provided a motive force, just as coal and electricity were powering the great machines of the age. This was surely a discovery that scientists and engineers of the future could exploit to their advantage.

It was later established that this was all just wishful thinking. When exposed to light, the black sides of Crookes' discs were warmed much faster than the white sides. It was this action of heat 'pushing' against the black that made the radiometer spin, and had nothing to do with the exposure to light.

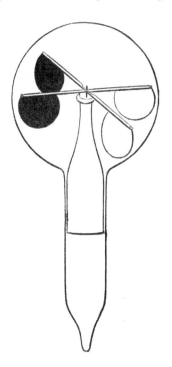

The Sunshine Fire Extinguisher (1875)

There was much discussion about the power of light during the 1870s, and one theory being bandied around suggested that the power of sunshine impeded combustion. This was based upon an old myth that sunlight, when directed onto a blaze, lessened the intensity of the flames and sometimes even extinguished them. The scientific explanation for this was that the sun's heat expanded the air, which resulted in a diminished supply of oxygen to feed the fire. Business-minded Victorians soon began to wonder whether it was possible to 'bottle' sunlight, for surely this would herald the discovery of the greatest fire extinguisher known to man.

In 1875, however, modern science condemned the theory once and for all. One experimenter explained that if a few pieces of charcoal were ignited and placed in a sunny room, the fire appeared to die away in the light. If, however, the shutters over the window were closed, and the room plunged into darkness, the coals would appear to burn brightly. There was no phenomenon at all, merely the illusion of one, which wasn't due to the sun's heat, but to the fact that its light, being stronger than that of the coals, simply subdued it.

The Temperature of the Solar Surface (1885)

Captain John Ericsson (1803–1889) was a Swedish mechanical engineer, best known for inventing *Novelty* in 1829, a steam locomotive believed to be history's first tank engine. He continued developing innovative machines throughout his career, and by 1885 Captain Ericsson had erected a solar pyrometer at New York, which he claimed could measure the temperature of the solar surface.

His device is shown in the diagrams, overleaf, and consisted of a polygonal reflector composed of a series of inclined mirrors, A, and provided with a central conical heater, B, acted upon by the reflected radiation of the sun in such a way that each point of its surface received an equal amount of heat in a given time.

The second image represents a transverse section of the instrument as it appeared when facing the sun, the direct and reflected rays being indicated by dotted lines. The heater was

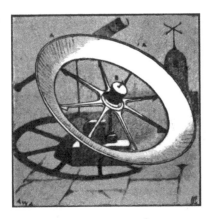

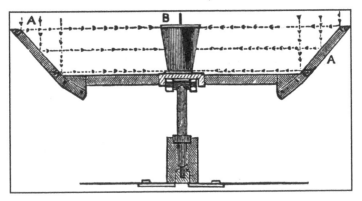

composed of rolled plate iron a fraction of an inch thick, with a head and bottom of non-conducting material. The whole apparatus was easy to carry and could be put in place or removed again in just a few minutes.

With this device, which recorded the amount of heat it received, the captain calculated that the temperature of the sun's surface couldn't be less than 3,060,727º F. This discovery stunned his contemporaries, for the figure was much higher than the former estimates of the likes of Herr Ernst Werner von Siemens (1816–1892), a German inventor who had placed the figure between 5,432º F and 18,032º F.

Scientists today have calculated the temperature of the solar surface to be about 9,941° F, or 5,505° C, suggesting that Captain Ericsson's solar pyrometer may have been slightly inaccurate!

How the Sun Grew Hot (1893)

Like so many others, Lord Kelvin began pondering the question of the origin of solar heat, and adopted the theory of the distinguished mathematician Pierre-Simon, Marquis de La Place (1749–1827), namely, that the sun was formed from a gaseous nebula.

Kelvin held two theories regarding the birth of the sun. His first was that an enormous number of small bodies, such as asteroids and meteorites, had begun bumping into one another and over time grew like a snowball. Alternatively, he hypothesised that the sun started its life as a smaller number of large bodies, such as planets and their satellites, which fell together by gravitation. Either way, if hundreds, thousands or even millions of these fell together in one mass, the heat generated by the shock of the collisions would combine everything together and form a burning nebula.

In the twenty-first century it is commonly accepted that the sun was moulded over millions of years by a collapsing cloud of gas, which became so dense that the atoms at the core started to fuse together, generating heat in the form of thermonuclear energy.

Thunderstorms and Sunspots (1893)

In 1874 a German meteorologist, Professor Johann Friedrich Wilhelm Von Bezold (1837–1907), began a series of weather experiments lasting two decades, and he eventually concluded that when the weather was hot and the sun's surface spotless, abounding thunderstorms would disturb the earth's atmosphere for several years. Fellow scientists arrived at similar conclusions, and Mr Alexander Baird MacDowall MA (1843–1939), a Scottish meteorologist, found a comparable correspondence in thunderstorms at Berlin and Geneva. He kept a record of his extensive observations by means of curved lines drawn from gathered statistics.

Mr MacDowall's graphs are reproduced in the accompanying figure and were derived from results obtained at both places since 1850 and 1852 respectively. The numbers of days of thunder were grouped in averages, and each yearly point of the

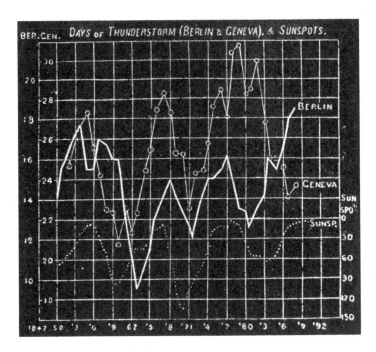

curve represents an average of five years. The scale figures are shown in vertical columns on the left. The dotted curve below is that of the minimum numbers of sunspots, with figures to the right, and it may be noticed that the heights of the thunderstorm curves coincide fairly well with the other curves, which represent the scarcity of sunspots.

The Colour of the Sun Is Really Blue (1885)

Professor Samuel Pierpont Langley (1834–1906) was an American physicist and astronomer who conducted his research at the summit of Mount Whitney in Southern California, where the atmosphere was dry and clear. He 'discovered' that as the solar light passed through the earth's atmosphere, it was robbed of a large proportion of blue rays, which scattered across the sky. In fact, Professor Langley calculated that the sun contained a greater proportion of blue rays than any other colour in the spectrum, meaning that the true colour of the sun, or in other words, as it would be seen outside of the earth's atmosphere, must have been bluish.

Despite the professor's assertions, modern scientists universally agree that the true colour of the sun is actually white. This is because the different coloured photons emanate from the sun at exactly the same time, producing a pure white light. As the rays pass through the earth's atmosphere, the sunlight is distorted into a spectrum, like a beam of light passing through a prism. Due to the angle of the sun, the shorter wavelengths of light, that is to say, blue and violet, are blocked from reaching the earth and are scattered away. The lack of these colours from the spectrum causes the sun to appear a warm orange – a mixture of the remaining colours – and the displaced wavelengths of light are what make the sky look blue.

The Death of the Solar System (1887 and 1893)

By 1887 Lord Kelvin had calculated that the sun was capable of supplying heat to the earth sufficient to sustain life for a total of 20 million to 40 million years, and it was already about half way through its life. The question on concerned Victorians' lips was: what would happen after that?

Nineteenth-century science told that the earth and other planets would eventually grow old and exhausted and, in short, would die. In the case of the solar system, astronomers presumed that the mysterious centrifugal force that kept the planets in their orbits round the sun would gradually become weaker owing to ethereal friction. This weakened force would ultimately fail to prevent everything being drawn into the sun, which by then would have become aged as well.

From the decrepit system a new one would eventually arise, and this process of birth and death could go on until the end of time, unless Lord Kelvin's theory of the 'dissipation of energy' proved correct. This, he explained, was the process by which energy was lost in the act of being used up, never to be recovered. He believed there was a universal tendency in nature for energy to run down like a clock, and thus time itself was numbered. This being the case, he described how the solar system would one day come to an end and the universe to a standstill, until an act of creative power decides to give it a fresh start.

Nowadays it is universally agreed that the sun and its solar system are 4.54 billion years old, and it will take roughly the same amount of time before the sun runs out of hydrogen and becomes a red giant, swallowing up the earth and the other inner planets as it expands.

The age of the sun wasn't Lord Kelvin's only flawed theory. In 1896 he claimed x-rays were nothing more than an elaborate hoax, and by 1902 he had declared that no kind of flying machine would ever get off the ground. Thankfully, his stark proclamation did nothing to discourage two American aeronauts, Messrs Orville (1871–1948) and Wilbur (1867–1912) Wright, who famously took to the skies in 1903 and flew straight into the history books.

2

DOWN TO EARTH

The Age of the Earth (1895)

While Victorian astronomers were gazing into the universe, geologists were focussing their attention on the Earth: how it worked and what it was made of. During the nineteenth century a school of scientists called the Uniformitarians were active in this field. For about 100 years these learned men had asserted that Mother Nature had been functioning in the same way for eternity, both on earth and throughout the entire universe, and would continue to do so forevermore.

Lord Kelvin was first to challenge this belief by attempting to calculate the age of the earth, and thus eliminate any suggestion that it had been in perpetual existence. Based on the assumption that the world began life as a molten globe, he calculated the time it would have taken for the surface to cool into a crust, thus creating a fitting environment for the evolution of life. He concluded that the earth couldn't have been less than 10 million years old or more than 400 million years old. These figures were openly derided at the time of their publication, but thirty years later, by 1895, many geologists had come to the conclusion that Kelvin's timeframe was probably sufficient after all.

Dr Clarence River King (1842–1901) was one of America's leading geologists. From existing geological data he calculated that all of the earth's stratified or sedimentary rocks could well have been produced by the eroding action of water over the course of 24 million years; a figure well within Lord Kelvin's allocation.

However, Professor John Perry FRS (1850–1920), mathematical assistant to Kelvin, questioned his master's estimate, certain his lordship had failed to allow enough time for the thermal conductivity of the rocks under the surface of the earth. The enthusiastic mathematician offered his own reckoning that the age of the world was far greater than Kelvin had made it, and raised the estimate to about 3 billion years.

Thus challenged, Kelvin returned to his laboratory and made further experiments, only to discover that, if anything, the lower figure of his former estimate was probably more accurate. These new findings concurred with Dr King's conclusions, and with the age of the sun calculated at somewhere between 10 million and 20 million years, give or take a few million, it was resolved that the earth must also be approximately the same age. This was in accordance with the nebular hypothesis of the Marquis de La Place, who put forth that the sun and planets originated in the same nebula.

Since the invention of radiometric dating in the early twentieth century, which measures the rate of the earth's decay, it was concluded that Lord Kelvin was mistaken. His junior assistant, however, was almost spot-on with his calculation, for the planet is approximately 4.54 billion years old.

Global Warming (1885)

By the mid-nineteenth century the Industrial Revolution had brought about a global consumption of fossil fuels on a scale far greater than in any previous period in the history of mankind. Some believed this had triggered a change in the earth's atmosphere, and in the late Victorian era a team of glaciologists began examining the effect of the sun's heat upon the surface of the earth. They studied the melting of the Great Glacier of Alaska, the front of which was a wall of ice 500 feet thick. Its breadth ranged from between 3 and 10 miles, while its length was recorded at 150 miles. The top was fractured, covered with ice-hills and small mountain chains. It was noted that every quarter of an hour hundreds of tons of ice broke from the glacier's facade and plunged into the sea, causing great waves. It was predicted that the ice was crumbling into the ocean at the rate of a quarter of a mile each year, meaning that if conditions didn't change, the entire glacier would vanish into its watery grave by the year 2485.

Some modern experts say the rate is now rapidly increasing and will only begin to slow once mankind halts its destructive ways and ceases pumping pollutants into the atmosphere.

The Discovery of Argon (1895)

Since as early as 1785 it was suspected that an inactive gas may be present in the air alongside the only two known existents, oxygen and nitrogen, though this third, theoretical element remained unidentified for more than a century. In 1894 the discovery of this new atmospheric gas, by prediction rather than accident, was an occasion so historic it reminded the older generations of the exhilaration they shared with the entire nation when a new planet, Neptune, was discovered in the solar system in 1846.

The noted English physicist, Lord Rayleigh (1842–1919), was led to infer the existence of a hitherto unknown gas in the air by observing that nitrogen extracted from the atmosphere was slightly heavier than nitrogen isolated from other sources by means of chemistry. In fact, an equal quantity of 'chemical' and 'atmospheric' nitrogen weighed 230 and 231 grams respectively, leading Rayleigh to presume that something else must also be present, albeit in tiny proportions.

With dogged perseverance and plenty of mathematical calculations, Lord Rayleigh and his collaborator, Professor William Ramsay (1852–1916), finally identified what it was. They attempted to isolate the element by passing atmospheric air over red-hot copper, which combined with the oxygen to form oxide of copper. They then passed the remaining gas over red-hot magnesium, which absorbed the nitrogen, and left the unidentified gas behind. 5 ½ litres of atmospheric nitrogen yielded 3 ½ cubic centimetres of the new element.

This colourless gas had an atomic weight of about forty. Remarkably, despite the scientists' best efforts, it refused to react with any other chemical or element on Earth, hence it was given the name 'argon', which meant 'inactive'.

It was difficult for people to believe, however, that argon was completely impractical, and it was hoped that one day science would discover a use for it. No doubt the Victorians would have been pleased to know that applications for their inert noble gas are now widespread, ranging from food preservation and incandescent lighting to cancer treatment and dark matter detection.

The Discovery of Helium (1895)

In 1868 astronomers identified a new type of gas in the sun's corona by means of its spectrum, as viewed through the spectroscope. They called the gas helium, and its spectrum was distinguished by a yellow band resembling that of sodium. Despite their best efforts, chemists were unsuccessful in their search for this new element on Earth. That was until 1895, when Professor Ramsay discovered it inside the rare Norwegian mineral, cleveite. When treated with sulphuric acid, the element emitted a gas which was initially believed to be nitrogen, until Professor Ramsay found it was actually a mixture of argon and another gas, which, when examined through the spectroscope, turned out to be helium, the same gas observed around the sun twenty-seven years earlier.

Molecular Music (1881)

In 1881 Sir William Crookes carried out a scientific trial known as 'molecular bombardment'. This involved causing gaseous molecules inside a vacuum to collide with each other, as the rarefied particles travelled back and forth in straight lines; an experiment not dissimilar to the ones currently underway in the Large Hadron Collider at CERN in Switzerland, where scientists are attempting to comprehend the Higgs boson, or so-called 'God' particle.

Crookes theorised that this bombardment of atoms could be rendered audible by means of a delicate microphone, though an American investigator named Mr C. R. Ross believed such a detector was unnecessary. He had been conducting his own molecular bombardment experiments and had found that if a stream of electrified particles in a vacuum tube was repelled from a concave metal mirror, so as to play on a sheet of thin platinum at the other end of the tube, the particles not only hammered the platinum red-hot, like the blows of a smith upon an anvil, but they also emitted a clear musical note. The pitch seemed entirely due to the vibration of the platinum under the impact of the molecules, and the sound resembled the pattering of rain upon a windowpane.

It was suggested that if Mr Ross could produce a musical scale of platinum sheets, each with the ability of emitting a different note, an entire atomic symphony could be composed.

Musical Gases (1881)

The previous year Professor Alexander Graham Bell (1847–1922) invented his remarkable 'photophone', a futuristic device that transmitted speech via a beam of light. This was the precursor to modern fibre-optic technology, and during its development Professor Bell discovered that if a rapidly interrupted beam from the sun, or a powerful lamp, was allowed to fall on a thin disc of any kind of material – such as glass, metal, rubber or wood – then the disc would be heard to give out a musical tone. Different shapes of discs emitted notes peculiar to themselves, and even tobacco smoke, bottled in a glass tube and held in the path of the occulted beam, was found to be in tune.

Dr John Tyndall (1820–1893) was a distinguished physicist who conducted interesting experiments on gases and vapours. It seemed to him that the audible effect discovered by Bell was due to the heat-rays in the beam expanding and contracting the substance on which they fell, and it was the vibrations within the material that could be heard. In other words, he believed the sound to be caused by the substance absorbing fresh heat each time a flash of light fell upon it.

For some time Dr Tyndall had been engaged in studying how effective different types of gases were at absorbing heat, though his contemporaries remained unconvinced by his findings. In Professor Bell's arrangement, Tyndall now had a novel plan enabling him to verify beyond reasonable doubt the absorptive power of gases by the intensity of the sounds they emitted when held in the track of light.

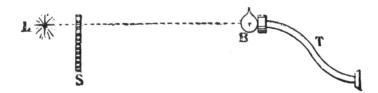

In the beam of an electric lamp, shown at L, which was rapidly eclipsed by a rotating screen, S, nicked round the rim, Tyndall placed samples of different gases and vapours, each confined in a thin bulb of glass, B. By listening through an ear-trumpet, T, which led to the bulb, he could readily hear the tones that were delivered by the gases. He concluded that the bulbs containing those gases and vapours that his earlier experiments had suggested were the best absorbers of radiant heat were found to ring out loud and clear, whereas the non-absorbent gases were either silent or produced only the feeblest tones. In this way he successfully proved that dry air was a bad absorber of heat, whereas moist air, charged with water vapour, was a good one. This yielded an important climatic bearing, for it followed that countries with a humid atmosphere would retain the solar heat far better than dry regions.

Liquid Air (1892)

At a lecture given at London's Royal Institution, the professor of chemistry, Sir James Dewar (1842–1923), presented to his astonished audience claret glasses full to the brim with liquid oxygen. Though this wasn't a first for science – small amounts of the gas having already been liquefied in 1877 – Professor Dewar astounded all when he revealed he had created a machine for yielding large quantities of the liquid, which could even be produced in pints.

At the lecture he demonstrated how an empty test tube, if plunged into a glass of liquid oxygen, would make the tube so incredibly cold that the air inside it, comprising mainly oxygen and nitrogen, would become liquefied.

Dewar went on to make a series of experiments to determine the properties of both liquid oxygen and liquid air. Curiously, the former was found to be strongly magnetic. When placed between the poles of an electromagnet it was forcibly attracted to them. The boiling point of liquid air was found to be -195° C, while that of liquid oxygen was -182° C. The liquid oxygen had a bluish tinge, though it and the air were clear and transparent.

Liquid Sky (1881)

One of the greatest triumphs of chemical science in the 1880s was said to have been the liquefaction of ozone, that peculiar form of oxygen that was present high above the clouds and could often be smelt in the atmosphere after a thunderstorm. A reservoir containing a sample of ozone was kept at a temperature of -9.4° F and was subjected to hydraulic pressure. The gas immediately turned an azure-blue colour, which deepened in shade as the compression increased, and eventually became liquefied. Its ethereal blue tint was said to be most beautiful and was believed to contribute to the colour of the sky.

During the experiments it was also discovered that liquid ozone was violently explosive, for unless carefully and slowly compressed at a low temperature it would detonate with a bright yellow flame.

Liquid Diamonds (1895)

Attention was later turned to another scientific conundrum: how to liquefy a naturally solid element. In about 1895 Monsieur Ferdinand Henri Moissan (1852–1907), the distinguished French chemist, caused a sensation by building an electric furnace so powerful it enabled him to liquefy carbon. He placed a specimen of the non-metallic element inside his furnace, and when the heat had become sufficiently intense, the carbon was vaporised. The professor was then able to liquefy the collected vapour by subjecting it to an immense atmospheric pressure. Once this had been achieved, drops of the liquid were found to solidify into a rare type of diamond found only in the mines of Brazil and South Africa.

This remarkable phenomenon was explained by the fact that the building blocks which make up a diamond are, in fact, carbon atoms.

The Underwater Atmosphere (1893)

While a select company of eminent chemists was busy examining the properties of different kinds of vapours prevalent above ground level, another group of researchers began conducting their own studies into what was coined the 'submerged atmosphere', which was alleged to exist deep beneath the earth's oceans. This theory was based upon the supposition that water, at great depths, contained a great quantity of air, for tests had shown that the air-absorbing power of water significantly increased under pressure.

An investigator named Mr A. G. Richardson calculated that at depths of 1,380 feet or more, a set volume of water would contain at least the same volume of air. Given that three quarters of the earth's surface was known to be covered by water, Mr Richardson concluded that there must be another atmosphere, as breathable as the one above the ground, far beneath the waves. Yet the wondrous varieties of air-breathing life forms that dwelled down there were left entirely to the imagination, for the task of building underwater technology capable of transporting mankind to this mythical water world was a mission left for future generations to undertake.

The Pressure of the Sea (1884)

It had often been asked, 'When an ocean-going vessel has been lost at sea, and it's supposed she has floundered, why does she not rise to the surface again and float, as wood would near the shore?'

Few could answer the enquiry with any degree of certainty, but by 1884 a scientific explanation was offered. It followed that once the sinking vessel had reached a certain depth, the pressure to which it was subjected would be so great that a quantity of water would be forced into the pores of the wood, thus rendering it so heavy that, even when detached from the ship, a piece of timber couldn't possibly rise back to the surface again. Instead it continued its descent to Davey Jones' Locker.

It was because of this constant and rapidly increasing pressure that a diver could never reach a great distance below the surface of the waves, as the weight of the water above him would crush his fragile body. Yet some remarkably durable species of fish were caught at a depth at which they would have borne a pressure of no less than 80 tons to each square foot of their bodies, implying they had evolved to endure such tremendous densities.

The Colour of Water (1882)

The beautiful colour of the sea has captivated the imagination of sailors and sightseers for centuries, inspiring many a romantic rhyme.

> I love, oh! I love the deep, deep blue sea,
> With its boundless waters so wild and free;
> Be it sweetly calm, or do dark storms rave,
> I love, ever love, the deep, deep blue wave.

In 1882 a scientific investigation was launched to explain the ocean's scenic hue, and two theories were advanced. One was put forward by the scientist Dr Tyndall, who theorised that there

were tiny, solid particles suspended in the water, which absorbed the longer, red rays of the spectrum, leaving the shorter, blue waves to be reflected back again, which were picked up by the human eye. The other theory supposed that there were no light-absorbing particles, but the colour was due to the absorbent action of the water itself, trapping the red light and releasing the blue.

Experiments by the Scottish meteorologist Mr John Aitken (1839–1919) upheld the latter theory, and he found that the greater the number of light-absorbing water molecules, the deeper the hue appeared to be. This, he explained, was why the sea appeared bluer, or sometimes greener, the further away one sailed from the shore.

Furthermore, he concluded that some water particles possessed greater powers of reflection than others, which was why different bodies of water reflected slightly different colours. The waters of the Italian Lake Como, for instance, owed their darkness to the absence of reflecting particles, while those of Lake Geneva owed their brilliant blue tinge to the presence of an abundance of them. Mr Aitken was able to reproduce a similar blue in the notoriously dark Lake Como by scattering powdered chalk on to the centre of the lake, which helped to reflect more blue light away from the water.

Others, however, supposed that Lake Como appeared dark because of its depth – at 1,300 feet deep, the lake is one of the deepest in the whole of Europe, thus little sunlight is reflected back out again.

The Speed of Tidal Waves (1884)

The greatest recorded eruption of Krakatoa took place at twelve minutes to noon on 27 August 1883. It was so powerful it triggered an enormous tidal wave in the Straits of Sunda, Indonesia, which claimed around 36,000 lives. At 1.30 p.m. the same day a wave was felt at Point de Galle, some 850 miles distant, and at Mauritius, about 3,400 miles away, a breaker was logged at quarter past two in the afternoon. Calculating from these observations, a French mathematician, Monsieur de la Croix, found the speed of the molecular wave through the sea to have been about 1,250 miles per hour, or 600 yards per second; in other words, more than one and a half times the speed of sound.

The Floating Reed Island (1884)

The accompanying illustration denotes one of the mysterious floating islands that were discovered on the Congo River by African explorers. Upon inspection, these moving landmasses were found to be made of naturally occurring aquatic vegetation that had become matted together, and were so strong they could even bear the weight of a man. The islands were borne along by the swift current of the river and were populated by various forms of vegetable and animal life.

Similar islands have since been sighted all across the globe,

as far afield as Peru, India, Africa and Australia, and may have even inspired the various vanishing island legends, such as King Arthur's mythical Avalon, that have peppered fairy tales since the time of antiquity.

The Island of Salt (1893)

Close to the Mississippi River, near New Orleans, there was an island known as Avery's Island, which, apart from the surface soil, appeared to be made entirely of rock salt. This natural resource had been known about since the days of the Native Americans, who used to distil the island's spring water and trade the salt to neighbouring tribes, until Western settlers began quarrying the rocks for their own profits.

The Greatest Waterfall on Earth (1892)

In 1891 two brave American explorers, Mr Henry Grier Bryant (1859–1932) and Professor Carlos A. Kenaston (1837–1905), set sail in a canoe along the hitherto unexplored regions of the Hamilton River in Labrador, Canada. After traversing perilous rapids and countless other dangers, they laid claim to the discovery of a magnificent waterfall in the wildernesses of Newfoundland. It was calculated to be 316 feet high and was described as the greatest cascade on Earth. Mr Bryant published a lengthy and detailed account of his discovery, including sketches of what became known as the Grand Falls of Labrador.

It had been assumed that no scientific explorer had succeeded in adventuring this far, and that the only human beings ever to set eyes upon the spectacle had hitherto been the native tribesmen who inhabited the land. Unbeknown to the explorers, however, the discovery had been forestalled by Mr John Maclean, a Scottish Highlander in the service of the Hudson Bay Company, as early as August 1849. In his diaries Mr Maclean described how, while exploring the country for purposes of trade, he descended the Hamilton River and came upon the falls. His description closely matched that of the two American travellers.

A few miles above the waterfall the river contracted from about 500 to 100 yards, and finally to 50 yards at the brink. After its leap, or rather series of leaps, the flow continued to foam and roar through a canyon 30 miles long, the walls rising in some places to a height of 300 feet. The vapour of the cataract could be seen for many miles around, and the rocks vibrated under the shock of the descending water. The great thundering of the falls was said to be audible for several miles.

Since the 1970s this once magnificent waterfall has ceased to flow, for the river was redirected from its natural course to the site of a massive hydroelectric power project, which today generates enough energy to power 35,000 homes in the region, making it the second largest hydropower plant in the country.

The Volcano-Lake (1880)

In January 1880 a novel geological effect took place at Ilopango, in San Salvador, Central America. So exceptional was the occurrence it was suspected that human eyes had never before witnessed anything like it. Inhabitants of the town were mesmerised to discover a volcano had suddenly appeared in the middle of a previously tranquil lake.

This manifestation was preceded by three tremors, not sufficiently violent to damage the houses of the district, but severe enough to create three volcanic vents in the lake, which spewed forth sulphurous gases into the air. After a time the three vents merged into one, and clouds of steam, dust and fiery cinders were discharged. As molten lava appeared out of the water, a young volcano was born.

The illustration below is from a photograph of the volcano, taken by the French Consul at San Salvador.

Attempts were made to reach the islet, but owing to the suffocating vapours and boiling temperature of the water, the people were repelled. Hundreds of dead fish and other aquatic denizens of the lake were found floating on the surface, partially cooked.

Like other lakes of the district, it was concluded that Ilopango must have occupied the crater of a dormant volcano. For hundreds of years it had been deceptively quiescent, yet all that time it had been primed to erupt.

The Mud Volcano (1887)

Exactly seven years after the Ilopango eruption, a volcano of boiling mud and water erupted at Lok Batan, Azerbaijan, very close to a busy railway station. The accompanying flames were estimated to have been 350 feet high, which rose vertically into the windless air like a gigantic pillar of light. At night the whole region was illuminated brighter than day, and the heat could be felt nearly a mile away. The thunderous explosion from the eruption drowned out the noise of passing trains, and the volume of muddy liquid that vomited from the volcano was spread, many feet deep, over a square mile around the perimeter of the crater.

The name Lok Batan translates into English as 'the place where the camel got stuck', perhaps in reference to the volcano's unusual appearance, which resembled the two humps on a camel's back, or maybe it epitomised a literal occurrence following a similar eruption some time in the distant past. Whatever its origin, Lok Batan remains one of the largest and most active mud volcanoes to this day.

The Astonishing Study of Earthquakes (1895)

Intrigued by such geological events, Monsieur Stanislas-Etienne Meunier (1843–1925), a well-known French geologist, began conducting experiments in order to determine the exact cause of earthquakes, and had the dubious good fortune of experiencing one at Nice.

'At first,' he reported, 'vague rumblings were heard, followed by distinct noises under the ground, which culminated in a series of irregular and indefinite shocks.'

In France only three shocks were felt, but across in Atlanta, Greece, as many as 365 shocks occurred that same day. This led Monsieur Meunier to deduce that earthquakes weren't isolated phenomena, but associated, and therefore shocks could be felt in different parts of the world at the same time, or soon afterwards.

The most powerful earthquakes in history have been known to wreck houses, bridges and other engineering works. At Seville, southern Spain, in 1884, a crack opened in the ground so suddenly it split a tree completely in two, leaving one half growing on each side of the brink. When tremors occurred beside the sea they were observed to send enormous waves across the land, strewing fish and vessels across the shore and destroying everything in its path. This once happened in Lisbon, Portugal, in 1755, when up to 100,000 people lost their lives. In 1886 a damaging earthquake struck at Charleston, South Carolina. It was so powerful it threw a train off the track, right up into the air, and at Riobamba, Ecuador, in 1797, a quake was so mighty it was even said to have unearthed the remains of the dead from their graves and launched them several hundred feet into the air.

Electrical Earthquakes (1887)

On 23 February 1887 a devastating earthquake struck in the Mediterranean. Many towns and villages were destroyed, and more than 2,000 people were killed in southern France and northern Italy. After the second shock, a soldier on duty at the French fort of Tête de Chien, Nice, was in the middle of sending a telegraph to a colleague, relaying his account of the tragedy, when he suddenly experienced a third shock and fell back in his chair, stunned. Since that day, he suffered excruciating headaches as well as an incurable trembling down the right arm.

His physician, Dr Onimus, investigated the matter, and concluded the soldier had received a strong electric shock through the telegraph key, which he was working at the time. It had long been known that earthquakes produced electric disturbances in telegraph lines, and the doctor believed in this case the current was so strong as to give an injurious shock.

Over the decades this curious electrical property of earthquakes has been exploited by science and today is utilised by early detection systems. Shortly before an earthquake occurs, a surge of low-frequency electromagnetic radiation is produced, which can be picked up, often by accident, by various types of machinery, warning that a quake is imminent. Geophysicists of the twenty-first century also believe earthquakes generate a huge quantity of static electricity underground, and are currently putting systems in place to monitor this level of activity in order to predict when and where an earthquake is going to strike next.

How to Detect Earth-Tremors (1882)

The microphone was one of the greatest inventions of the nineteenth century, having been patented by the illustrious engineer Mr Thomas Edison (1847–1931) in 1877. By 1882 this new device had been applied to detect earthquake disturbances.

Such technological fads, however, were deemed by some to be an unnecessary extravagance, and an American expert in seismology, Professor H. M. Paul, introduced an alternative method of investigating the phenomenon. His plan involved sinking a stout wooden post 4 or 5 feet into the ground and supporting upon it a dish containing mercury. The brilliant surface of the metal acted as a reflector, and the image of a suitably placed object, or perhaps even a nearby landmark, was mirrored in it. When the ground was still, the image was clear and well defined, but even the slightest tremor of the earth blurred the reflection. In this way the severity of the quake could be measured by the intensity of the disturbance upon the surface of the mercury.

The Glass Cliff (1887)

One of the most curious natural wonders to be discovered during the era was a spectacular cliff in Yellowstone National Park, Wyoming, which had been formed almost entirely from obsidian, or natural glass. In 1887 it was stumbled upon by Western explorers who calculated it to be half a mile long, varying in height from 150 to 200 feet. The quality of the glass was considered as good as any that could be artificially manufactured, and the discoverers believed this unusual cliff to be a relic of an ancient eastward flow of obsidian.

At its southern end prismatic columns of shining black glass, several feet in diameter, shimmered in the sunlight. Though the cliff was primarily a dark tint, it was also mottled in places with red, yellow, purple and olive-green glass, and in some spots even displayed a fine satin lustre, while in others there was a golden sheen.

Since its discovery, scientists have confirmed the cliff was formed around 180,000 years ago from a thick lava flow, which eventually crystallised, providing a natural source of obsidian for the Native Americans who used to mine the material for constructing spears and knives long before the Western explorers came. In 1996 the cliff was officially recognised by the US Government as a National Historic Landmark.

The Exploration of Mount Roraima (1885)

The flat-topped mountain, or tableland, of Roraima, in the forests of South America, was a great curiosity to the Victorians. Though this geological wonder had been discovered as early as 1596 by the famous English adventurer Sir Walter Raleigh (*c*. 1554–1618), the mountain had never thoroughly been explored. This was rectified in the December of 1884 when Mr Everard Ferdinand Im Thurn (1852–1932), a London-born botanist, bravely ventured into the unknown, promising to return with a full account of his findings.

The mountain was of specific scientific interest to researchers, as the flat top had been isolated from the rest of the world for an indefinable span of time, leaving it to cultivate its own unique world of plants and animals, high up in the clouds. It was widely expected Mr Im Thurn would find many unknown species during his foray, and from the few lines that reached the British press from the travelling botanist, this hope was not entirely misplaced.

'The scenery is in the highest degree wonderful,' he declared upon reaching the summit, after a long and tiring ascent. 'We went to the highest point – 8,089 feet above the level of the sea – and saw the highest pinnacles. We saw no animal life of any kind; no cover of any kind, and no tree of any kind.'

He described the rock formations as being 'of every shape imaginable – weird, strange and fantastic', while the ground vegetation was 'most wonderful, but somewhat scanty and quite dwarf.' Of these plants he managed to sketch and collect between 300 and 400 new species and found the orchard gardens on the lower slopes to be exceedingly fine. The absence of trees, coupled with the altitude, made the temperature feel bitterly cold, though he pressed on with his exploration and returned home some months later, armed with fascinating tales of his adventures.

A full description of his findings was published in a book, *The Botany of Roraima Expedition of 1884: being notes on the plants observed; with a list of the species collected, and determinations of those that are new.*

The Mammoth Caves (1892)

In the National Park in Kentucky was a prehistoric mammoth cave, said to have been discovered by a European bear hunter in 1797. This cave, the longest known in the world, was then largely forgotten about until the nineteenth century, when it became an attraction for tourists who had heard about its existence and its ancient artefacts that lay inside.

The American people were always on the lookout for new delights, and rumour had it there was another cave, deep in the heart of Josephine County, Oregon, in which one might wander for months without reaching the end, but no Western eyes, save for the occasional hunter or trapper, had ever seen it. By 1891 this legendary mammoth cave was officially discovered by a team of reporters from a San Francisco newspaper. The party explored miles and miles of tortuous passages, which seemed to go on forever. Inside they espied beautiful galleries adorned with translucent stalactites and milk-white columns of alabaster, and the caves were diversified with ponds, streams and falls of clear water, one of which was 30 feet high.

These sensational discoveries prompted a team of explorers, led by Mr Frank Miles Rothrock (1870–1957), to survey a third mammoth cave, Indiana's prehistoric Wyandotte Cave, believed to be one of the largest limestone caverns in the state. The explorers took with them a stock of candles, and after hours of taking perilous risks to life and limb, advancing for miles into parts of the cave never before visited, they lost their way just as their light began to fail. They were down to their last candle as they descended into a cavernous pit in search of an exit, only to find it was a dead end. There would have been no way of clambering back out again had they not chanced upon a ladder they had left behind earlier in the day and eventually recovered their way out.

The Luray Cavern (1880)

In Page County, Virginia, a family of local men accidentally discovered a remarkable cavern in the town of Luray, which promised to become one of the world's greatest wonders.

Exploring the endless chasm by candlelight, the party happened upon a vast collection of early human remains, including the complete skeleton of a Native American girl, which had become embedded within the glistening stalagmites as the centuries passed. The air of the cave was cool and pure,

untainted by the smog of the outside world. There were great chambers and crystal clear pools all around, and one of these was so still and pure it reflected the overhead stalactites like a mirror. It was christened the Dream Lake, and though not very deep, the reflection of the stalactites made it seem as though hundreds of stalagmites were rising out of an abyss. One of the most spectacular stalagmites in the cave rose 25 feet from the floor like a huge marble tusk.

For two years the men kept their amazing find a secret while they bought up the land around the cave, fitted it up with boats, bridges, guards and lights, and then opened the cavern to visitors, making a small fortune.

Black Gold (1887 and 1890)

In 1887 a new type of metal, labelled 'black gold', was found in the Nuggety Reef of Maldon, Victoria, where would-be prospectors had been flocking since around 1856. The metal was

mined from granite veins in the quartz of the reef, and when freshly excavated the gold assumed a crystalline silvery-white appearance, but became black on exposure to the air.

Though quite rare, this striking metal was adopted by jewellery makers, who began turning black gold into rings, necklaces, earrings and other adornments.

Three years after the discovery, reports came flooding in from America that pure gold had been discovered in a meteorite that had fallen there. This caused quite a stir, and today it is broadly accepted by scientists that the earth was originally delivered of all its precious metals, such as gold, platinum and osmium, by impacting meteorites, which embedded their extraterrestrial offerings into the crust of the planet around 4 billion years ago.

Masrium (1892)

In 1890 a member of the Royal Geographical Society, Mr Johnson Pasha, discovered a curious mineral in the bed of an old river in Upper Egypt. Though the river had long since dried up and had become known as Bahr-Bela-Ma, or 'the river without water', a few isolated lakes on the riverbed were celebrated for their medicinal value. Curious to learn the remedial secrets of the former watercourse, the gentleman began studying the earth and rocks beneath the dried up bed, and came across a mineral containing a hitherto undiscovered element. Upon analysis, scientists at the Khedivial Laboratory of Cairo discovered that the ordinary constituents of the mineral were accompanied by a small quantity of the oxide of another element, possessing properties entirely different from any others known to man.

The new element was dubbed masrium, after the Arabic name for Egypt, and adopted the atomic symbol Ms. Its atomic weight appeared to be about 228, and chemists of the age conducted a series of experiments to learn more about its curious nature. Despite their efforts, metallic masrium was never isolated, and no further evidence of its existence ever materialised. Masrium's assigned place in the periodic table was later filled by the chemical element radium, discovered in 1898 by the noted chemist Mme Marie Curie (1867–1934) and her husband Pierre (1859–1906).

Hiddenite (1881 and 1887)

Mr William Earl Hidden (1853–1919) was an American geologist and mineralogist. In about 1879 he set out on an exploratory expedition to North Carolina in search of platinum, which he intended to sell to the great Victorian inventor Thomas Edison, famed for his electric light bulb. During his journey a local mineralogist, Mr John Adlai D. Stephenson, approached him and showed him some unusual gemstones that had been discovered at Stony Point, Alexander County. They took the form of slender green crystals, similar to emeralds, but with a more ethereal tint. The mineral's green lustre was of a rare brilliancy, peculiar only to itself.

Mr Hidden was intrigued by the finding and sent a sample to be examined by his colleague and fellow chemist Mr John Lawrence Smith (1818–1883), who officially declared that a new type of precious stone, of the spodumene classification, had been discovered. It was given the name 'hiddenite' in honour of the official discoverer, and the gemstone became so sought-after that the area where it was first found was also bestowed with the same title. In just a few short years it took rank as one of the most precious gems in the world, equal in price only to the diamond.

Until recent times it was believed this rare treasure was only to be found in North Carolina, and its high value was partly due to the fact that it was the first known gem of pure American origin. Since then, however, hiddenite has also been found as far afield as Brazil, Madagascar and Afghanistan.

Giant Crystals (1887)

In 1883 the Etta Mine was opened for business in Pennington County, South Dakota. Though the excavators who worked there were primarily searching for tin – a lump 'as big as a small boy' having been discovered there shortly after its opening – by 1887 something else had been unearthed down in the depths of the mine. Public imagination was stirred when a set of sizeable spodumene crystals, the largest known natural crystals ever to be found, were uncovered. One of them was over 36 feet long, around six times the height of the average man, and all were up to 3 feet thick. Prospectors flocked to the mine in search of larger specimens, and a few years later a spodumene crystal was unearthed, which was an astonishing 47 feet in length. It weighed 90 tons, breaking all records and becoming the largest known crystal in the universe.

In France, miners from the Loire Valley discovered their own peculiar minerals in the form of large, hollow pebbles, almost 2 inches in diameter, among the Quaternary gravels. Curiously, the pebbles contained water. No trace of cracks could be seen by even the most powerful magnifying glass, so the question was, how did the water get inside?

Measuring Irregular Solids (1887)

Herr R. Kleemann of Halle, Germany, was said to have devised a useful little method for measuring the volume of bodies of any

shape without bringing them into contact with water or even weighing them. His equipment consisted, as shown in the figure, of a cylindrical copper box 6 cm high and 10 cm in diameter. A long, graduated tube, 3 cm in diameter, was jointed into the top of this, which was closed at the top by a rubber cork. The base of the box was removable and had a sharp point inside to support the solid to be measured.

To gauge the volume of an object, fine sand was poured down the tube into the empty box until its level reached the zero mark of the instrument. The cork was then inserted and the instrument inverted. When the solid was put in place, the sand was turned back again, and the difference of level reached gave the exact volume of the body, since it showed the displacement that the latter had produced.

Squaring the Circle (1884)

In 1884 the mathematician Mr Charles Elmes Parker Rhodes (*c.* 1831–1907) introduced a simple method for facilitating certain geometrical calculations. His instrument consisted of a shallow square trough, an adjustable right angle and a quantity of small shot, or pellets. To find the square of a given circle, the latter was cut out of some hard material, such as card, and the circle thus made was placed on a level slab and carefully filled in with the shot, none of which was allowed to overlap. The shot was then poured into the shallow trough and the right angle adjusted until the shot just filled the square formed by the right angle and the corner of the trough. This area was thus equal to the square of the circle on which the shot were first placed.

Similarly, if a surveyor wished to know the exact area of an irregular piece of land, he simply had to cut the plot to scale out of cardboard and cover it with shot, then find the square in the trough in the same manner.

Finding the Poles (1895)

Modern machines of the nineteenth century had opened hitherto unknown doors into the wider world. The steam locomotive, for

instance, had made it possible for the humblest of families to step aboard and take the ride of their lives to almost any destination imaginable. Tourism was booming across the globe, and intrepid explorers, keen to feast their eager eyes upon thrilling new discoveries, had set about reconnoitring the wildest depths of the planet. Yet there were still two regions on Earth that remained untrodden by human feet. These were the poles. For many decades mankind had strived to reach the elusive North and South Poles without success, and now, as a bright new century dawned, the race to the axis of the world began hotting up.

First, however, the pioneers needed a way of finding them. The ordinary navigational instruments used by nineteenth-century mariners and travellers weren't up to the task, so Monsieur Nicolas Camille Flammarion (1842–1925), the well-known writer on astronomy, devised a photographic method of calculating their position. He theorised that the stars would appear to take a circular path round the zenith, or the point immediately overhead each pole, as the earth span on its axis. Therefore, by exposing sensitive plates to the night sky, the true and exact position of the poles could be identified quite easily by the curves of light traced by the stars upon the photographs.

The Nansen Polar Expedition (1893)

In 1879 the would-be arctic explorer Lieutenant Commander George Washington DeLong (1844–1881) set sail aboard USS *Jeannette*, bound for the North Pole. His journey, however, was doomed to failure, and the crew never reached their destination.

For several years afterwards, the appearance in Greenland waters of driftwood and flotsam from the ill-fated vessel, which was wrecked off the Siberian coast, planted an ingenious seed of thought into the mind of Dr Fridtjof Nansen (1861–1930), who won his fame in 1888 by becoming the first voyager to cross Greenland. Trusting a theory that the currents of the Arctic Ocean could be harnessed to carry a ship towards the North Pole, just as the wreck of the *Jeannette* had drifted towards Greenland, he organised a novel type of polar expedition that was due to commence in 1893.

The *Fram*, or 'Forward', as his ship was called, wasn't as large as other Arctic vessels but was strongly built, her timbers being over 4 feet thick at the bows. Her hull resembled a

longitudinal section of an egg for buoyancy. Dr Nansen took enough provisions to last five years and fitted an electric arc lamp on his masthead for use during the long winter nights. A dynamo, driven either by the wind or by the members of the crew when taking their walking exercise on deck, supplied the current for the lamp. The doctor also took with him a captive balloon for reconnoitring purposes, and in the event of having

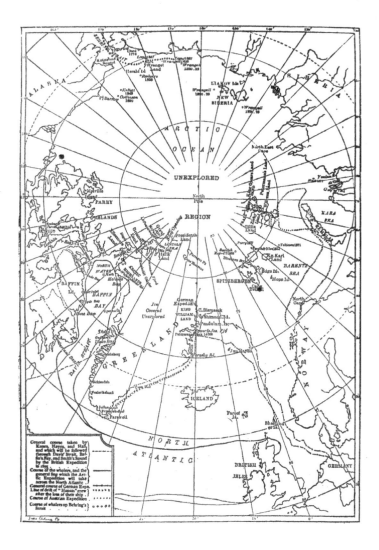

to abandon the *Fram* and take to the ice, he had acquired several smaller boats for getting home.

With a crew of twelve men Dr Nansen proceeded to the New Siberian Islands to begin his voyage. Once there, he allowed the *Fram* to become frozen in the ice, and then waited to catch a current from Siberia, in the hope of floating across the roof of the world, over, or at least very close to, the North Pole. After a lengthy wait, the vessel finally began its long journey.

The expedition was a long and hazardous one, and back home the riveted public waited with bated breath, eager to hear stories of success, as they pictured Nansen's electric star of civilisation venturing over the frozen wasteland.

The journey, however, wasn't as speedy as Nansen had anticipated, and after eighteen months or so he was forced to abandon the *Fram* and continue his journey by sled, pulled by a pack of dogs. Though he never made it to the pole, he succeeded in venturing further north than any man had gone before, reaching an impressive latitude of 86° 13.6" N.

The Balloon Trip to the Pole (1895)

In 1895 the Académie des Sciences in Paris was considering a proposal by the Swedish engineer Herr Salomon August Andrée (1854–1897) for travelling to the North Pole in a dirigible balloon. It was estimated that the aerial vessel would have to be capable of raising and supporting over 6,000 lbs in cargo, including three travellers, various apparatuses and enough provisions to remain airborne for thirty days. After considering the pros and cons, permission was granted, and Herr Andrée duly began constructing his airship.

The explorers intended to depart from the Norwegian island of Spitzbergen in the summer of 1896, and, if there was a fair wind, they expected to reach the pole in just a few days. After making their observations and taking photographs they would refill their balloon and set off back to civilisation.

After months of preparation and an array of unexpected technical issues, Andrée and his two companions finally departed in July 1897, bound for the record books. Tragically, they never arrived. Just days after departing the balloon began losing hydrogen and crash-landed in the Arctic. With no backup plan,

the three men were forced to make their return journey by foot; but, inadequately equipped for the gruelling climate, the glacial winter closed in on them, and the trio perished.

Sketching the Arctic (1895)

Lieutenant Julius von Payer (1841–1915) was one of the celebrated explorers who had participated in an Austro-Hungarian expedition to the North Pole in the 1870s. Though they had failed to make it as far as the pole, the party returned home jubilant, for the scientific discoveries they had made and the spectacular sights they had witnessed had made the trip worthwhile in the end.

In 1895 the lieutenant proposed a return to the Arctic the following year for further exploration. This time, though, his purpose wasn't so much to discover new territory, but to obtain a series of sketches of Arctic scenery. Pictures made by artists after they had returned home were, according to Payer, imperfect, conveying a false impression of reality. He believed on-the-spot sketches were the only way to properly capture the weird and

fascinating beauty of the polar landscapes, with their delicate effects of atmosphere, light and snow.

Since conceiving of the idea, the lieutenant spent many months learning how to draw, but owing to his inexperience he was accompanied on his trip by a band of professional artists who made studies on the spot, working them into pictures while the impressions were still fresh in their minds. For this purpose portable studios were taken on the voyage so the artists could ply their brushes under shelter and in comparative comfort. Furthermore, the paints were mixed with a special oil that didn't freeze, and Payer expected to return home with a veritable gallery of Arctic landscapes and scenes of Eskimo life, which he hoped would be an acquisition to the civilised world.

Atlantis Discovered (1892)

With so much exploration underway, the ancient legend of the lost land of Atlantis was once again revisited by learned men of the late nineteenth century, keen to learn its true location at last. It had long been suspected that the New World was key to unlocking the mystery, so it was here that attention turned.

At a meeting of the French Academy of Sciences, the notable zoologist Monsieur Charles Emile Blanchard (1819–1900) read a paper setting forth an array of facts seeming to prove that at some point within the human geological period the region of Labrador in Canada was once connected to Europe by a now subterranean link of land that ran from Scotland, through the Orkney and Faroe Islands, to Iceland and Greenland. Upon investigation, the sea over this supposed tract of land was found to be comparatively shallow, and the islands in questions were therefore, Monsieur Blanchard deduced, vestiges of the lost land.

His theory was supported by the fact that European animals and plants existed in America alongside species that were atypical to the Western continent. Anemones, violets, roses, orchids and lilies were common to both. Certain beetles, spiders and other insects of slow gait were also to be found on either side of the Atlantic. The reindeer of Lapland was plentiful in Hudson Bay; the beaver was a native of the two continents, and so was the river perch, which never left fresh water. This being the case, how did this fish cross the saltwater of the Atlantic Ocean if the two continents were never connected?

By identifying this lost land, Blanchard firmly believed he had pinpointed the precise location of the place known by the ancients as Atlantis.

All Things Great and Small (1893)

The author and scientist Professor John I. D. Hinds (1847–1921) of Lebanon, Tennessee, was so awed by the diversity of the earth that he took time to draw the public's attention to the extremes of the world, from the gigantic trees of California to the unseen microscopic bacteria. Some of the world's largest trees, he explained, stood nearly 400 feet high and 90 feet in girth. Conversely, some species of bacteria escaped even the most powerful Victorian microscope. Thousands could swim side by side through the eye of a needle, and a person could hold billions of them in the hollow of his hand. A giant sequoia tree was therefore thousands of millions of millions of millions of times larger than a bacterium. That meant there was roughly the same ratio between the two species as that of the earth to a football.

Furthermore, the average life of many bacteria was about an hour; that of a giant tree was probably 3,000 years. Hence a single tree outlived 26 million generations of its invisible kindred.

'As many bacteria can be laid side by side on a linear inch as earths upon the diameter of its orbit around the sun,' Professor Hinds elucidated. 'Compared with the tree, the bacterium is almost infinitesimal; by the side of the earth the tree is insignificant; in the solar system the earth is but a small factor, and if the solar system were annihilated it would be millions of years before its loss would be felt on distant stars.'

Magnitudes were therefore relative, he concluded, and things were only great according to the standpoint from which they were viewed.

3

BOTANICAL STUDIES

Red Water (1892)

'Red snow' was a phenomenon occasionally heard of in the nineteenth century, such as the time when it fell over the Crimson Cliffs, and was spotted by the arctic explorer, Sir John Ross (1777–1856), on the south-west coast of Greenland during an expedition he undertook in 1819. The snow had fallen thick and red, yet underneath this crimson blanket was a layer of pure white snow. Ancient records, like the *Annals of Ireland* from the eleventh century, spoke of water running red, and the Old Testament described how the River Nile was once turned into blood by the hands of God. Victorian scientists supposed, however, that the phenomenon wasn't a miracle at all and had perhaps been caused by the reflection of a red aurora in the sky. By 1892 it was declared more likely that, like red snow, these rare occurrences were due to the presence of a microscopic type of seaweed in the water.

It was around the same time when the water of Port Jackson Harbour, in Sydney, was found to have mysteriously turned a deep shade of red. Upon investigation, the British naturalist Mr Thomas Whitelegge (1850–1927) discovered that the colour had been produced by a species of *Glenodinium*, a type of poisonous algae that killed most of the fauna that came into contact with the water.

The Glowing Mushroom (1893)

In Tahiti there once grew a rare species of tree fungus that was luminous and remained so for about twenty-four hours after it had been harvested. When kept in the dark, the light it emitted resembled that of a glow-worm or firefly. In fact, these mushrooms were so beautiful they were often collected and used by the women of the island as articles of personal adornment, either arranged delicately in their hair or attached to their dresses, like luminous brooches. They were also carried in bouquets of flowers.

This natural fairy lamp was given the scientific name *Pleurotus lux*.

Fairy Rings (1884)

The dark green circles of grass known as 'fairy rings' have long attracted the imagination of young and old, and over the centuries many theories supposing the origins of their formation have been shared. Some said they were gateways to the supernatural realm, into which no human being had ever set foot, while others told their children the curious circles were actually footprints of dancing gnomes who had gathered the previous night to frolic in the moonlight.

By 1884 the agricultural chemists Sir John Bennet Lawes (1814–1900) and Sir Henry Gilbert (1817–1901), founders of the Rothamsted Agricultural Research Station in Hertfordshire, offered what they deemed to be the true explanation of the phenomenon. Contrary to popular folklore, it was found that the luxuriance of the grass was actually due to the presence of nitrogen, a potent fertiliser, which was extracted from the surrounding soil by the fungus plants that grew in the ring. The grass, in turn, fed on the nitrogen collected by the fungi, thus growing greener and more fulsome than the grass outside the ring.

Lawes and Gilbert thus became the first scientists to prove that vegetation could feed directly on the organic nitrogen of the soil, and it was hoped that the explanation of fairy rings would lead to further advances in agricultural chemistry. Their research station continued to deliver knowledge and new practices to British farmers, and today it lays claim to being the longest running agricultural research station in the world, providing cutting-edge science and innovation for the past two centuries.

The Fish-Eating Plant (1885)

The common bladderwort, or *Utricularia*, which thrived in the ponds of Victorian England, had long been distinguished for the tiny, peculiar bladders on its leaves. These were thought to serve as floats, as the plant was usually found just underneath the surface of the water, as shown in the figure. However, by 1885 it was discovered that these little bladders had a more sinister application, for they also served as stomachs for the plant, which turned out to be carnivorous. The organs were so constructed as to catch and trap passing food, such as carps' eggs, insects and even small fish! The animal matter was then allowed to digest before the juices were absorbed.

The small figures, A, B and C, serve to illustrate the process, with B showing a tiny fish in the closed bladder.

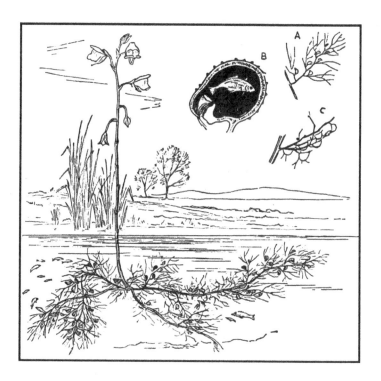

The Travelling Plants (1882 and 1893)

A plant that had the curious habit of wandering from place to place, or, rather, propagating itself by bending its branches to the ground and taking root in a new spot, was discovered in the Indian district of Kashmir by Monsieur Gérard Ermens, director of agriculture to the Maharajah of that province. This unusual plant, known scientifically as *Adiantum edwarthi*, was found to grow abundantly in the Jummoo and Kashmir territories. It flourished best during the rainy season, and a representation of this botanical curio is shown in the engraving.

Over in America, a similar plant, which had the peculiar property of migrating, or shifting its position by 2 or 3 cm every year, was dubbed *Aplectrum hyemale*. This unusual orchid began its journey when a new tubercle sprouted from the old root, planting itself in the ground and eventually taking the place of the original root, which would die and decay. It was in this way that the plant took its annual leave.

The Laughing Plant of Arabia (1890)

In Arabia there was a plant that possessed all the properties of laughing gas. It grew up to 4 feet tall and had woody stems with wide-spreading branches. The flowers were bright yellow, and each soft and woolly pod yielded three seeds resembling black beans. These were collected, dried and crushed into a fine powder, while the leaves were sometimes made into tea. When the brew was drunk or the powder ingested, the person to whom the dose had been administered felt an overwhelming desire to laugh like a madman, sing and dance, and generally cut all manner of fantastic capers until exhaustion supervened. Sleep overcame them after about an hour, and when they awoke, they remembered nothing of what had happened.

The plant was aptly known as 'the laughing plant of Arabia', and it was said that the extravagances of gait and manner experienced by those under its influence were unmatched by any other drug.

The Deadly Coca Plant (1880)

Rumour had it in Victorian Britain that a species of tropical plant, native to Peru and Bolivia, was used by the indigenous people as a nervous stimulant. It was said to enable them to stave off hunger for long periods, and also gave them energy to undergo strenuous labour without fatigue. This miraculous plant was called the coca plant, and although it had been introduced to Western culture as early as the 1500s, it remained relatively unheard of until the mid-nineteenth century when the taking of experimental drugs and stimulants became popular.

The natives of these South American countries were known to chew the leaves, which had an aromatic taste and made their tongues go numb, due to the poisonous cocaine that was contained inside. Like tea and coffee, the plant occasioned indisposition to sleep, though it had a more decided influence on the heart, increasing its rate and giving elasticity to its action. Taken in larger doses, the drug was believed to invigorate both muscle and intellect, producing what was described as a remarkable sense of satisfaction.

Coca leaves sounded truly wondrous to the Victorians, who hoped the plant would prove invaluable to the pharmaceutical world. Indeed, the drug steadily increased in popularity as the century progressed, and in 1886 the American pharmacist

Colonel John Styth Pemberton (1831–1888) added 'a pinch of coca leaves' to his original recipe for Coca-Cola, which he had named after the noxious plant. By the 1920s, following a series of high profile deaths linked to the use of cocaine, the lethal drug was banned in America and the UK.

The Electric Plant (1885)

In 1885 a German publication described the discovery of an unusual tropical plant termed *Phytolacca electrica*. When in full bloom, this extraordinary species generated a strong current of electricity that flowed all the way through it, from root to tip. The natives who lived on the torrid plain of Hindustan, where the plant was indigenous, regarded it with awe and reverence, never daring to get too close. Birds and insects coming into contact with the tree were killed at once, but most had learned to keep well away from this natural generator, too afraid to perch on the electrified branches.

When the stem or a twig was snapped by hand, an intense electric shock was felt, causing even the strongest man to stagger backwards, and magnetic compasses, even at a distance of 40 feet, were affected by the plant's power.

Curiously, the electrical influence was said to vary throughout the day, being at its strongest at about two o'clock in the afternoon and most feeble during the night. In the rainy season the plant became completely dormant, yet the energy of its action increased to a marked degree during thunderstorms.

The Ink Plant (1890)

A useful new South American plant, known as *Coriaria thymifolia*, was discovered in Colombia. Its sap was found to serve as a capital ready-made ink, earning it the name 'the ink plant'.

When pen was put to paper, the ink was a reddish colour, but it quickly turned black as it dried. The substance, known as *chanchi*, was free from the corrosive properties of ordinary ink. Furthermore, documents written in this new vegetable juice

could be soaked in water for the longest period and would still be entirely legible once dried.

However, *chanchi* never succeeded in taking over from normal ink. Despite their best efforts, botanists failed to introduce the plant to the European climate for cultivation, and it was later discovered that the plant was actually poisonous.

The Boot-Polishing Plant (1882)

The world had suddenly become full of natural curiosities, with new testimonies from across the globe chronicling Mother Nature's latest wonders. In Australia, in 1882, the public took a fancy to a remarkable new flower that was capable of polishing boots, granting the finest lustre that would rival even the best boot-blacking brand of the day. This was achieved by simply rubbing the leather on the flower, which secreted a gummy juice that gave a glossy coating to the footwear.

The plant was a species of hibiscus, known as *Rosa sinenus*, which grew in New South Wales, and four or five of its flowers were found to be sufficient for each boot.

Seaweed and Vegetable Leather (1882 and 1887)

Seaweed, one of today's so-called superfoods, was an abundant and cheap commodity in the nineteenth century, but its uses were few and far between. That was until a French chemist, Monsieur

Alexandre Saint-Yves, succeeded in extracting from the aquatic plant a sugar-like substance, which could be used to manufacture leather.

After being washed and then dried, the seaweed was pounded and treated to a steam bath inside a conical boiler. A soluble substance was thus extracted, and the residue, on cooling, assumed a leathery consistency.

By 1887 a comparable process for turning vegetables into leather was developed and introduced in France. This new material was strong, durable and suitable for manufacturing the soles and heels of shoes.

Vegetable Pearls (1887)

In the East Indian Islands, the endosperm of certain coconuts was found to contain precious pearls in the form of round or pear-shaped stones. These gems possessed a brilliant lustre and were believed to be the rarest botanical jewels in the world. So unique were they that even today there is dispute over whether or not they actually exist, with some authorities dismissing them as nothing more than a hoax. The Eastern natives, however, vowed that the gems were genuine and highly valued as charms or trinkets. A few stones of the sort were allegedly discovered inside pomegranates and other similar plants.

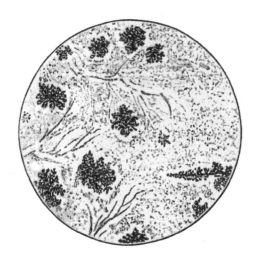

Certain types of bamboo, too, were found to contain within their stems a type of opal, similar in nature to amber and pearls. Specimens were subjected to microscopic examination, and the accompanying figure shows their peculiar structure as seen with a magnifying power of 250 diameters. 'Tabasheer' was the name given to this new mineral, which rattled inside the bamboo on being shaken.

Though new to the Western world, Eastern natives had known of its existence for centuries, and venerated it for its medicinal virtues. In fact, health officials still consider tabasheer to be beneficial for the heart, lungs, joints and immune system. It is also an aphrodisiac and is even said to slow the ageing process.

The Vegetable Barometer (1881)

In 1880 Professor Bentley, a Fellow of the Royal Botanic Society, drew attention to the interesting properties of the so-called 'rose of Jericho', a moss-like vegetable that grew under the Eastern sun. During the dry season the plant was observed to curl up into a tight ball, as if dead, and for months on end would blow about like tumbleweed across the sandy deserts of Egypt and Syria. Then, as soon as the first drops of rain began to fall, its leaves would open out and the plant would spring into life again. It expanded in a like manner when placed in water, or on moist earth, and was so sensitive to damp that the slightest presence of moisture was at once detected by its leaves.

The plant earned the nickname 'the vegetable barometer', or weather detector.

Edible Ferns (1880)

Green and leafy ferns were a common sight in Victorian woodlands, and when properly prepared by the finest culinary experts, they were found to be extremely palatable.

Throughout the ages France has always been celebrated for its culinary brilliance, and by the 1880s a collective attempt was made by Gallic chefs to popularise ferns as a chief ingredient in food. The tender shoots of the common braken fern were

exceedingly fleshy, white and tender, and it was said that a famous French painter was known to pride himself on his fern omelettes, made from such shoots.

At the other side of the world, in the hill-tribes of Japan, the locals lived on ferns all the year round. In spring they ate the tender young leaves, and later in the season they consumed the starch that was extracted from the roots.

Fern Perfume (1890)

At an assembly of the Royal Botanic Society, the secretary exhibited a sweet-scented fern that he had grown in the society's gardens. Its fragrance was compared to that of freshly mown hay, which lingered long after the fronds were dried. The secretary remarked that the specimen, a little-known species from Mussorie, in the north-west provinces of India, could be cultivated for its perfume. During the rainy season, the oaks and rhododendrons of the region became covered with ferns, one of which was the *Phymatodes normalis*. It resembled the European 'hart's tongue', and emitted from its leafy spores its delicate scent.

Aromatic ferns were also found in Britain, particularly in Totnes, Devonshire, where specimens of the *Lastrea recurva*, or 'hay-scented buckler fern', were collected. This variety secreted its aroma when the leaves were rubbed.

The Wind Flower (1885)

In about 1885 a new type of cactus shrub was discovered in the wildest desert lands of South America. Its great peculiarity was that its flowers were only visible when the wind blew.

The plant, which was said to resemble a black walking stick, grew 3 feet in height, and on the stalk were a number of diseased-looking warty lumps. In calm weather the cactus seemed entirely unremarkable, but the warts needed only the slightest breeze to unfurl into large, creamy-white flowers of great beauty. As soon as the desert wind subsided, the flowers would close up and appear as dead warts once more.

Dyeing Flowers (1881, 1882, 1884 and 1892)

By soaking the stems of cut flowers in a weak solution of dye, Mr Nesbit, a well-known Victorian botanist, discovered that their colour could be altered without affecting their scent or freshness. Rumour had it this method was found entirely by accident, and through trial and error it was determined that the most striking effects could be produced.

In 1882 tinted hyacinths were all the rage, an experimentalist having achieved some beautiful blooms sporting all manner of colours never before attained by even the most dedicated gardener. By 1892 novel bouquets of green carnations were seen adorning the windows of the most stylish flower shops of Paris and London. Their unusual colour was achieved by placing the stems of white carnations in an aqueous solution of the aniline dye known as malachite green – the use of which is regulated today, the chemical having been designated a health hazard in the 1990s. After cutting the bottom of the stem and soaking it

in the solution for twelve hours, the petals became tinged with a glorious green hue. A longer immersion deepened the shade.

Meanwhile, Professor Schnetzler, of the Vaudois Society of Natural Science, conducted his own, rather curious experiments into the colour of flowers and leaves, and concluded that a multitude of shades could be obtained by feeding spirits of wine to the plant. For instance, a peony would adopt a reddish-violet hue when placed in alcohol. If salt of sorrel was added it became a pure red, and by the addition of soda the red changed back to violet.

Chinese Garden Plants (1885)

An exciting new fashion of importing and cultivating Chinese garden plants was growing across the United States of America, and Victorian futurists predicted the fad would extend to Britain in the coming years. By 1885 American agriculturalists had introduced the Chinese water-lily, or *Nelumbium speciosum*, which bloomed with brilliant flowers. Its roots and seeds were edible, while its leaves could be used to make excellent wrapping paper.

The Americans also favoured varieties of water celery, which they planted on bamboo rafts covered with mud to form floating gardens. A strange type of plant known as the iron-tree, or *t'ieth-shu*, purportedly had the property of absorbing iron to keep itself sustained. It was said that the Chinese used to drive nails into its wilting branches to provide it with a mild tonic whenever it showed signs of drooping.

The *tiao-lan* was a type of plant that only flowered when it was taken off the ground and suspended from the ceiling, and the *chi-shu* was a tree with a golden varnish, used for decorating signboards in China. However, the varnish had one slight drawback: it contained an irritant that caused acute inflammation of the skin. Only one antidote was known to exist, and this comprised dried crab's liver mixed with a decoction of pine-shavings, which was applied directly to the affected area.

Cultivating Water-Lilies (1880)

The introduction of so many new and glorious plants to Western gardens had whetted the public's appetite for exotic blooms. Fashionable ladies, particularly, were desirous to obtain water-lilies when out boating. Luckily, the pond-lily, or *Nymphoea adorata*, could be cultivated to glorious effect with just a little effort.

It quickly became popular to prepare one's garden by sinking a large wooden barrel into the ground and placing inside it some soil collected from the bottom of the lake, or pond, or river, in which the lilies had been observed flourishing. Then, once the lily roots had been gathered, they were placed in the soil, and the barrel was filled to the brim with water. Buds would start to appear in due course, and by August the surface of the water would be blooming. In the autumn a little manure was added to the barrel and a lid was placed over the top. Thus protected during the winter, the lilies would return in abundance the following year.

Vegetables Rewired (1892)

Professor L'Arbalétrier, of l'Ecole d'Agriculture in Pas-de-Calais, France, was one of the first scientists to prove by experiment that nitrates, brought into the leaves of plants by the ascending movement of sap, were transformed into growth by the action of light. If the plant was kept in darkness, the nitrates simply accumulated in the leaves and roots and did nothing. Transformation was thus arrested, and the development of the plant was seriously checked.

The professor's experiments helped to explain the blossoming of flowers and fruits by the action of the recently introduced electric light, which was the subject of many investigations during the late Victorian era. Reports came flooding in that trees, plants and flowers that grew close to an artificial light source, such as a streetlight or house lamp, were observed to flourish to a greater degree than those that lived solely within the bounds of natural light. Market gardeners began to utilise electricity, in addition to heat and manure, in their cultivation of fruit and vegetables.

A Russian horticulturalist named Gospodin Spechneff succeeded in growing some fine vegetables by electrifying the ground in which he had planted them. He constructed his radical 'earth battery' by burying copper and iron plates in the soil, some distance apart from each other. The plates were connected above ground by an iron wire, and the current generated by the moisture of the earth circulated through the ground between each plate.

Spechneff sowed various seeds and raised exceptional crops. One of his radishes, for instance, grew over 17 inches long and almost 6 inches thick, while his carrot was just over 10 inches in diameter and weighed a whopping 6.5 lbs. Spechneff concluded that electricity, when applied in this way, would increase the yield of root-crops fourfold and of ordinary vegetables twofold.

Hearing Plants Grow (1881)

At a Silesian Botanical Society conference, in Prussia, two German gentlemen claimed to have discovered a method that allowed a listener to actually hear plants grow. To demonstrate, a plant was connected to a metal disc which had an indicator in the middle. This indicator moved visibly and regularly, and, upon a highly magnified scale, registered the growth of the plant to which it was attached. The apparatus was also connected to an electrical hammer, and whenever the indicator moved to the following measurement on the scale, it was made to interrupt the electrical current. This caused the hammer to strike a small bell, and thus the growth of the plant was perceptible to the ear.

Homicidal Houseplants (1875)

A popular fallacy in Victorian times was that houseplants were deadly organisms, poisoning the air of the room in which they dwelled by their exhalation of carbonic acid during the dead of night, while the unsuspecting occupants of the home were sleeping.

This terrifying myth was finally debunked in 1875 when Professor Kedzie, of the Michigan Agricultural College, tested the air of a greenhouse that housed more than 6,000 plants. Three samples of the greenhouse gases were gathered shortly before sunrise, from different parts of the room, and the analysis of each proved that the air in the greenhouse was even more wholesome than pure country air.

Over the coming decades it became common knowledge that plants actually remove the noxious gas carbon dioxide from the air and release life-giving oxygen into the atmosphere.

The Fountain Tree (1882 and 1895)

In 1895 it was said that a rare type of tree had been discovered in Mexico, which possessed the remarkable property of absorbing atmospheric vapour through its leaves and converting it into water, which was secreted through its trunk and branches. In fact, the tree released its water in such quantities that the ground

around it became saturated. Explorers in one of the arid Mexican deserts were startled to find a forest of this species had turned the earth into a quagmire, which they had to wade through.

Around the same time ramblers in Madagascar discovered a comparable tree, which filtered a supply of fresh water when the bark was cut. It earned the title 'the fountain tree' and was believed to be a cousin of the 'milk' or 'cow' tree, which yielded a quantity of rich, milky liquid; however, the water from the Madagascan variety was both colourless and tasteless, affording a refreshing drink to travellers in arid regions.

In 1882 an Australian outback explorer saved himself from dying of thirst by thrusting the ends of branches from the Mallee scrub into a fire and catching in a cup the sap that was driven out at the other end. A dozen Mallee sticks, 4 feet long by 2 inches in diameter, yielded a pint of water, and the explorer hoped this information would prove useful to other travellers who found themselves in desperate situations.

The Cold-Curing Tree (1875, 1880 and 1892)

In 1880 the eminent orchidologist Mr Thomas Christy FLS (1831–1905) published an interesting pamphlet about new types of plants, in which he stressed to British subjects residing in foreign parts the importance of observing the uses to which the local plants were put by the natives. By acting upon this advice, travellers were able to introduce to the British Pharmacopoeia plants possessing invaluable medicinal properties.

In the same year an Italian professor, who had travelled to Australia to conduct some experiments, was suddenly seized with a severe attack of catarrh. He had heard about the fabled eucalyptus oil, which for centuries had been revered by the Aboriginals for its ability to treat a variety of minor health complaints. Happening upon a copse of eucalyptus trees, the professor proceeded to chew one or two of the twigs before swallowing the excreted sap, which had a bitter, aromatic flavour. Much to his surprise, within an hour his symptoms had entirely disappeared. A subsequent attack was cured in the same way, and he administered the remedy to several of his friends with like success.

The custom of placing green boughs of this tree in sick rooms soon began to spread across Australia. It was stated that the volatile perfume had a favourable effect on consumptive patients, and the leaves were able to promote a restful night's sleep. Furthermore, medical practitioners expressed the opinion that if placed under the sick bed in cases of scarlet fever, the boughs would have the power to disinfect the room.

Some years earlier, in 1875, an outbreak of malaria affected certain parts of Italy, and the monks who lived at the monastery in the Roman Campagna region began planting in the surrounding marshes a woodland of eucalyptus trees as part of an organised attempt to overcome the terrible malady. At that time nobody knew how malaria was spread, and as the eucalyptus was believed to absorb foul gases through its leaves, it was presumed that the surrounding air would be purified.

The monks hoped that if their experiment proved successful, entire forests of eucalyptus trees could be planted in the sickliest regions of the world, thereby eradicating every disease known to man.

The Yucca Arch (1887)

The accompanying illustration was taken from a photograph of a remarkable yucca tree that was discovered in the Mojave Desert, near southern California. The trunk had bent over and taken root again, thereby forming a complete arch, under which four or five horses could pass abreast; its height being from 12 to 15 feet at its crown. From the top sprung a similar limb like a plume.

The Giant Cypress and the Fairy Horse (1893)

At Saint-Rémy-de-Provence, in the French province of Bouches-du-Rhône, there stood a magnificent pyramidal cypress tree of Crete, said to be the most spectacular specimen of its kind. It stood over 19 metres high, with a 5-metre girth, while the foliage covered a space of 33 metres in diameter, making it large enough to shelter two waggon-loads of hay. This magnificent tree was estimated to be about 700 years old.

In his book *Dernier Roi d'Arles* – or *The Last King of Arles* – the French historian Monsieur Amédée Pichot (1795–1877) asserted that the tree was planted on the tomb of Passeroun. He was the legendary flying horse belonging to Dragonet de Montdragon, a twelfth-century crusader who was said to have ridden into battle on his faithful steed and slain the most fearful monsters of France. After one particularly heroic victory, Passeroun began whinnying with pride, but the excitement was too much for him and his magical powers began to wane.

'Dragonet' Monsieur Pichot wrote, 'assisted a peasant to transplant on the grave of Passeroun a young cypress, and surrounded it by a hedge of woven reeds. This sacred tree, whose trunk resembled an enormous cable of serpents, attests today the renown of the fairy horse. Its vigorous age has defied the centuries. In vain the lightning has struck it, for it covered its scars under new vegetation; in vain the hostile axe has mutilated some of its branches, for it has only pushed forth more.'

The cypress was a celebrated tree in ancient times, and doctors of the nineteenth century still sent those who suffered from chest affections to breathe the balsamic odour of the Cretan cypress.

The Tree of Hippocrates (1884)

At a meeting of the Berlin Medical Society, photographs were exhibited by the illustrious pathologist Professor Rudolf Virchow (1821–1902) depicting a gigantic plane tree on the island of Cos. Tradition held that the great Hippocrates (*c.* 460 BC – *c.* 370 BC) held medical consultations beneath the shade of its branches. The tree stood in the marketplace of the town of Cos, on the eastern side of the Greek island, and its limbs, supported by marble pillars, spread over almost the entire market.

In recent years it was discovered that this mythical tree of Hippocrates was only 500 years old, yet it is believed to have grown from a sapling that sprouted from a much older tree on the same site, dating back 2,400 years to the time of the ancient Greek physician.

The Oldest Tree on Earth (1885)

In 1885 it was claimed that the oldest, and at the same time largest, tree in the world had been discovered. It was a giant old chestnut that was growing near the foot of Mount Etna, Sicily. This remarkable specimen was said to be hollow and large enough to admit two carriages driving abreast; the circumference of the main trunk was measured at a staggering 212 feet. It was given the nickname 'the tree of 100 horses', owing to a local legend that told of the time when the same number of medieval knights, and their horses, took shelter underneath the enormous branches during a torrential storm. Remarkably, the tree was large enough to ensure that every one of them stayed dry.

Today it is believed that a Norwegian spruce, discovered in Sweden in 2004, is the oldest living tree in the world, having taken root at the end of the last ice age, nearly 10,000 years ago. The tree at the foot of Mount Etna, though certainly the oldest known surviving chestnut tree, has only been flourishing for a mere 4,000 years, and is still going strong.

4

THE ANIMAL KINGDOM

The Silurian Scorpion (1885)

The Silurian era dawned around 444 million years ago. This was the geological age when sea levels began to rise. The temperature of the earth was warm and stable; fish had begun to evolve in the sea, and small, moss-like plants were starting to grow on land. A race of water-dwelling scorpions was also evolving, but terrestrial life didn't begin to diversify until the following age, known as the Devonian period.

All of this was thrown into doubt in the summer of 1884, when, on the remote Swedish island of Gotland, a palaeontologist, Professor Gustav Lindström (1829–1901), discovered a fossilised specimen of a giant terrestrial scorpion in the Silurian rocks. The illustration shows this remarkable discovery, which proved the existence of air-breathing land animals long before they were believed to have existed. The scorpion's most peculiar feature was the four pairs of pointed feet, which jutted out from its throat, a characteristic lacking in later varieties of the arthropod.

A year earlier, the Scottish geologist Dr Hunter of Carluke unearthed a similar fossil in the Upper Silurian rocks of Lesmahagow, Lanarkshire, but didn't realise its importance until after the announcement of Professor Lindström's discovery. Dr Hunter's scorpion closely resembled that of the Swedish rocks, though it was only about half the size.

A fossilised beetle was also discovered in the Silurian sandstone of Calvados, France, thus supplying more evidence of the existence of terrestrial, air-breathing creatures during that era and perhaps even answering the vexing question of what did the scorpions find to prey upon?

The Silurian scorpion rose to fame in the twenty-first century, when it was cast as one of the people-eating monsters in ITV's popular sci-fi drama *Primeval*. The creature was responsible for the death of six people including Stephen Hart, the lab technician.

The Dinosaur-Eating Bird (1895)

Geological explorations in Southern Patagonia, South America, made by the palaeontologist brothers Señors Carlos (1865–1936) and Florentino Ameghino (1854–1911), revealed the existence of a large deposit of fossil birds and herb-eating mammals. These were exhumed from gravel beds dating back around 40 million years to the Eocene age of Earth's history, the period that saw prehistoric life begin to diversify. Dozens of species of extinct birds were discovered in these gravels, and among them was a monstrous winged creature, the largest avian specimen known to man. Up until then the *Dinornis*, an extinct 12-foot bird from Madagascar, had been regarded as the largest bird that ever lived, but the discovery of the *Brontornis burmeisteri*, shown in the illustration,

was believed to surpass even this. It wasn't only taller but also thicker; it was calculated to have stood over 13 feet tall – more than twice the height of an average man – and was of stocky build. Its beak was armed with two teeth near the hook and its scaly feet with powerful claws. Its wings, however, were too small to allow it to fly.

The *Dinornis* and its congeners lived on vegetables, but the *Brontornis* was carnivorous, and no doubt fed on molluscs, reptiles and perhaps even larger animals, such as the dinosaur *Hadrosaurus* as imagined in the picture. The bird in the distance is a *Phororhacos longissimus*, another extinct bird of Patagonia, discovered by the Ameghino brothers in the Eocene gravel.

Titanotherium Robustum *(1890)*

The following illustration represents the skeleton of a *Titanotherium robustum*, an extinct monster allied to the rhinoceros, whose bones were discovered in Dakota, USA. Professor Othniel Charles Marsh (1831–1899), a palaeontologist

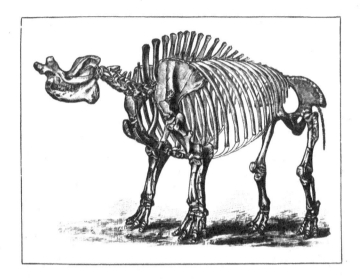

from New Haven, presented a finely executed model of the skull of this mammal to the British Museum for further analysis.

It seemed to Victorian experts that the *Titanotherium*, which thrived around 56–34 million years ago, was about the size of an elephant, and its skull differed from that of the rhinoceros by having two large bones projecting out from the nose, one above each nostril. The rhinoceros was well known for having either one or two horns above the snout, but placed one behind the other and having no bony connection with the skull itself.

The Devil's Corkscrew (1892)

The accompanying figure represents a peculiar kind of fossil that was discovered in the walls of a canyon in the Badlands of north-west Nebraska, USA. These bizarre formations, or 'devil's corkscrews', as they were dubbed, were up to 40 feet long, and were usually found in a vertical position in the crumbling sandstone from which they were excavated. The specimen shown in the figure resembled a thick vine, twisted round a pole, which spiralled down into the bed of an ancient lake. The skin or shell of the relic was found to be siliceous, but the core was formed from the soft sandstone of the district.

Following further research, it was deduced that semiarid grasslands once covered the area over 20 million years ago. However, American geologists were unable to determine what these unusual fossils were, but judging by their appearance they believed the most likely explanation was that they were the petrified shells of some prehistoric plant, sponge or even some kind of worm. A set of bones belonging to an extinct beaver-like rodent had been unearthed alongside one of the corkscrew fossils, leading experts to believe that the formation was most likely a sponge in which the creature had accidentally become entangled before it died.

As more corkscrews were excavated, more sets of rodent bones were discovered, and it was eventually understood that the giant fossils weren't extinct plants or sponges after all, but were, in fact, the fossilised remains of ancient burrows made by the beavers in order to provide shelter for their families in the blistering grasslands. The engineering work was a remarkable feat for the creature, known as the *Palaeocastor*, as chambers and side passages were constructed within the burrows, providing the rodents with cool living quarters as well as water and food stores and even a toilet! This beaver became extinct about 23 million years ago.

The Fossil Mammal from the European Chalk (1892)

By slow degrees, gaps in the earth's geological record were filled as the Victorians brushed away the creationist beliefs of old and strived to learn more about the life forms that once inhabited the planet millennia before the age of man.

Until Victorian times, no remains of mammals had ever been found in the European chalk, the rocky deposits dating back to the Upper Cretaceous period when dinosaurs still roamed the earth. It was an almost indisputable fact that mammals only began evolving after the dinosaurs were wiped out, so the nation was stunned to learn that several genera of small, mouse-like mammals, known as *Plagiaulax*, which once lived side by side with the giant reptiles, had been discovered in the Purbeck beds of Dorset. The most curious finding of all was that one of these extinct creatures was closely related to the kangaroo rat of Australia, hitherto believed to be unique to that continent. No other traces of mammals were discovered in the rocks until the Tertiary period, after the terrestrial dinosaurs had become extinct.

In a quarry near Hastings, however, a bed of bones in the Wadhurst Clay yielded evidence that the *Plagiaulax*, or, rather, a closely allied genus, survived in Britain much earlier than the Dorset discovery suggested. In 1892 it was announced that an amateur palaeontologist from Uckfield, East Sussex, had discovered a tooth resembling those belonging to the little mammal, dating from 140 to 100 million years ago. This man's name was Mr Charles Dawson (1864–1916), and he had spent a great deal of time in carefully examining the deposit. He forwarded the tooth to the Natural History Museum at South Kensington, and the authorities there named the animal to which it belonged *Plagiaulax dawsoni* in honour of the palaeontologist who had officially discovered the first Cretaceous mammal in the European chalk.

Mr Dawson went on to make more remarkable archaeological discoveries during the late nineteenth and early twentieth centuries, including an ancient boat, a subterranean cave, a 'toad in a hole', and, perhaps most notably, the 'missing link' in human evolution. In 1912 Dawson laid claim to the discovery of a new kind of early human skull during a dig at Piltdown, near Hastings. The skull was found buried along with iron-stained flints and carved elephant bones, seemingly proving that this early human, named *Eoanthropus dawsoni*, could think. This was a revolutionary breakthrough, and Dawson received much praise and appreciation for his find.

Immediately after his death in 1916, these remarkable Sussex discoveries mysteriously ceased, and no further remains of the 'Piltdown Man' were ever found, despite the best efforts of scientists, archaeologists and palaeontologists of the day.

It transpired almost half a century after his death that Dawson was nothing more than a fraudster who had faked at least thirty-eight of his alleged discoveries, including *Plagiaulax dawsoni* and the Piltdown Man, which took rank alongside the greatest hoaxes in history. The mammal tooth had simply been filed down to resemble that of the *Plagiaulax*, and the skull was found to be a hybrid between those of an orangutan and a 50,000-year-old human.

The Kangaroo-Lion (1887)

In the 1880s a fossil jawbone was discovered in the Wellington Caves of Australia and submitted to Sir Richard Owen (1804–1892), the well-known palaeontologist, for inspection. He astounded all when he announced that it belonged to a lion, an animal that was never supposed to have existed on the Australian continent. However, this particular lion was even more extraordinary, for it was, in fact, a marsupial, possessing a pouch similar to that sported by the native kangaroo.

This extinct carnivore was known as *Thylacoleo carnifex*, and roamed Australia about 2 million years ago. It was about the size of a tiger and had the strongest bite of any known creature of its build. It fed on large animals such as the extinct giant kangaroos, and, like its prey, carried its young in its pouch.

In 2008, about 30,000 years after the kangaroo-lion became extinct, an Aboriginal cave drawing was discovered in Kimberley, Western Australia, which is thought to be a depiction of the beast as portrayed by ancient man.

The Leech Barometer (1881)

For centuries it had been well known that the leech was a creature highly sensitive to atmospheric changes, and in 1881 an imaginative gentleman named Mr A. W. Roberts explained to his Victorian contemporaries how a leech storm-glass could be made in order to predict the weather. Leeches were easy to come by, as nineteenth-century physicians regularly employed them for remedial purposes, so it was easy for anyone to participate in this weather experiment.

The bottom of a tall candy jar was carpeted with peat, and two or three smooth stones were laid down inside. The jar was then filled with water, into which, after the peat had settled and the water had become clear again, two or three leeches were placed. A tin lid, in which several air holes had been bored, was then used to cover the jar, which was kept in a cool, shady spot in the garden. To ensure the creatures' health and wellbeing, the water was changed once a fortnight.

So long as the weather remained calm and pleasant, the leeches would lie motionless at the bottom of the vessel, but on the approach of snow or rain, they would rise to the top, where they would rest until the weather became settled again. A forthcoming windstorm caused them to gallop about the jar in a lively fashion, while an approaching thunderstorm was a source of great uneasiness, causing them to try to seek a lodging above water, and in clear frosts they would lie quietly at the bottom.

The Honey-Bearing Ant (1882)

The Reverend Henry Christopher McCook (1837–1911) was an American naturalist who travelled to New Mexico in 1877 to study the indigenous insects. His researches brought to light a peculiarity of ant life, for among the honey-ants of the region was a caste of working ants who gathered food from a species of vegetable gall during the night, but instead of eating it themselves, they fed it to another caste belonging to the colony. These were the honey bearers, and their sole function in life was simply to convert the food into honey, which was stored inside their oversized abdomens until the other members of the community wanted to feast upon it. For this purpose their bodies were abnormally developed, and when swollen could reach the size of a grape. The reverend calculated that it required about 1,000 'rotunds', as these ants were dubbed, to yield a troy pound of the produce.

The honey was described as pleasant to taste, like ordinary honey but runnier and more aromatic. The honey could be harvested and consumed by itself, but in New Mexico the entire ant was considered a rare delicacy.

Suicidal Wasps (1895)

Benzine was a type of chemical found to be a potent insecticide and particularly suitable for driving away wasps and mosquitoes. It was rubbed on one's face, hands and other parts of the body exposed to the insects, and was sometimes spread in a film over the surface of reservoirs in the hope of repelling the large swarms that often congregated over the water.

The health implications of human contact with benzine weren't fully understood in the nineteenth century, and the chemical has since been labelled a carcinogen by the US Department of Health; however, in the 1890s a French experimenter named Monsieur Henry, curious to see the effect of this chemical on insects, put a quantity of it under a glass in which a wasp was imprisoned. The insect immediately showed signs of great annoyance, darting around in a frenzied manner. Finally accepting there were no means of escape, the wasp appeared to submit in despair, for it lay down on its back, and bending up its abdomen, planted its sting thrice into its body and died.

Monsieur Henry allowed his scientific interest to overcome his humanity and repeated the experiment with three more wasps, only to find that the trio acted in exactly the same way. He was, therefore, of opinion that wasps, under desperate circumstances, committed suicide.

It had also been said that snakes and scorpions took their own lives, but this assumption didn't seem to take into account the fact that snakes were immune to snake poison, unless one supposed they weren't impervious to their own.

The Fish-Killing Mosquito (1887)

Contrary to the familiar belief that freshwater fish generally fed upon mosquitoes, a bulletin of the United States Fish Commission stated that mosquitoes were actually a deadly enemy to young brook trout. In June 1882, while sitting underneath a willow tree by the Tomichi Creek in Gunnison Valley, Colorado, where the water was clear and shallow, a gentleman named Mr C. H. Murray witnessed a number of newly hatched mountain brook trout exploring their surroundings. When one of them came to the surface of the cool water, a mosquito flew at it and stabbed its trunk into the little creature's brain. When the mosquito flew away the fish turned over and died. In the course of half an hour, the observer saw some twenty trout slain in this way. This was a startling and unheard-of extermination of fish, and Mr Murray was believed to be the one and only witness to this peculiar occurrence.

Electrical Insects (1880)

For centuries the generating properties of the electric eel had been renowned, but few Victorians were aware that there were also certain insects that had the ability to give comparatively powerful electric shocks.

The *Reduvius serratus*, or wheel-bug, of the West Indies, was alleged to send a smart discharge into the flesh of any person brave enough to touch it. One curious naturalist allowed the insect to rest on his hand and immediately felt a shock that was so powerful it extended to his shoulder. When the bug was dropped on the floor, he observed six red marks on his palm where the feet had stood.

It was also proven that the same mysterious power was wielded by a beetle, one of the common *Elateridae* genus, and by a large, hairy lepidopterous caterpillar found in South America. One Captain Blakeney was unfortunate enough to receive a strong jolt, which paralysed his arm for some time, when he attempted to pick up one of these electrical larvae. The shock was so severe it even put his life in danger for a while, though he eventually made a full recovery.

Insects and the Electric Light (1885 and 1887)

Though the electric light had been around since the early nineteenth century, it wasn't until Thomas Edison developed the first practical light bulb in 1879 that this modern convenience was introduced to an astonished, yet somewhat cautious, society. By the 1880s electric lights had been installed in front of the Treasury and other public buildings in Washington, USA, and a curious consequence of their introduction left the public baffled. Almost overnight, a congregation of hundreds, if not thousands, of spider-webs was discovered covering the new lamps and neighbouring buildings. Upon investigation the leading academics of the city found that these cunning arachnids had worked out that an abundant food source, in the form of flies and moths, could be found near the bright electric light, owing to the attraction it had for these nocturnal insects. Hence they built their webs over the city's streetlights, and in some places the webs were so thick that the architectural ornamentations were no longer visible.

Meanwhile, in New Orleans, the new electric streetlights, which were infested with moths and other night insects, unintentionally led to their destruction in vast numbers. The bright lights had allured them in the same way as a candle flame, and each morning the streets were found carpeted with a thick layer of dead moths, eradicated, the citizens presumed, by the heat from the electricity.

It was also interesting to entomologists that the new lights led to the discovery of several rare insects that had been thus attracted by the brilliant new radiance.

The Mimicking Caterpillar (1882)

A curious example of animal mimicry was introduced to the British public from Assam, near Bangladesh, where the naturalist Mr Samuel Edward Peal (1834–1897) discovered a rare type of caterpillar with an extraordinary personality. Instances were common enough in which insects were observed to mimic each other, or different kinds of seeds, leaves, flowers or stones to assume a camouflage, but the curious caterpillar discovered by Mr Peal had apparently adopted a habit unique only to itself. When alarmed, shocked or surprised, this wiggly larva assumed the pose of a shrew, as may be seen from the accompanying sketch.

Mr Peal was passing through a dense forest when he saw the caterpillar standing in front of him on a stout creeper, and actually mistook the insect for a mammal. It was entirely motionless, allowing a closer look to be had. Its stance was perfected by stretching out two prolongations on its head, to

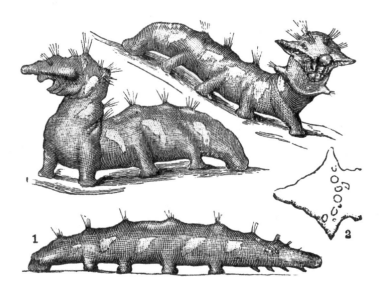

resemble ears, and sticking out its pointed nose to mimic a long, shrew-like muzzle, in the hope of scaring away predators. When the perceived danger had passed, the caterpillar resumed its normal posture, as in diagram one. Diagram two shows a detailed plan of the head.

Innumerable creatures on the planet were renowned for their gift of mimicry, from the eye and nose of a crocodile, resembling lumps of dirty foam on the water, to the tiger's hunting call, which was remarkably similar to the cry of its prey – the sambar deer – but Mr Peal's account of the caterpillar was perhaps the most singular and amusing instance of mimicry in Victorian record books.

The Singing Snake (1895)

In 1895 Sir William Macgregor (1846–1919), the governor of British New Guinea, drew the public's attention to a small, black species of snake that was discovered in the region. Remarkably, instead of issuing the conventional hiss, this snake could sing like a bird. So convincing was the deceitful serpent's call that a local boy, mistaking it for a cockatoo, was lured into the bushes and bitten to death.

The account was reminiscent of the discovery of the 'fiddling' spider of Australia's Macdonnell Ranges in the Northern Territory, which composed musical notes by drawing its leg across its jaw, as a violinist would caress the strings with their bow.

The Water-Carrying Tortoise (1882)

Certain strains of giant cactus plants that grew in Mexico's deserts were known to contain a great quantity of drinkable water in their soft, fleshy lobes, and tales of these natural water stores relieving thirsty travellers had captivated Victorians for decades. However, in the 1880s another living water-bearer was observed in the deserts of Arizona and California. This unlikely specimen was a tortoise, a fine example of which was presented to the Academy of Science at San Francisco. The tortoise was said to be the size of a large bucket, and upon

examination a store of water was found inside a bag under the shell, and a pint of the liquid could be extracted from a fully grown specimen.

The creatures were highly prized by the Mexicans, not only for their water but also their flesh, as this could be used to make delicious soups.

The cacti and tortoises were the only living residents in these arid wastelands, where rain was scarce. As water was almost non-existent in this part of the world, Mother Nature had doubtless found it necessary to endow these two species with their amazing water-bearing gifts.

The Shell with Eyes (1885)

In 1885 a Victorian professor named Moseley made the intriguing discovery that a sea creature known as the *Chitonidoe* lived inside a shell endowed with eyes. No other molluscs thus far examined possessed any kind of sensory organs in their shells, making the finding a first for biology.

In some specimens as many as 11,000 eyes were counted, providing the shellfish with a remarkably wide view of its surroundings. Each organ had a calcareous cornea and a lens of soft tissue, with a retina similar to that of the common snail. New eyes were constantly formed at the edge as the shell grew. There were also organs of touch across the surface, each being capable of protruding through tiny pores, making it a truly sensory shell.

Wool from the Sea (1887)

The Victorians discovered that an innovative type of material called bisso, or 'golden wool', was utilised on the island of Maddalena, northern Sardinia, for making cravats, shawls and other such garments. The wool, however, hadn't come from any sheep, goat, llama or any other type of land mammal; it had, in fact, been obtained from a shellfish, the *Pinna nobilis*, which attached itself to the sea bottom by a tuft of woolly hair.

The fibre was a golden yellow hue and was exceptionally rare. The collected tuft was washed, dried, combed and spun, before being woven into a silk-like cloth. The dark 'old gold' variety was the most prized; besides being pretty, it was said to be extremely durable.

Though this seemed a remarkable new discovery to the Victorians, this type of marine wool had actually been woven since ancient times, the Egyptians using the material to wrap bodies during the mummification process. There was also a mention of 'byssus cloth' on the Rosetta Stone, inscribed in the year 196 BC.

Flying Shellfish (1895)

The Victorians were accustomed to hearing about fish out of water and crabs on dry land, but stories of flying crustaceans were an unexpected novelty to naturalists. It was Dr Ostroumoff, of the Sebastopol Biological Station, who was perhaps the first person to report this rare phenomenon. He and his son were taking a boating expedition along the Malay Peninsula, southeast Asia, on a calm, clear morning in July 1894 when they observed a tiny green crustacean, the *Pontellina mediterranea Claus*, hovering just above the level of the water. A number of them were springing from the surface and travelling in a long curve in the air before falling back into the water again.

Their efforts reminded the doctor of Herr Otto Lilienthal (1848–1896), the eccentric aeronaut who invented artificial wings and could often be spotted gliding across the landscape strapped to his invention.

The House-Building Shrimp (1895)

A variety of shrimps could commonly be espied in rock pools, filled at each incoming tide, and these crustaceans often formed the basis of many a collector's sea aquarium. In around 1895 one rarer species of shrimp was observed to have the peculiar

habit of building for itself a house in which to find shelter. The little creature in the illustration was sketched from life as he was perching outside the entrance to his tubular dwelling, fastened against the side of the aquarium in which he lived.

The tube inhabited by the shrimp was semi-circular and was built of sand and small pieces of seaweed, cemented together with a glutinous matter, secreted by the builder. When commencing its project, the shrimp lay on its back, and with its long antennae began gathering a small heap of decaying vegetable matter and sand. Upon this it poured the cement secretion from its mouth and used the front pair of legs as tools, adding bit by bit to the structure until it was large enough to form a secure dwelling where the creature's offspring were born and nurtured.

The species was named *Amphithoe littorina* and differed from other shrimps in that its eyes were set in the head rather than at the end of stalks like those of the lobster and crab. They could be found among the threadlike green seaweed in any rock pool, and the fronds of carrageen moss were often studded with the mud-tubes of the species.

The Monster of the Deep (1890)

One blustery morning in 1889, the villagers of Blacksod Bay, on the west coast of Mayo, Ireland, were startled to find the washed-up remains of one of the most curious sea creatures they had ever seen. It was assumed at first to be the carcass of a large whale, but upon examination it was deemed more likely to be either a giant squid or a king cuttlefish. Though shrunk and maimed when it was examined, the body of the beast measured 60 feet in circumference. The length of each tentacle was 30 feet, and the girth in some parts 4 feet. The total span of the animal was at least 70 feet, making it 27 feet longer than the largest giant squid ever recorded by scientists.

The residents of Ireland had, until then, only heard of these ocean monsters from returning mariners who told of fearsome creatures from the deep, rising out of the water with outstretched tentacles, ready to drag a vessel down to the depths of the abyss. One such sea monster, which could easily have been mistaken for the great mythical sea serpent, was cast ashore at County Kerry more than 200 years earlier, another was reported on the banks of Newfoundland, a third from Shetland, and a fourth was picked up off Boffin, Isle of Mayo, in around 1875, portions of which were proudly exhibited in Dublin Museum. The locations of these beached bodies confirmed to marine biologists that the North Atlantic Ocean was probably a breeding ground for gigantic sea monsters.

The Trout that Wore Cologne (1895)

In the vicinity of Geneva there was once a great chemical works that manufactured musk, a key ingredient in nineteenth-century perfume. The factory stood on the banks of the River Rhône, into which the waste products were regularly dumped. Consequently, the trout and other fish that lived in the river assumed a musky taste. It was never ascertained whether the fish were attracted by the scent of the musk and ate the waste products, or had simply become impregnated with the perfume.

The Muzzled Fish (1882)

It would be safe to assume that a rubber band secured tightly round the gills of a fish would be enough to strangle it.

Nevertheless, Mr Charles Clarke, of Plymouth, caught a living trout in the River Plym which had a rubber band slipped over its head, as shown in the sketch. The band was so tight it had compressed the gills and deeply indented the horny part of the lower jaw. How the band got there, and how long it had been around the head of Mr Clarke's curious catch, was a question on everyone's lips. Whether the young fish had accidentally become entangled in the band, and had grown so large it couldn't be undone, or whether it had been put there by the wanton mischief of some unscrupulous person, the Victorians never knew, but the fact that the creature continued to live was truly remarkable.

The Sword-Swallowing Fish (1887)

In 1887 the United States Fish Commission reported the capture of a large, live codfish at Gloucester, Massachusetts, on 15 September 1886. Upon examination by Captain John Q. Getchell (*c.* 1836–1898), master of the vessel, the fish was found to contain a pocket-knife of curious workmanship that had become embedded inside its flesh, as if it had been swallowed whole. The knife possessed a curved and tapered brass handle with a slit in the hollow side for the lance-shaped blade to fit inside. The weapon measured more than 6 inches long, and it was thought, judging by the unique design, that the owner must have been of Aboriginal descent, or perhaps a sailor from a foreign land.

How the knife had come to be inside the fish, how long it had been there, and how the fish had survived, were questions that were never answered.

Fish Leather (1882 and 1887)

In Germany the skin of the catfish was found to be a suitable material to tan into leather. The material was tough, supple and of good appearance, and was made into purses and shoelaces. Similarly, the women of Castries Bay in St Lucia used to make dresses out of salmon skins.

In 1882 a process was discovered that could render leather, sourced from any animal, transparent. Ordinary skins were shaved of their hair, cleaned, then stretched on frames and rubbed with a composition consisting of glycerin and three types of acid. Before drying the skins were taken into a dark room and impregnated with a solution of bichromate of potash. After this they were coated with varnish, and once dry were ready for use. As well as being novel, transparent leather was found to be several times stronger than the ordinary variety.

The Aquarium and the Wicked Fish (1875)

Since the 1840s families across Britain had been adorning their homes with glazed tanks in which all manner of aquatic life were kept, and by the middle of the century the keeping of fish had become a popular pastime. Public aquariums were opened around the country, and by the 1870s the fish house at London Zoo had amassed a sizeable collection of treasures from the deep.

The fact that aquariums were coming into fashion was a hopeful sign of a growing interest in scientific research. The Victorians were waking up to see that the world was full of more wonders than could ever have been imagined, and curiosity was urging them to go prying even deeper into the ocean.

In 1875 a native of the sea was captured and conveyed in triumph to Manchester Aquarium. This was the 'devil fish', or the angler fish, *Lophius piscatorius*, so unattractive that there was no demand for the species at Billingsgate fish market. It was over 4 feet in length, weighed about 80 lbs, and resembled an enormous, severed head. Its mouth was wide and toothy, while its large, goggle eyes gave the fish a meditative expression.

The name 'angler fish' was well bestowed, for the species was, effectively, an angler, possessing its own line, hook and bait. Its piscatorial equipment consisted of two long erectile filaments growing out of its head, like a fishing line. Aided by these, the fish would lie among the rocks and weeds at the bottom of the water, waiting for an unsuspecting victim to pass by. The end of the 'fishing rod' would glow, thereby attracting smaller fish towards the hidden predator.

The Victorians imagined that the angler fish was the terror of its homeland, and dubbed a 'mean fellow', 'glutton', 'cannibal' and 'assassin' by all its neighbours.

Luminous Coral and the Electric Light in Aquaria (1882)

By night, and with the aid of old-fashioned gas lamps, it was very difficult for Victorians to inspect their aquariums. It followed, therefore, that one of the most interesting and novel applications of the electric light was thought to be its introduction into household aquariums, with the object of illuminating the tanks.

At a public aquarium six bright lights were submerged, with the result that every fish and plant was shown with great clarity. The fish didn't appear to pay any attention to the lamps, nor was their health affected. In fact, this new form of lighting was deemed pure and wholesome to the heath of every living organism, as noxious products, such as those yielded by the combustion of gas, didn't accompany the use of the electric lamps. Furthermore, the light could be made more or less intense as required, and coloured filters could be applied, producing spectacular effects.

In 1882 a natural sea-lamp in the form of phosphorescent coral was sourced by Mr C. F. Holder, a Fellow of the New York Academy of Sciences, and placed in his aquarium. The remarkable reef comprised five branches, each terminating in a luminous cell, which glowed with a greenish light sufficient to illuminate the water in his tank. The light was intermittent, like that of a firefly, and he described the effects as quite charming.

The Fish that Lived Underground (1884)

There was once a civil engineer from Rome named Signor
Cavalier Moerath, who devoted his labours to the improvement
of water supplies in his home country. In 1884 he was engaged in
prospecting for water in mainland Italy. During the construction
of a well, he tapped an underground spring, deep below the
surface of the earth. To his surprise, out shot a tiny, living fish.
The creature, which was just a fraction of an inch in length,
didn't have any eyes. Nothing of the like had ever been seen
before, thus it was believed to belong to a hitherto undiscovered
species of fish intended to inhabit deep, subterranean waters,
never seeing the light of day.

The Fish that Breathed Air (1892)

At a conference of the Australasian Association for the
Advancement of Science, which was held in Hobart Town,
Tasmania, Sir Walter Baldwin Spencer (1860–1929), professor of
biology at Melbourne University, read an interesting paper on
the 'lungfish', which inhabited the Burnett and Mary Rivers of
Queensland. Inside this curious creature was a fully functional
lung, enabling it to breathe air at will, despite being a fish. During
the dry season when the rivers were parched, the fish was able
to cover itself with mud and live by means of its lung. In the wet
season, when the rivers were flooded and the water polluted with
mud and sand, the lung proved very useful to the creature, which
would pop its head out of the suffocating river and breathe the
fresh air, just like the beasts on the land and the birds in the sky.

The Rain Bird (1890)

In the skies of Africa was said to dwell a brightly coloured
species of bird known as the plantain-eater. Its beautiful crimson
feathers were said to be coloured by a natural red pigment,
which, incredibly, washed out, hence the bird would conceal itself
under thick foliage whenever it rained.

Some ornithologists doubted this fact, but Mr Frank Evers

Beddard (1858–1925), of the Zoological Society, where a number of these birds were housed, claimed to have obtained a pink solution from the feathers of a dead plantain-eater by steeping them in ordinary tap water.

By the 1890s visitors were flocking to the London Zoological Gardens to see for themselves whether or not the anecdote was true. It was even suggested by some sceptics that the zookeepers, or some other authority, had dyed the birds' feathers to make them more attractive to the public, hence the reason why the pigment used to run in wet weather.

Whether there really was such a species of rain bird, or whether there was simply some trickery afoot, still remains a mystery.

The Four-Legged Bird (1885)

Since the days of Charles Darwin (1809–1882) mankind has been captivated by the theory of evolution. Testament to the fact that science is still completing the chain of evolution came in 1885 when an American naturalist, Mr Edward Morris Brigham, took great pleasure in announcing the discovery of an astonishing type of bird that lived on the island of Marajó by the Anabiju River, at the mouth of the Amazon. The bird's most incredible characteristic was that it was born with four feet.

The existence of a quadruped bird was so contrary to the accepted order of things that the discovery came as a baffling revelation to scientists of the age, with many refusing to believe it. Even more curious was that this South American creature, known scientifically as *Opisthocoma cristata*, was four-footed only in its early life, one pair of legs developing into a set of wings a few days, or even weeks, after hatching, making it the only known member of the higher vertebrates to display post-natal metamorphosis in primary organs. This was a trait akin to the regenerative power of lizards, which had the ability to regrow lost limbs. Its discovery, therefore, seemed to confirm the evolutionary theory that birds are descended from dinosaurs, or similar reptilian ancestors.

Though the winged creature was seldom seen by human eyes,

Mr Brigham was lucky enough to catch a glimpse, and compared its likeness to a pheasant. The bird, commonly known as the 'cigana' or 'gypsy bird' by the locals, was thought to inhabit the beds of semi-aquatic plants with large leaves, which grew in the flat, muddy margins of the island. The bird would build its nest there, rather than in the treetops, and would rarely fly far from its peculiar haunt, especially during the day.

Unlike other birds, the cigana couldn't sing; instead it uttered doleful and demonic cries, as if it was deep in mourning. This was an eerie sound in the dead of night, when the bird was at its most active.

The New Ostrich (1892)

By the kindness of Mr Keith Anstruther, of the Imperial British East Africa Company, a new species of ostrich was granted to the Zoological Society of London. The donor intended to grace the gardens with a pair, but sadly the male perished during the journey.

Up until the arrival of the female the management at the zoo had met with a great deal of difficulty in keeping their ostriches alive. According to one authority, the problems arose because the

birds couldn't discriminate between what was helpful and what was harmful to their digestion, and a curious public, accustomed to the novelty of slipping pennies into automatic machines, couldn't resist the temptation offered by the long, omnivorous throats of the ostriches, and filled them up with poisonous copper.

It was hoped that a better fate was in store for the new visitor from East Africa, for she was the first example of the species *Struthio molybdophanes* to be exhibited in England. Her general appearance was much like that of the common ostrich, but the parts of the skin not covered in plumage were a greyish blue colour, while in the common form they were flesh-coloured. There was also a difference in the eggs, as those of the new species were said to be larger and more rounded.

Vultures and Telephone Wires (1884)

In Rio de Janeiro, the beautiful and flourishing capital of Brazil, there existed a scavenger bird that was permitted to inhabit the

town by law because of its sanitary usefulness; its staple diet consisted of dung. However, this vulture had the unfortunate habit of flying low over the houses, and, being a heavy bird, caused all sorts of havoc with the newly installed telephone wires, either by breaking them or becoming entangled in them. The result was that the telephone company was forced to employ a team of assistants to wave the vultures away whenever they saw one approaching.

There seemed no remedy for the disorder except to wait until the birds had learned that it was better to fly a little higher and over the wires, or until new technology developed, allowing communication cables to be carried underground.

The Sorcery of the Electrical Telegraph (1882)

From August to November 1881, the city of Paris hosted a spectacular exhibition at the Palais de l'Industrie showcasing a spectacular display of electrical innovations from around the world. It was known as the International Exposition of Electricity, and alongside some of the electrical marvels of the day, including Edison's incandescent light bulb and Bell's telephone, was a battered old telegraph pole from Norway. Though seemingly unremarkable, the extraordinary thing about the stout piece of wood was a hole bored right through the centre of it, large enough to admit the fist of a man.

The woodcut illustrates the irregular nature of this cavity, which had been pecked out by the European green woodpecker. At first their behaviour was unfathomable, a mystery even to the shrewdest ornithologist, until the reason for their attack eventually became clear. The truth was they were being duped by the electrical humming of the pole, caused by the vibrations of the wire, into believing that insects were lurking inside, hence they spent several hours pounding a hole right through the middle of the pole.

This also explained why the Norwegian bear was regularly spotted attacking the poles; they were apparently under the impression that a swarm of bees had made their honeyed nest within.

Another instance of the witchery of the telegraph in Norway

was the disappearance of the wolves that once lived in the mountains. Since the introduction of the wires across the region their numbers began to dwindle. It was believed they had been driven away either by the humming noise made by the poles or the ensnaring appearance of the wires.

The Elderly Falcon (1875)

Dr Christoph Wilhelm Friedrich Hufeland (1762–1836) was a German physician who published a number of medical essays during his career. In particular he devoted considerable time and attention to the study of the duration of life. After his death, a forgotten paper he had written came to light, in which he asserted, as an undeniable fact, that in 1793 a falcon was brought to London from the Cape of Good Hope, South Africa, by a gentleman named Mr Selwand. The falcon was wearing a golden collar, inscribed with the words 'To His Majesty James, King of England, 1610.' If genuine, that would have made the bird at least 183 years old, when they were rarely known to make it to twenty!

It was assumed the captive must have escaped from the

custody of its royal keeper, and in order to avoid recapture had spent its long years negotiating the remotest regions of Europe and Africa. It seemed that the Fates were not to be resisted when the bird was recaptured during its dotage and returned to England.

Carrier Falcons (1893)

In Russia, an inspired naval officer, Lieutenant M. Smoiloff, succeeded in training falcons for carrying top-secret despatches in lieu of carrier pigeons. The falcon was deemed to have many advantages over the pigeon for this purpose. For a start, it was able to fly much higher, could defend itself against enemies, and was capable of performing longer journeys in a shorter time. In fact, it was calculated that the falcon's powers of expedition were about 30 per cent better than the pigeon's.

Some of the lieutenant's birds successfully carried a heavy despatch a distance of 250 miles in just over seven hours.

The Doctor's Carrier Pigeon (1880)

The relationship between man and pigeon has changed wildly over the centuries, with some cultures valuing the birds as food and others regarding them as nothing more than vermin. There have always been plenty of pigeon fanciers, however, who breed the birds specifically for their homing abilities, and in the late nineteenth century the British physician Dr Harvey John Philpot (*c.* 1833–1913) put these birds to good use by employing them as his 'unqualified assistants'. While out on his rounds, Dr Philpot would take along with him half a dozen birds in a small basket, and after seeing a patient, he would tie the prescription round the neck of one of them and let it go. The bird would fly straight home to the surgery, where the medicine was prepared by the chemist and sent directly to the patient without loss of time.

Postman Cat (1880)

The wonderful instinct of locality, which the domestic cat shared with the homing pigeon, had been put to practical use in Belgium by 1880.

Some time earlier thirty-seven cats who lived in the city of Liege were put into baskets and taken many miles into the country. They were liberated at two o'clock one afternoon, and by quarter to five on the same evening one of them had returned safe and sound to his family, while his companions arrived at their respective homes within twenty-four hours after being set free.

Following the success of this experiment it was proposed to establish a regular system of cat communication between Liege and the neighbouring villages by strapping letters and small parcels to the backs of cats, thereby relieving the overworked postman of some of his duties.

The Dog Battalion (1887)

The Kingdom of Prussia was a powerful European state in the nineteenth century, one that asserted itself as a force to be reckoned with. Following a Prussian victory against the French in the Franco-Prussian War of 1870–1871, the kingdom began strengthening its army with every fortification imaginable. The Victorians were curious to hear, in 1887, that Prussia had formed a 'watchdog battalion', made up of military dogs that were highly trained to carry news from the advance posts to the main body of the army in despatches tied round their necks. The dogs were also employed to warn the outposts of an advancing enemy during the night, and to hunt for wounded men or stragglers.

This wasn't the first time dogs had been employed to serve the military. Since at least the seventh century BC mankind has been furnishing its armies with canine allies, and still does so today. In 2011 the United States' Navy SEALs used a Belgian Malinois, called Cairo, as part of their operation to track and kill Osama Bin Laden.

Rearing Puppies in Coloured Light (1885)

A researcher named Dr Ernst Horbacewicz decided to undertake various experiments to better understand the effects different colours had on life on Earth. It had long been understood that light affected the development of living things, notably plants, which responded visibly to the sun's action. The doctor began his studies by rearing a litter of puppies, all of the same breed, in different shades of light, to determine whether or not the colours influenced the characters of the animals as they grew.

According to the results, the puppies reared in green light were of extreme cheerfulness and playfulness; those reared under an orange light were also playful, but their movements were heavy and awkward and their tempers cross and quarrelsome. Contrary to the expectations of Dr Horbacewicz, red puppies were lethargic and uninterested, highlighting the difference between a dog and a bull, as far as colour awareness was concerned. Blue and violet rays appeared to have a soothing and taming influence on the dogs, instilling in them a genial disposition. The blue light, especially, afforded steady, serious, and even studious personality traits, affirming the old belief that there was an infallible yet mysterious connection between learnedness and the colour blue.

The Affection of Dogs (1875)

In the 1870s a dog owner from America drew attention to the affectionate behaviour of man's best friend by relating how emotional his own pet, Don, a fluffy black Newfoundland dog, could be. He recalled that

> His affection for our family was very great. To be allowed to come into the house and lie down close to us was his chief happiness. He was very fond of my son, who played with him a good deal; and when the young man went away during the American Civil War, Don was greatly depressed by his absence. He'd regularly walk himself down to the station, where he'd stand until a train of cars came in; and when his friend didn't arrive in it, he'd come home with a melancholy air.
>
> At last the young man returned. It was in the evening, and

Don was lying on the piazza. As soon as he saw his friend, his exultation knew no bounds. He leaped upon him, almost knocking him to the floor, and ran round in circles, barking and showing the wildest signs of delight. All at once he turned and ran up into the garden, and came back bringing an apple, which he laid down at the feet of his young master. It was the only thing he could think of to do for him.

The Dog that Could Read (1887)

In England, the Right Honourable Sir John Lubbock MP (1834–1913) successfully taught his own pet poodle, Van, 'a little light reading'. He achieved this remarkable feat by taking identical pieces of cardboard and painting upon them a variety of simple words such as 'food', 'out', 'bone', 'tea', and so on. Then, by associating food in the dog's mind with the card bearing the word 'food', Sir John was able to train the little black poodle to pick out the card bearing that word whenever he was hungry, thereby prompting his owner to feed him. Again, when needing to go outside, Van successfully picked up the card bearing that

particular word and dropped it at his master's feet, repeating the trick with the other words accordingly.

It took the Liberal MP a considerably long time to apply this method of teaching, but his persistence allowed him to show the world what might be achieved with certain breeds of dogs when employing the correct approaches.

The Horse that Knew the Days of the Week (1875)

There was once a man from Massachusetts who owned a horse named Ruby. After being in possession of the creature for a long time, the gentleman became convinced that Ruby could tell the days of the week.

On Sunday the man used to drive his horse to church in the city of Boston, but during the rest of the week he drove to his neighbouring village, where he would call at the shops, the Post Office and various other stores. To get to Boston, he would always turn right at the end of his driveway, and to go to the village he would bear left.

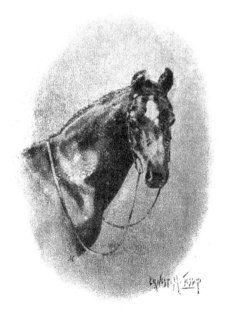

After a time, the gentleman found that on a Sunday, if he left the reins loose so Ruby could do as he pleased, he invariably turned to the right and headed to church and on other days he would instinctively turn left and take his master into the village. Ruby did this so constantly and regularly that none of the gentleman's family members were in any doubt that their horse knew when it was Sunday.

Zebras in Harnesses (1895)

Unlike horses, zebras have always been notoriously difficult to domesticate, owing to their impulsive nature and nervous disposition. There was one species of zebra, however, that was found easier to tame, and by the 1890s a merchant from the Transvaal Province, South Africa, succeeded in breaking to harness a number of Burchell's zebras. This variety was not only pretty but intelligent too. The merchant found that with a combination of gentleness, patience and firmness, it was relatively easy to train the zebras to pull a carriage.

The First Waterbuck Born in Captivity (1893)

It wasn't often that the rarer species of antelopes ever bred in captivity, and not until the late nineteenth century had the waterbuck done so. In 1893 the London Zoological Society announced that a waterbuck had been born in its gardens at Regent's Park. Not only was the calf the first of its species to be born in England, it was the only one known to have been born outside of Africa. The little creature saw the light on 4 May, and when photographed was about nine weeks old.

Its parents had come from the territories held by the East African Company, where they were captured and transported to Britain. These large antelopes were plentiful all over Africa, particularly near large swampy plains overgrown with coarse grass, tall reeds and papyrus. Their build was stout, the legs short and thick, and the hair coarse. The adult male stood about 4 feet at the shoulders and bore large ringed horns, some 30 inches in length. The female was hornless and smaller than her mate.

Both of the calf's parents seemed happy to come to the railings of their stalls to be fed by visitors to the zoo, and it was expected

that the young one would soon begin to trot up whenever he espied a biscuit bag as readily as his parents did.

The Gibbon from Borneo (1893)

At around the same time, the house near the kangaroo dens at the Zoological Gardens acquired a new resident. She was a gibbon, a *Hylobates muelleri*, who had come all the way from Borneo. The arrival of this remarkable new creature attracted considerable attention and visitors came from all over the country. Not only was she the first of her species to visit England, she was also the only known gibbon to have been captured on camera. This hadn't been without its difficulties. No matter the methods attempted by her keepers, they couldn't entice her to sit for her likeness. In the end her attention was attracted for the briefest of moments by the offer of some fruit, and in that instant the camera did its work.

Besides giving a good likeness, the photograph distinctly showed one of the chief characteristics of the gibbons: the extraordinary length of the arms, which came in most useful when swinging through the trees. Gibbons were native to the forests of south-east Asia and the Malay Archipelago, and were the only monkeys that habitually assumed an erect position when walking, just like humans. Full-grown specimens of the largest kind were about 3 feet in height, and, though gibbons were the lowest of the anthropoid apes, the skull resembled that of man more closely than any other type of primate.

5

VICTORIAN ANTHROPOLOGY

Land of the Giants (1890)

Mankind's oldest legends are dotted with tales of giants who once roamed the landscape, causing unspeakable mayhem for the regular-sized inhabitants of the Earth. From David and Goliath to Jack and the Beanstalk, so frequent were the references to oversized beings that by the end of the nineteenth century the Victorians had opened a serious inquiry as to whether or not a race of exceedingly tall men once existed on Earth but later became extinct.

One of the investigators was Count Georges Vacher de Lapouge (1854–1936), a French archaeologist who made a remarkable discovery in a prehistoric burial ground at Castelnau-le-Lez, near Montpellier. In 1890 he uncovered portions of two human skeletons from the Neolithic period, so large they must have belonged to veritable giants. One piece was from the skull of a youth, no older than eighteen years old, who stood around 7 feet tall.

In this Bronze Age burial ground, Monsieur de Lapouge also found parts of three other human bones, namely the tibia, femur and humerus, which, by his calculations, came from a man who stood nearly 12 feet tall. The remains were sent for examination by a team of professors at the Montpellier School of Medicine, who confirmed that the bones appeared to belong to a race of 'very tall' men. They concluded, from the age of the bones, that the giant must have lived at the beginning of the present geological period, and, strangely enough, an old French fable placed the cavern of a giant in the same valley of Castelnau.

The Neanderthal Bone Cave (1887)

In about 1887 explorers in Belgium were travelling through a region close to the River Meuse when they stumbled across a magnificent bone cave of great scientific interest. Upon entering, they found the floor of the cave to be made up of several beds of clay and calcareous matter, which contained ancient flint weapons revealing traces of use. They began to dig further and unearthed fragments of pottery, weapons made of bone and plates made of mammoth ivory with images of men carved into them.

Among various remains of elephants, rhinoceros, mammoths and deer were also found human skeletons, which had evidently been laid there for sepulchre. The skulls were uncommonly thick and similar in shape to that of the Neanderthal, the first example of which had only been discovered four decades earlier in Gibraltar.

Anthropologists believed that this type of skull was compatible with a high degree of intellect. The evidence found in the cave supported this theory, suggesting that these past inhabitants were capable of working the flint, utilising the bones and tusks of animals to create living utensils, making and firing clay vessels and ceremoniously burying their dead. In short, they were possessed of the rudiments of civilisation.

Contrary to the evidence revealed by this Victorian discovery, the popular belief in the twentieth century was that the Neanderthal was dim-witted, and it was supposed that the evolution and migration of modern humans around 40,000 years ago drove this simple-minded man to extinction. Yet twenty-first-century anthropologists have returned to the Victorian theory that this species of primordial hominoid was greatly astute. A study of Neanderthal skulls recently revealed that the brain was anatomically identical to that of the modern human, and, in fact, was 20 per cent larger. The Neanderthal could also process complex ideas, had the same thinking patterns as humans and could even speak.

The Nampa Figurine (1890)

In 1889 a well-drilling mission was underway in the United States to tap a source of fresh water for the new and developing frontier town of Nampa, Idaho. Work was started near the railway station where a deep borehole was drilled, running 320 feet into the earth.

The engineers engaged in the task were startled when a crude figurine of a man, carved in pumice stone and coated with rust, was flushed to the surface from the bottom of the hole. Its appearance left no doubt that it was made by human hands, and given the depth at which it was found, its age was placed many eons before the estimated arrival of men in that part of the world. Astonishingly, this made it the earliest example of human artistry ever discovered.

It had been assumed that prehistoric artwork only dated back to the Middle Palaeolithic era, which spanned from 300,000 to 30,000 years ago, but staggeringly, having been sent for examination, it was concluded that this rudimentary doll dated back to the early Quaternary Period, which began around 2.6 million years ago. To this day, the figurine remains an enigma to modern science.

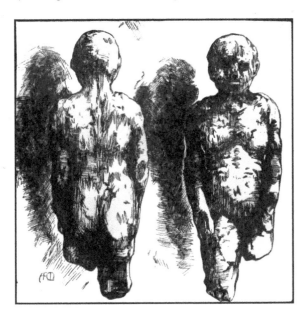

Tombs of the People of the Sea (1895)

The illustration shows an example of one of the strange prehistoric monuments that were discovered on the Balearic Islands and on the Italian island of Pantelleria. The former structures were known as *talayots*; the latter, *sesi*. These round buildings, made of rough stone, were constructed about 60 feet in diameter and up to around 25 feet high. They contained cells, or chambers, connected by passages, and after exploration it was concluded that they were ancient tombs, for skeletons were discovered inside, along with small clay vessels.

Given the similarities between these and other constructions, such as the megaliths of North Africa and the *nuraghi* of Sardinia, it was suggested that the men who built the *sesi* may have been the 'People of the Sea', a mythical race of seafaring raiders who were driven out of Egypt by Pharaohs Merneptah and Ramesses III in the thirteenth or fourteenth century BC, following several failed invasion attempts. History tells that the vanquished men were driven back towards Libya, and from there they would have passed first to Pantelleria and thence to Sardinia and onwards to the Balearic Islands.

The World's Oldest Trumpet (1893)

The woodcut represents an old Scandinavian *lur*, a type of giant, ceremonial trumpet dating back to the Bronze Age, which was discovered, almost perfectly preserved, in a bog in Sweden. This was just one of many to be found along the Baltic coast of north Germany. Each instrument, made of cast-bronze, measured between 6 and 7 feet in length and was twisted, as shown. It was believed that there were no musical instruments of the kind left in existence, making the discovery a unique find.

To play the *lur*, it was held in front of the musician, generally during a military or religious festival, and was blown into, in much the same way as a modern brass instrument would be, though it lacked any keys or finger holes. Some of these ancient trumpets were heard playing once again, 2,000 or 3,000 years since they were lost to history, at a concert given by Dr Angul Hammerich (1848–1931), the Danish music historian, in the Royal Chapel, Copenhagen.

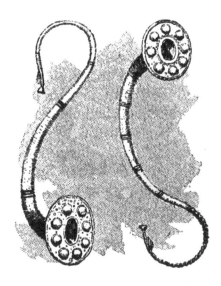

The Cave Villages of Mexico (1892)

During the 1880s the Norwegian explorer Mr Carl Lumholtz (1851–1922) was engaged in a five-year study of the ancient cave dwellings of New Mexico. By 1892 he had published an account of his researches, explaining that the most remarkable caves he had visited were situated in the state of Chihuahua at the headwaters of the Piedras Verdes River, 6,850 feet above sea level. They opened in the walls of a canyon, and some were 50 feet from floor to ceiling. Inside were entire villages, though the houses had long since been deserted. Some of the properties, constructed from volcanic rock, were three storeys high and provided with windows, cruciform doors and stone staircases. Many contained collections of large, intricately decorated jars, standing exactly as their past owners had left them.

On the shady side of the canyon the caves were reserved for burial grounds, and the bodies discovered there had become mummified by the saltpetre of the rock. In some instances the remains were so well preserved that the hair, eyebrows and features were nearly perfect. The hair was said to be softer and wavier than that of the indigenous Mexican, and the features resembled those of the existing Moqui and Zuni tribes.

The Moqui Indians were so unlike the ordinary Indians of the north that the American trappers used to call them Welsh Indians, believing them to be the descendants of the followers of Prince Madoc, who, according to legend, sailed from Wales to America in the year 1170, hundreds of years before Signor Christopher Columbus (*c.* 1451–1506) had even been born. It was certainly of interest to Mr Lumholtz that the Moquis weaved a striped blanket similar in appearance to the traditional Welsh blanket.

The Underground City (1893)

Caesar, Pliny, Tacitus and other authors of the ancient world once spoke of secret underground cities in the European region formerly known as Gaul, where the inhabitants of the land retreated in times of war. Though the Victorians suspected such notions were nothing more than pagan legends, by 1893 the foundations of some of these sanctuaries were at long last excavated, and the figure shows a plan of one discovered deep below the modern-day streets of Brétigny-sur-Orge, south of Paris.

These buried metropolises were elaborate works built on a

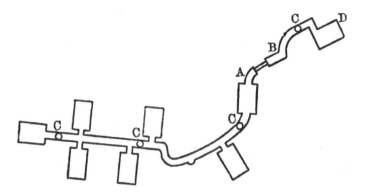

symmetrical plan, with main galleries branching from a common centre and connecting galleries spreading out like a web. The winding character of the gallery was all part of the design, and the rectangular side chambers were used as stores and living rooms. The galleries were, on average, about 5 feet high and 3 feet wide. At A B there was a constriction in height for defensive purposes. A foeman entering the refuge at D was obliged to crawl like a snake through a narrow passage raised above the ground between A and B, so that a sentinel at A could cleave the intruder's head off as soon as it appeared. Holes were also pierced through the walls at sharp angles, to enable the defenders to stab their enemies as they passed along the tunnels.

For the citizens of the towns, these refuges were well equipped for sustaining life for a considerable period of time. The air-vents, C, C, C, C, were round holes penetrating to the surface of the ground, and filled with loose stones for purifying the air. Underground wells, or springs, provided the inhabitants with fresh water, and fireplaces were cut in the soft rock. Such artificial caves would have been cool in summer and snug in winter, with the roaring fires crackling as the villagers seated themselves on the benches that were also carved out of rock.

The Hittite Inscriptions (1887)

Until the nineteenth century the Hittites were nothing more than a legendary race of ancient people from Anatolia, or Asia Minor, who supposedly lived during the Neolithic era. These men were said to have been ahead of their time, possessing skills and knowledge that other civilisations didn't acquire until centuries later. Yet the only evidence as to this nation's existence were passages in the Old Testament, and many scholars doubted that the Hittites ever existed at all. That was until archaeologists in Syria finally stumbled upon the first physical clues left behind after the Hittite Empire collapsed at the end of the Bronze Age. These were carved tablets, written in a mysterious, ancient language, similar to Egyptian hieroglyphics, that nobody could read.

By 1887, however, the key to deciphering them had at last been found by Captain Claude Conder (1848–1910), a British explorer and antiquarian. He published the formulae for translating the ancient hieroglyphics as well as the rules of grammar, phonetic values, the history of the discoveries and the legends of the Hittite gods and goddesses.

STONE BOWL FOUND AT BABYLON.

INSCRIPTION ON A STONE BOWL. **SILVER BOSS.**

The Lost Dwarfs of the Atlas Mountains (1893)

Just as tales had been abound since time immemorial about a giant race of men that once roamed the earth, so too were there stories of a forgotten tribe of tiny people who inhabited the southern regions of Morocco. It was said that only a handful of Europeans had ever caught a glimpse of these fabled dwarves, and in about 1892 the Victorian adventurers Mr Walter Burton Harris (1866–1933) and the Right Honourable Robert Bontine Cunninghame Graham MP (1852–1936) embarked on a journey to catch a glimpse of the mythical people for themselves.

The locals of the region attested that these tiny citizens inhabited the upper ranges of the Atlas Mountains, and they brought good luck to anyone fortunate enough to spot them.

'The dwarfs are very brave and active,' one observer affirmed, 'and are great hunters of ostriches, having small, swift horses that are known by a name meaning "those that drink the wind", for they are fed on a diet of dates and camels' milk. The dwarfs are so agile that they can jump over three camels standing side by side. They use fire arms, and sometimes bows and poisoned arrows.'

During their travels through the remote region at the foot of the snow-capped mountains, the two explorers did indeed encounter a handful of men who were no more than 4 feet tall. After speaking to the dwarves and meeting some of their family members, the travellers learned that they ranged from 3 feet 7 inches to 3 feet 9 inches high, and were otherwise characterised by a yellow skin, broad, square faces, Mongolian eyes, and red hair of a woolly texture.

Following a comprehensive study, Mr Harris concluded that the tribe was descended from the native *Shleh* clans, and over the course of evolution their growth had become stunted due to the altitude at which they lived, their poverty and a relative scarceness of food.

Old Hats, New Fashions (1875)

Far across the Indian Ocean was a remote archipelagic chain known as the Nicobar Islands, which fell under the jurisdiction of the British Empire. It was said that the indigenous Nicobarese people, who had relatively little contact with the Western world, developed a passion for the cast-off hats of European explorers of the region. In fact, so great was their interest in the white man's headdress that a regular trade in old hats was established between Calcutta and the Nicobars. The value of the article was measured in coconuts, the only produce of the islands, and the Nicobarian's ideal hat was said to be a tall white one – the taller the better – with a black band round it. Such a specimen was worth from fifty to sixty-five coconuts, and no native would be seen without his top hat on whenever he went fishing.

The Stupendous Statue (1893)

In 1881 a British railway contractor, searching for ballast in a jungle of the province of Pegu, Burma, accidentally came upon an enormous recumbent statue of Buddha which had been lost to sight and memory for over a century. The illustration represents this curious work, which was examined by an expert who at first dated its construction to the fifteenth century, though other authorities believed it was created much earlier, way back in the first century AD. In fact, many historians suspected King Migadepa commissioned the work in about the year 994 in honour of his conversion to Buddhism.

The whole effigy measured 181 feet long and 46 feet high at the shoulders, making it the second largest Buddha statue in the world. It was finely proportioned and built of brick, and, following its rediscovery, work was begun to restore it to its former glory. The statue was dubbed the 'Shwethalyaung Reclining Buddha', and remains a popular tourist attraction to this day.

It wasn't just the jungles of Pegu that were filled with lost treasures. Indeed, the whole of Burma offered the Victorians a rich field for archaeological exploration. On the shores of the Irrawaddy River, at a place called Akauk Taung, there was a cliff 2 miles long and 300 feet high, which was carved with innumerable statues of Buddha, tier upon tier from top to bottom. Some of the figures were 20 feet high, making the cliff a spectacular sight indeed.

The Human Foot (1890)

Dr Thomas S. Ellis was a surgeon who was fascinated by the form and function of the human foot. He conducted many studies into its anatomy, and his results were published in a book, *The Human Foot – Its Form and Structure, Functions and Clothing*, in which he pointed out some curious facts.

He noted that in some ancient statues the second toe was depicted as being much longer than the great toe. Dr Ellis affirmed that while this feature sometimes occurred in modern humans it wasn't the rule, for in general the big toe was longest. This phenomenon, like the difference in length between the ring and the index finger, was therefore a variation.

It was, however, a fact known to biologists that primitive primates tended to possess longer middle toes and shorter big toes. During the act of walking, the line of leverage passed through the animals' middle toes, particularly the second digit, signifying its importance for movement and balance by its greater length. It was perhaps a sign of the evolution of *Homo sapiens* that prehistoric sculptors depicted their contemporaries with longer second toes than the Victorians possessed, indicating a distinct change of gait in modern men.

With regard to walking, Ellis advised that the manner which kept the big toes almost parallel to each other was best for steady progression, since it allowed the joints and muscles of the foot to rest during the brief intervals between steps. He condemned the military position, with the toes turned outwards, as much more fatiguing, as this method of walking kept the joints and muscles under continual strain. Moreover, he assured that those who suffered from flat feet would find that the condition would eventually disappear by adopting a springing motion from heel to tiptoe when the foot was kept straight. Dancing, too, was declared beneficial in correcting this defect.

The doctor also observed that the North American Indians walked with a straight foot pointing forwards, or with the toes turned slightly inwards, while the Europeans tended to walk with their toes vaguely outwards. Since the red man lived by the chase, the doctor deduced that the white man's habit was a physical shortcoming produced by the effects of Western civilisation.

Many readers found Dr Ellis' advice regarding footwear the most valuable part of his book. His opinion was that ill-made stockings and badly fitting shoes did much mischief to one's feet. A stocking, he instructed, should be made with a separate stall on each foot for the big toe to slide into, in order to promote unrestricted movement. As these digits aided balance, it was essential that the toes weren't confined too tightly. Furthermore, in order to make a perfectly fitting shoe or boot, in addition to measuring the length and girth of the foot it was also desirable to obtain contour lines of the foot. For this purpose the author devised a foot-stand and pedistat, which were illustrated in his work. From these measurements a cast could be made, representing the foot as it stood on a level surface, and from this a shoemaker could construct the perfect pair of shoes, the most comfortable the owner would ever wear.

The Disappearing Little Toe (1890)

Dr Ellis wasn't the only medical man engaged in the study of podiatry. A German investigator named Herr Pfitzner made a number of noteworthy observations on the small toe. He found that in the case of 31 per cent of men and nearly 42 per cent of women the foot's fifth digit was in the process of becoming extinct, owing to the terminal bones slowly fusing into one piece. The phenomenon was equally common among children, and wasn't a consequence of wearing ill-fitting shoes.

As humans continued evolving from primates, the line of leverage, through walking, shifted from the middle toe over to the big toe. This prompted the big toe to evolve as well, growing in size in order to bear the body's weight, with a progressive decrease in size and function of the other toes, right the way down to the smallest at the end. The increasing loss of function in the little toe was proved by the fact that in a large number of cases investigated by Herr Pfitzner it had become nothing more than a stump, sometimes without even a nail, or often just the merest trace of one. Pfitzner believed it was only a matter of time – perhaps a few tens of thousands of years or so – before the small toe, completely devoid of functionality, would vanish from the human race.

Mankind's Lost Magnetic Sense (1884)

On 3 October 1883 Lord Kelvin delivered a lecture before the Midland Institute in Birmingham on the 'six gateways of knowledge', using the word 'six' as a supposed improvement on the 'five gateways of knowledge', or, more commonly, the five human senses. As was commonly known, these were sight, sound, smell, taste and touch. Lord Kelvin argued that the sixth or additional gateway was the sense of heat. This, he suggested, probably extended to magnetism as well, and was thus dubbed the 'magnetic sense'. As such, the phenomenon of clairvoyance could be easily explained by the fact that some people were in tune with their magnetic sense much better than others, and could sense the presence of magnetism acting upon their person. Unaware of what they were picking up on, they interpreted the sensation as the presence of some invisible being, perhaps even a spirit from beyond the grave.

The notion of a magnetic sense was first propounded around 100 years earlier, but until Lord Kelvin's lecture it hadn't been well publicised. His address thus prompted a series of experiments under the sponsorship of the Physical Society. In consequence, several people were found who, when their heads were placed between the poles of a strong electromagnet, could tell when it was turned on by the sensation of an unpleasant feeling in the head. A person suffering from neuralgia also felt this pain increase when they were standing in the magnetic field.

Whether this indicated a real magnetic sense, or merely a strain produced in the head through their ordinary sense of touch, remained a mystery until the 1970s, when a team of researchers revisited the subject. Through their experiments they discovered that the human nose consists of bones and sinews that may once have been receptive to the earth's magnetic field, thereby acting as a kind of in-built compass, which, during the course of evolution, became functionless. The presence of such magnetic bones offers an explanation for how homing pigeons and other migratory animals manage to successfully navigate vast distances across the globe, and also points to the likely etymology of the old expression 'follow your nose'.

An Extraordinary Swimming Feat (1875)

Mr Thomas Topham (c. 1710–1749) was once known as 'the Strong Man of Islington', for he was famed throughout the land for his incredible feats of strength. He could lift 2 hundredweight on his little finger, raise a 6-foot-long oak table from the ground with his teeth and heave a horse over a turnpike gate. Since his death there had been few contenders to claim his legendary title, and by the 1870s the Victorians were clamouring to crown another present-day Hercules. A gauntlet was thrown down to members of the public, challenging anybody brave enough to swim a distance of 20 miles in one go; a deed so incredible the victor would be pronounced the new Thomas Topham.

This remarkable achievement was successfully executed on 3 July 1875 by Captain Matthew Webb (1848–1883), an amateur swimmer in the mercantile marine. He swam along the River Thames from Blackwall Pier to Gravesend, and arrived at his destination at the end of his 20-mile journey in just four hours and fifty-three minutes.

From first to last the captain touched nothing but water and had no aid of any kind, except that about halfway through he received a swig of brandy. His style of swimming was a slow, steady stroke of the arms and a vigorous action of the legs, the head being kept down so that the water flowed over his mouth at every stroke. He never once rested, and only now and then varied the performance by taking a few strokes on his right side. There was a strong current down river in his favour, but in spite of this the public was amazed by his efforts and wondered how on earth anyone was able to remain so long in the water without cramp or exhaustion.

Not content to leave it there, the following month Captain

Webb made the courageous decision to double the distance by attempting to swim the English Channel, completely unaided.

'Why should anybody do such a thing?' was the general response when the British public read about the captain's plans in the daily newspapers. 'Why would a man imperil his life in the middle of the sea, or perhaps lay the seeds of some future illness by such a prolonged immersion in cold salt water?'

'I thought I might have a try,' was the daring merchantman's response.

On 25 August 1875, rubbed down with porpoise oil, he dived off a crowded Dover Pier and began his long swim. Several small boats, filled with food and ale to sustain him during the twenty-two-hour journey, and newspaper journalists to keep track of his every stroke, accompanied him. His trek was far from smooth, and after being stung by jellyfish, battling the rough sea and suffering from cold and exhaustion, Webb finally landed on the shores of Calais. At 10.41 a.m. the valiant captain made history by becoming the world's first person to have swum across the English Channel.

By 1883 the daredevil had set his sights on an even greater swimming challenge, deemed by many to be the greatest – and most foolish – attempt of his life. Amid cheers and waves from the gathered crowd, on 24 July the thirty-five-year-old plunged into a terrific whirlpool 2 miles below the clashing Niagara Falls, having resolved to become the first swimmer to navigate these treacherous waters. Sadly, the freezing currents were too strong, and Captain Webb paid with his life.

Watching the Circulation of Blood (1880)

By the 1880s a German physician, Dr Carl Hüter (1838–1882), of Greifswald, had discovered a simple but ingenious plan for observing the blood circulating through the vessels of a living person. The head of the patient was first slotted into a frame, which carried a support for a lamp and microscope. Next, the lower lip was drawn out, and, with the inner surface facing upwards, was fastened by clips to the table of the microscope. A strong light was then directed upon the exposed lip-surface, and when viewed through the powerful objective lens the fine network of vessels could be examined.

At first sight Dr Hüter observed that the veins and capillaries seemed to be filled with a red injection, and on focussing in closer the flow of the current was clearly detected, being made apparent from the movement of the red blood cells. White cells were spotted now and again, visible as tiny specks in the blood stream.

The doctor felt sure that his discovery would prove most useful in medical practice, as it was able to indicate with sufficient accuracy any irregularity or abnormality in the circulation of the blood.

The Brains of Men and Women (1892)

At an assembly of the Medical Society of London, the illustrious British psychiatrist Sir James Crichton-Browne FRS (1840–1938) expressed his opinion that there was a measurable difference between the intellects of men and women. Furthermore, he had firm evidence to back up his claim, discovered as a result of his examinations of the structure of the two types of brain.

He was able to demonstrate that the average female brain was significantly lighter than the average male organ, and he had calculated that this would still be so if women were as large and heavy as men. Moreover, he explained that the gravity of the 'grey matter' of the male brain was higher than that of the female, while the specific gravity of the 'white matter' was the same in both. The former matter was known to be where the 'thinking' functions of the brain took place, whereas the latter acted merely as the intermediaries between the different parts of the organ.

Though the total supply of blood to the brain was found to be much the same in men and women, the distribution of blood was different in the two sexes: the larger part going to the front of the male brain and to the back of the female brain. The front, Sir James explained, was where natural impulses, decisions and unconscious thoughts took place, while the back was mainly concerned with the perception of sensory functions.

Convinced by the accuracy of his research, he uttered a warning to all men against over-educating women. 'Instructing them as if they are men is a grave mistake, for their brains are not designed to function like a man's,' declared the small-minded psychiatrist.

The Brain of Laura Bridgman (1892)

Miss Laura Bridgman (1829–1889) was a remarkable American lady who shot to fame in the 1840s. Her remarkable life story moved many a reader of Mr Charles Dickens' *American Notes*, in which the author described Miss Bridgman's revolutionary education.

When she was young, long before her childish mind could realise the meaning of what she saw and heard, she tragically lost her sight, hearing, ability to speak, and nearly all sense of taste and smell after contracting scarlet fever at the age of just two. All hope for her future was lost, and many members of her family wanted little more to do with her; but in 1837 the director of the Perkins Institution for the Blind, in Boston, heard about the young girl's plight and felt his institution could offer her a form of education. Over the years she was taught how to speak using sign language; read; sew; carry out domestic duties; recognise individuals, and even point out locations on a map.

Consequently, visitors in their thousands flocked to the school in order to catch a glimpse of this remarkable woman at work, and Miss Bridgman became a household name all across the world.

Over the years she embraced her family's Baptist religion, and even penned inspirational poems. In fact, she became quite fond of writing, and in 1881 composed an articulate and sensitive letter to Mrs Garfield, the widow of the assassinated President James Garfield (1831–1881), expressing her deepest sympathy for the death of the president who Miss Bridgman had held in the highest esteem.

In 1878 the American teacher and psychologist Professor Granville Stanley Hall (1844–1924) began to carefully examine this incredible lady. He noted that although she could feel mechanical vibrations, she couldn't hear even the loudest noise. Rotation made her giddy, and her sense of touch was thrice acute. In her mind she was eccentric, lacking the data of thought but not the power to reason, and was exceptionally emotional.

When Miss Bridgman died, at the age of sixty, her brain was subjected to thorough examination by Dr Henry Herbert Donaldson (1857–1938), of Clark University, who found it to weigh 1,200 grams, which was a little below the average weight of 1,275 grams for the female Anglo-American brain. However, as she was a small woman, it wasn't considered abnormally small. Upon careful dissection there was found a defect in the centre known to regulate the power of speech, and also in the occipital lobe, which controlled the eyesight. The temporal lobe, in the part of the brain that governed the retention of optical memories, was also faulty around the tips. Other defects were observable as well, but it was concluded there was nothing of a criminal or insane character about them.

The Calculating Boy (1892)

Another exceptional person who lived in the nineteenth century was Signor Jacques Inaudi (1867–1950), a young shepherd from Italy whose feats of mental computation astonished academics from across the world. This young man was found to be possessed of the incredible gift of what was termed 'double action of the brain'. Signor Inaudi could perform the most problematic calculations while speaking or listening to others 'as though there was a calculating machine inside his head.' At a demonstration in front of members of the French Academy of Sciences, he was asked to subtract the following numbers, which were simply called out to him:

$$4,123,547,238,445,523,831$$
$$1,248,126,138,234,129,910$$

While in the middle of a conversation with those around him he gave the answer correctly. When requested to multiply 452 by 538 he did so at once, and almost immediately gave the answer to the puzzle what is the number whose cube added to its square makes 3,600? He was then asked to square the number 4,801, cut away a figure, divide the difference by six and give the square root of the result. While explaining to the meeting how he performed the first subtraction he suddenly announced 'I have found the answer,' and gave it correctly.

Inaudi, who was born in Piedmont, was entirely self-taught. His methods of computing were peculiar even to himself, and he could solve questions in his head that would ordinarily require a person of average intellect to use algebra, and even then it would take several minutes to work out the answer. The young man was declared a prodigy, and he was thoroughly examined by a commissioner of the academy in order to attempt to understand him in greater depth. He later embarked on a world tour with travelling showmen who had heard of his incredible gift.

The Danger of Mental Excitement (1875)

'Bad news weakens the action of the heart,' the Victorians were warned by the learned medical men who had conducted detailed studies into the physical effects of mental excitement. 'It oppresses the lungs, destroys the appetite, stops digestion and partially suspends all the functions of the system.'

It was also found that an emotion of shame flushed the face, while the sensation of fear blanched it, joy illuminated it and an instant thrill electrified a million nerve endings. Surprise spurred the pulse into a gallop. Delirium infused great energy, though too powerful an emotion often killed the body by triggering a heart attack or a stroke. Scribes of the ancient world warned that Chilon of Sparta, Diagoras of Rhodes and Sophocles the playwright all died of joy at the Olympic Games. The news of a military defeat killed the Spanish king, Philip V (1683–1746), while the doorkeeper of the United States Congress expired upon hearing of the surrender of Lord Cornwallis (1738–1805) at the Siege of Yorktown on 19 October 1781, an event that paved the way for American independence.

Over the centuries eminent public speakers had often been known to die in the midst of impassioned bursts of eloquence, or else shortly afterwards, when the deep emotion that spurred their speech suddenly subsided. All this considered, Victorian health officials generally dissuaded periods of mental overexcitement in members of society.

A Study of Dreams (1890)

In New York, Dr Julius Nelson made an interesting study of his dreams, having recorded and analysed no fewer than 4,000 of them during his lifetime. He found that the evening and nightly

dreams were more or less connected with the events of the day, those of the night generally being the more alarming or terrifying. Dreams of the early morning were the pleasantest and most vivid, perhaps because the dreamer's mind was rested and therefore more composed.

Furthermore, the doctor concluded that a person's dreams varied with the seasons: those at the end of the year, in December, being the most vivid, and those of March and April the dullest.

His findings tended to concur with those of a German investigator, who also found that sleeping on the left side was apt to cause bad dreams. It was therefore advised that people prone to night terrors should try sleeping on their right, or else on their back.

The Explanation of Inspiration (1895)

The inspiration of genius has been a mystery to the greatest minds of every era, but the Victorians lived in the first truly scientific age, when psychologists began striving to elucidate the complex processes of the human mind.

The distinguished German author Herr Johann Wolfgang von Goethe (1749–1832), who was widely admired by the late Victorians for his scientific spirit, expressed the surprising opinion that 'no productiveness of the highest kind, no remarkable discovery, no great thought which bears fruit and has results, is in the power of anyone: such things are elevated above all earthly control, and man must consider them as unexpected gifts from God, which he must receive and venerate with joyful thanks.'

Herr Goethe argued that inspiration had nothing to do with the human mind at all, and was, in fact, an invisible force of nature, akin to divine inspiration, influencing mankind however it pleased. A man thus blessed unconsciously resigned himself to the care of this heavenly force, all the while believing he was acting from his own free will and impulse, though in actuality he was being guided down a specific pathway in life. In such cases a man could thus be considered an instrument in a higher government of the world; a vessel found worthy for the reception of a divine influence.

He believed there was also a productiveness of another kind, one that guided the contemplative man through the execution of a plan, or in other words, helped him link together a long chain of thought, the end of which had already been predetermined. This same method was applied to artistic and literary souls engaged in the production of a work of art.

Contrary to this stance, messieurs Jacques Passy and Alfred Binet (1857–1911), two French psychologists, interviewed the most eminent French writers and dramatists of the day – including messieurs Alphonse Daudet (1840–1897), Victorien Sardou (1831–1908), François Coppée (1842–1908) and Edmond de Goncourt (1822–1896) – and asked them about their experiences of influence. Literary composition, the psychologists concluded, didn't manifest itself in the way Goethe described. The belief in some form of artistic hallucination, or artists being influenced by the seasons, the environment or artificial excitants, was, in their opinion, unfounded. Instead, the work of artistic creation demanded full self-possession and depended not only on the imagination but also on the artist's reason and common sense.

The drive to work, they explained, was entirely of a psychological nature: the composer would find himself in a particular emotional state, which arose directly from the subject matter, and would feel compelled to express his ideas in some medium or another. An author would either give his own thoughts to a character, or else he would seek to forget his own personality and try to enter into that of the fictitious character. When in the right frame of mind, he would have the ability to enter into a state that might be called inspiration, in which he could almost listen to the conversation of his characters. Mental images were thus, in the view of Messieurs Passy and Binet, of little or no importance in composition.

Though Victorian scientists found this study interesting, the findings were in no way conclusive, for they were based upon the experiences of just a handful of authors. It was well known to nineteenth-century philosophers that where genius lacked, art was used to supplement it, and although most, if not all, of the writers examined were consummately creative, none were considered to possess the highest order of genius, like that of Shakespeare, or Goethe, for example. They were, therefore, likely to fail in the diviner kind of inspiration, which Goethe described, and to work rather by an earthlier form, which didn't necessitate self-surrender and relied merely on common sense.

As to an 'artistic hallucination', some authors claimed to have experienced it. Monsieur Gustave Flaubert (1821–1880), the great French novelist and amateur psychologist, was one such person, and he described his experiences to the art critic, Monsieur Henri Taine, in a letter.

'In pathological hallucination there is always terror,' he explained. 'You feel your personality escape you, and believe you are going to die. In poetic vision, on the contrary, there is joy: it is something which enters into you. It is none the less true that one no longer knows where one is.'

As Monsieur Flaubert was subjected to both types of hallucination, his testimony was therefore considered reliable.

Regarding mental images, Mr Charles Dickens (1812–1870) and several other eminent authors described how in their minds' eyes they actually saw the scenes they so vividly depicted in their literary creations. As for the environment and the influence of the seasons, the biographies of great men were full of evidence that proved their productivity was much affected by the weather and their surroundings. The deductions of Passy and Binet were therefore dismissed, and investigations into the workings of the mind – and, indeed, the influence of inspiration – continue well into the twenty-first century.

Absorbing Studies (1875)

The French mathematician Monsieur Joseph Privat de Molières (1677–1742) was well known for absorbing himself in his studies to such an extent that he became almost insensible to everything surrounding him. One famous incident was the time when he paused in the street to follow up an intricate problem, and a shoeblack removed his silver shoe-buckles, replacing them with a pair made of iron, without the mathematician being aware of it. On another occasion, when he was in the midst of his midnight studies, an armed burglar suddenly appeared demanding money. Without even rising from his chair, Monsieur Molières pointed out where it was kept, and when the man had taken it and gone, he forgot to raise the alarm.

This, and no doubt countless other incidents, served to prove that the mind can become so absorbed in a particular activity that it doesn't have the capacity to process anything else.

Honest Men (1875)

Monsieur Alexandre Dumas père (1802–1870) was an illustrious French writer of novel expedients, perhaps most famous for composing *The Three Musketeers*. Whenever he gave a dinner to a company of commercial worthies, he devised the following method for deciding the time when the inferior wine was to be produced. He instructed his servants to put the best bottle on the table at the beginning of the meal while his guests' heads were clear.

'Then,' he said, 'watch the conversation, and as soon as you hear any single one of the company say, "I, who am an honest man ... " you may be sure that all their heads have gone astray, and you can serve up any rubbish you choose.'

Judging by Appearances (1892)

Mr Henry Frith (1840–1910) was an Irish author who published several books on the art of evaluating a person's character by simply observing the lines on their hand, reading their body language or analysing their handwriting.

'Every action of an individual is characteristic of that particular individual,' Mr Frith explained, 'and indicates the character of his mind; it is the outward and visible sign of the inward spirit. The gait, the mode of carrying the head, the movement of the arms, all indicate the manner of men we are, and all these traits must be studied from the living models we see every day.'

Despite the proverbial folly of judging a person purely by their appearance, Frith asserted there was no doubt a person's involuntary actions offered a significant insight upon which their character might be judged. However, certain authorities believed that a great danger lay in 'dabbling' in the art of character reading and the drawing of definite conclusions about

a person's character under what were only ever meant to be general, non-specific laws. Frith was unmoved by the barrage of criticism he received, citing the forehead as the ideal feature from which one could form the basis of an opinion pertaining to one's character.

'When we were young,' he elucidated, 'a high forehead was always pointed out to us as a type of great intellect and natural talent. A low forehead was taken to represent a want of cleverness.'

Following a period of study into this belief, Frith deemed that the reality was somewhat different. The reading man, who was stored with knowledge and had the faculty for learning, was generally possessed of a high forehead, the various bumps indicating his natural or acquired tastes. He was the complier: the industrious, well-informed man, a good preacher, perhaps, and a man of cramming. He was full of information from reading and not necessarily from observation or life experience.

The low, wide band of forehead, previously supposed to belong to a man of lesser intellect, was in fact quite the opposite. These foreheads belonged to men of imaginative, clever and intuitively sharp characters, and were, curiously, often the writers of adventure literature.

In short, it was concluded that there was more natural talent inside the low forehead than behind the high one.

Colour Music (1895)

The influence of colour on life was a subject that received considerable attention from psychologists and physiologists of the late nineteenth century. Through various tests it was proved that red light stimulated the human senses, whereas blue light soothed the nerves. Curious particulars were also collected regarding the influence of colour on intellectual activity. The great musical composer Herr Wilhelm Richard Wagner (1813–1883), for example, draped his study with satin hangings of rose or blue colour, depending on the type of inspiration he craved, and always took them with him on his journeys.

In 1879 professors William Edward Ayrton (1847–1908) and John Perry (1850–1920), the well-known physicists, read a paper before the Physical Society of London, in which they proposed the introduction of a new form of Japanese art into civilised Europe, having recently returned to England from the East. This consisted in throwing coloured lights on screens, or even onto the clouds, and compounding or harmonising the colours in an artistic manner so as to excite an emotion of pleasure similar to that derived from hearing fine music. The pair had been inspired by the people of Japan, among whom this visual art was practised. At first, however, their idea fell on unresponsive ears, but it soon caught on in the form of electrical fountains, devised by the engineer Sir Francis Bolton (1831–1887), in which different coloured lights were projected on the rising and falling spray, producing a pleasurable and harmonious effect.

In 1893 the British artist Mr Alexander Wallace Rimington (c. 1853–1918) introduced another incarnation of the art. It had long been known that a certain analogy existed between the spectrum of light and the octave of sound, and that both were based on waves of vibration through the air. Mr Rimington thereby devised what became known as a 'colour organ' to throw harmonious beams of coloured light on a screen by playing a musical keyboard, thus composing what he termed 'colour music'.

The Secret of Longevity (1875)

Over the centuries there have been people from every walk of life who would complain about being tired of living, hardly caring to hear about growing to a grand old age. Such readers are advised to skip to the next article, for the Victorians laid claim to the discovery of a recipe for longevity, outlined herewith.

An Indian contemporary related the story of a native gentleman who died at the respectable age of 109. He was a votary of the holy shrine of Brindabun, an ancient town in the north of the country, and passed the last four decades of his life in deep meditation underneath a tree. Sustenance simply comprised *peera* – a type of Indian sweetmeat – and milk. Quiet contemplation, fresh air and a modest diet were therefore all that were required to grow old in the most inexpensive yet effective way.

The Electrical Test of Death (1875 and 1880)

Although cases of burying people alive were rare, they nevertheless happened every now and again when a person fell into a deep, death-like sleep. It was therefore rather fortunate that the late Victorians discovered a reliable way for testing whether someone was alive or dead. This was dubbed 'the electrical test of death', and claimed to indicate the total absence of vitality in a corpse.

It was observed by some medical men that two or three hours after the heart had stopped, all the muscles of the body completely lost their excitability, that is to say, when stimulated by electricity they no longer contracted. It followed that if the muscles of the supposedly dead person's limbs and trunk were subjected to a strong electric shock, say five or six hours after the alleged time of passing, and no contractile response ensued, it was safe to certify that death had occurred. It was believed that no faint, trance or coma, however deep, could prevent the manifestation of electrical muscular excitability, so the electrocution of a suspected corpse proved an infallible method for preventing any more unfortunate people being buried alive.

For occasions when an electricity supply wasn't at hand, a medical gentleman of Cremona, northern Italy, proposed an alternative death-detection method. He had discovered that if a drop of ammonia was injected beneath the skin, a red spot appeared if the patient was still alive. If they were already dead, no such effect followed.

Handy Marks of Handicraft (1890)

In the days before fingerprinting technology and DNA testing were available, the identification of dead bodies often proved problematic. Many were the cases of parish clerks and civil registrars, unsure of what names to enter in their register books, simply declaring that the corpse of 'a stranger' had been found and duly buried in the local churchyard, or that the body of 'a drowned sailor' had been washed up on shore and provided with a decent Christian burial.

The field of criminal forensic science was still in its infancy prior to the turn of the twentieth century, but in France Monsieur Alphonse Bertillon (1853–1914), the director of the identification department at the Prefecture of Police, Paris, began applying photography to study the physical peculiarities engendered by different occupations. He theorised that if the trade of a murdered person could be determined by examining his hands, it would be an important clue as to his identity.

Monsieur Bertillon found that the hand of a navvy lost its fine lines, and a callosity appeared where the spade handle rubbed on the skin. Tin-plate workers had hands that were covered with little cracks produced by the acid used in soldering. The hands of lace-workers were, on the contrary, smooth, but callosities were apt to grow on the front of their shoulders, and blisters to appear upon their backs, owing to the friction of the loom straps. The thumbs and first joints of the right hands of metal-founders often sported large blisters, while their left hands were scarred with sparks from the metal.

Thanks to Bertillon's dedication, the technique known as anthropometry was introduced to the police force in order to help identify both victims and criminals by examining their physical irregularities. This was the first forensic scientific system to be adopted by the police in the solving of crime, and Bertillon soon earned a first-class reputation in the world of criminology. Even the great fictional detective Sherlock Holmes was credited in *The Hound of the Baskervilles* as being the 'second highest expert in Europe' after Monsieur Bertillon!

Pictures in Dead Eyes (1895)

It was often noted that the mechanics of the camera were similar to those of the eye. Indeed, the inventors of the former took their inspiration from the structure of the latter, and by 1895 it was supposed that a final picture might be found imprinted on the retina of a dead person, just as the camera fixed an image on to photographic plates. If true, this fact would have proved particularly beneficial in the solving of murders, as the likeness of the culprit would have become imprinted in the victim's eye.

A researcher named Dr Ellerslie Wallace began investigating this supposed phenomenon, though he didn't expect a positive outcome owing to the fact that a certain amount of time was required for the picture to make a lasting impression on the retina. Furthermore, the difficulty of transferring the image onto a viewable medium, such as a photographic print, would have been great.

That being said, an experiment was carried out where a condemned man on the scaffold, whose eyes had been kept in darkness, was told to fix them on a certain object before the trapdoor opened. Miraculously, a microscopic examination of his lifeless eyes showed an inverted image of the object in each, though they were only faint. It was hoped that technology would one day find a way of photographing these final imprints and convert them into useable images.

This hypothetical phenomenon became known as optography, and though it was a prevalent subject of study in the twentieth century, forensic science has so far failed in every attempt to verify the theory.

6

MEDICAL RESEARCH

Projecting Microscopic Views (1887)

The development of medicine was emphatic during the Victorian era. A new understanding of science was invalidating the medical practices of days gone by, when mercury was thought to heal wounds and bloodletting was seen as a cure for many ailments.

By 1887 Professor Salomon Stricker (1834–1898), an experimental pathologist from Vienna, had succeeded in projecting, on to a white screen, the views of objects as seen through the microscope, magnified from six to 8,000 times. This was a revolutionary breakthrough and was achieved by means of an arc lamp, enclosed in a camera that had powerful magnifying lenses. The light of the arc lamp, the equivalent of 4,000 candlepower, was shone through the microscopic bodies, which were placed on glass slides, and by means of the camera lenses, their images were projected on the white screen. In this way it was possible to teach to a whole class at once the secrets of anatomical structure.

Breeding and Killing Microbes (1895)

Thanks in part to the development of the microscope, scientists of the nineteenth century were able to glean a greater understanding of microbiology. Experts in the field, including Herren Ferdinand Cohn (1828–1898), Robert Koch (1843–1910) and Monsieur Louis Pasteur (1822–1895), were able to prove that pathogenic microorganisms spread diseases, when it was hitherto supposed that such afflictions were the result of breathing bad air. This prompted an investigation into the world of microscopic organisms, and by 1895 a French bacteriologist, Monsieur Physalix, had succeeded in breeding his own variety of microbe. As its name suggested, *Bacillus anthracis claviformi* had the appearance of a short, club-like rod. It was an offspring of anthrax, and the properties of the original bacillus, as well as its shape, were found to have completely altered in the process of cultivation.

The experiment was a first in bacteriology, and many hoped it would have important consequences in the future.

In America, the microbiologist Dr Benjamin Meade Bolton (1857–1929) conducted experiments which proved that copper coins killed bacteria, whereas coins of gold, silver, nickel or other metals that resisted chemical reagents didn't seem to cause them any harm. His observations were instrumental in connection with the spread of disease by means of money.

As library books were also often blamed for spreading germs, it was proposed, in the wake of these investigations, that these items be submitted to disinfection on their return to the library. Barbers of high standing began to employ disinfectors for their brushes and razors, but a series of French experiments seemed to show that ordinary soap and water was just as effective in killing bacteria.

Inoculating for Disease (1895)

Diphtheria was a common respiratory disease in the nineteenth century. Indeed, Queen Victoria's own daughter, Princess Alice, died from the illness in 1878. As there was no known cure, microbiologists from all over the world began collaborating in an attempt to better understand and ultimately eradicate the disease.

In the 1890s a new method of vaccinating against diphtheria had been introduced by Monsieur Pierre Paul Emile Roux (1853–1933) and Herr Emil Adolf von Behring (1854–1917), the famed immunologists, following their discovery that it was possible to create an antibody by cultivating the bacterium of the disease in beef tea then inoculating horses with it. At the end of eighty days a horse thus treated was able, without suffering, to supply lymph for inoculating humans. The serum of the horse's blood, drawn from the jugular vein, was capable of resisting the bacterium of diphtheria, and when injected under the skin of diphtheritic patients, it worked a remarkable change in their condition. In the course of a few hours the fever declined, the face resumed its healthy tints, and the subject felt much better – lively, even.

By 1895 the remedy had halved the number of deaths from diphtheria in the regions where it had been trialled, and hopes were entertained of further reductions as the years went by.

Over in Geneva, a scientist named Dr Viquerat claimed to have discovered a treatment for even the most desperate cases of consumption, a disease that killed thousands of men, women and children throughout the era. His twenty-seven test subjects, all of whom were suffering so terribly that they had been written off by their own physicians, were inoculated with the serum of donkeys that had previously been immunised against the dreadful scourge. Remarkably, at the end of the treatment, twenty-five of the patients were entirely cured and able to return to work.

Today diphtheria is treated by a combination of antibiotics and antitoxins, while TB generally requires a specialist team of medical experts and a lengthy course of antibiotics.

The Cure for Hydrophobia (1884)

Hydrophobia, or rabies, was a fatal disease affecting the brain and nervous system of those unfortunate enough to contract it.

Its victims suffered paralysis, delirium, paranoia and a fear of water so intense they were unable to quench their burning thirst. For centuries there had been no known cure, and as such, the disease was feared across the globe.

During his distinguished career, Louis Pasteur had succeeded in discovering vaccines for chickenpox, dog distemper and a series of other contagious diseases, and before the dawn of the twentieth century he had added hydrophobia to his long list of triumphs.

He deduced that no case of hydrophobia in man or dog occurred naturally, but instead originated in the bite of an infected animal. Though he wasn't an accredited physician, the determined Frenchman began searching for a cure nonetheless. His theory was that a diluted form of the disease, if administered to one infected, would stimulate the body to develop immunity to the potent kind. With the assistance of his fellow immunologist Monsieur Pierre Paul Emile Roux, Pasteur began searching for a vaccine using infected rabbits to cultivate a weak version of the disease. His earliest trials were conducted on dogs, which, after being inoculated with the virus, were found to be completely resistant to hydrophobia. The dogs were all vaccinated under chloroform, so the operation was painless.

The vaccine was first administered to a human in 1885, when a nine-year-old French boy named Joseph Meister (1876–1940) was bitten by a rabid dog. The inoculation was a success, and the boy failed to contract the disease. In a cruel twist of fate, however, Joseph Meister committed suicide at the age of sixty-four, having been overcome with despair following the Nazi occupation of France during the Second World War.

Pasteur's development of the hydrophobia vaccine was an important breakthrough for mankind, and by 1922 the disease was completely eradicated from the United Kingdom.

How to Treat a Weak Heart (1893)

According to the principle of medicine advocated by the Mauritian physiologist Mr Charles-Edouard Brown-Séquard (1817–1894), every organ of the body took from the blood the nutriment it required, and no more. If, then, the blood was unable to supply the correct amount of nutrients, the organs would begin to languish; so instead of focussing attention directly on a weak organ, treatment could instead be administered by supplying to the blood, through the skin or stomach, the essential elements that were required to sustain the body.

In the case of a weak or failing heart, a new remedy was applied by Dr Hamilton, of New York. He had discovered a nutritious substance called 'cardine', which was extracted from the fresh heart of a bullock. The animal's heart had derived the nutriment from its blood, and when administered to a patient in proper doses (the doctor recommended five or six drops) it supplied nutrition to the blood, which in turn provided vital sustenance to the heart. The results in strengthening his patients' hearts were said to be thoroughly remarkable.

In light of Dr Hamilton's findings, a bullock's heart as an ingredient of everyday cookery was proposed, in order to keep the nation's hearts healthy.

The Railway that Cured Malaria (1882)

Prior to 1897, when the British medical doctor Sir Ronald Ross (1857–1932) categorically proved that mosquitoes were responsible for transmitting malaria, there were a number of hypotheses as to the cause of this deadly parasitic infection. These ranged from bad weather, or infectious transmissions in the breeze, to the notion that it didn't exist at all, and was, in fact, nothing more than a mere chill!

In 1882 Dr King of Philadelphia was struck by the absence of malaria fever in New York and his local neighbourhoods, and duly propounded another theory. He supposed that, as these great metropolises were places where the railways ran, the immunity was due to the continual passage of trains disturbing the air and soil, effectively blowing away the contagion.

The Malaria Inhaler (1890)

Africa's Gold Coast was reputedly one of the most unhealthy places in the world; a place where malarial fever was the cause of the sickness and death of about 80 per cent of the region's residents. In 1890 one of the inhabitants, a gentleman named Mr A. McSwiney, claimed he had discovered a method for proofing against this terrible malady.

'Malaria is due to the poisonous germ-laden vapours rising from the swamps and gullies that are filled with decaying vegetable matter,' he explained. 'These germs, taken into the lungs with the breath, poison the blood and thus produce malarial fever.'

It was similarly accepted that eucalyptus oil was one of the most powerful antiseptics on Earth, for it had been 'proved' that microbes couldn't exist when this potent substance was present in the atmosphere. Acting on this principle, Mr McSwiney procured a device known as the Pinol Eucalyptia Dry Inhaler. This was a small, glass tube resembling a cigarette holder. Its insides were packed with wood shavings, and into the end of the tube a few drops of eucalyptus oil were poured. Once the sawdust had absorbed the liquid, the user was required to inhale the vapours, thus supplying the lungs and nasal passages with the antiseptic properties of the oil.

McSwiney used his inhaler every morning on leaving his house, with the result that he was completely untouched by malaria, even though the fever was raging in the district. He thereby recommended its use to anyone living in climates where the disease was rife.

Malaria Screens (1890)

Sir Henry Morton Stanley (1841–1904) was a nineteenth-century African explorer, who rose to fame in the 1870s following his recovery – and celebrated greeting – of the lost medical missionary Dr David Livingstone (1813–1873). Stanley spent many years exploring the darkest depths of the country and formed the opinion that malaria was borne on the winds far inland, across open plains, or up the course of rivers, but that a belt of trees or high shrubs acted as a screen against its effects.

Seven years before the true cause of malaria was revealed, the German physician Emin Pasha (1840–1892) adopted the discerning plan of sleeping underneath mosquito nets. This, for reasons

that hadn't occurred to him, appeared to ward away the disease. Furthermore, Stanley suggested that thin veils constructed from mosquito nets should be worn as respirators in districts affected by malaria, as these, too, seemed to prevent infection.

The Insect Repellent (1887 and 1890)

The Victorians believed that carbolic acid sponged liberally onto the skin and hair, and even on the clothing, was an effective protection against the bites of gnats and other insects. It was recommended that people who were prone to insect bites should always keep a bottle of the acid in their home, which could be readily and safely applied with a sponge before venturing outside.

While it may have repelled insects, carbolic acid has since been found to be highly toxic, and prolonged exposure to the skin can cause serious burns, as well as internal damage from ingesting the acid or inhaling the vapours. Today carbolic acid is used in disinfectants and certain kinds of antiseptics, as well as weed killers and paint strippers.

Insect repellents were also discussed at a meeting of the

Entomological Society in 1890, with particular emphasis on how to preserve the beams of churches from the ravages of beetles. It was duly recommended that the wood, which was undoubtedly surrounded by lighted candles, should be well soaked in the highly flammable liquid paraffin oil, as this was deemed to be a particularly potent insect repellent.

Valerian Dressing (1885)

A new type of lotion for dressing fresh wounds was brought to notice by a French surgeon named Monsieur Arragon who had been studying the health benefits of the root of the valerian plant. The lotion thus derived was said to considerably hasten the body's natural healing process and at the same time provide swift pain relief. Bandages containing a decoction of thirty parts of valerian

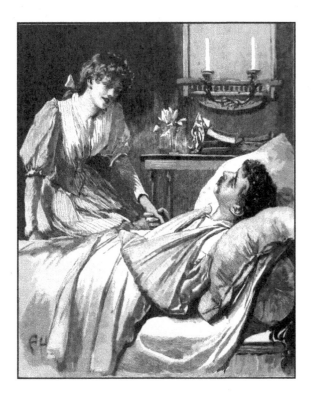

root to 1,000 parts of water were applied to patients' wounds. Of fifty test subjects only two failed to benefit by the treatment.

Today the root of the valerian plant is sold in many health food supplement shops in the form of drops or capsules, though instead of healing cuts and grazes it is more commonly used to treat insomnia, irritable bowel syndrome and stress-related illnesses.

The Cure for Nosebleeds (1890)

The Victorians were curious to hear that ham fat had been deemed a successful remedy for stopping nosebleeds. Several aggravated cases of this bothersome haemorrhage had occurred at the University Hospital of Pennsylvania, and as a last resort Dr D. Hayes plugged the sufferers' nostrils with cylinders cut from raw bacon fat. Remarkably, the bleeding ceased within moments, and the remedy was said to be as simple as it was effective.

The Cure for Catarrh (1880)

An easy and successful remedy for chronic catarrh was discovered in seawater gargling. Professor Mosler claimed to have treated numerous patients in this way, and recorded his experiences in a Berlin paper. In fact, the treatment became so popular towards the end of the nineteenth century that special gargling huts were erected at some seaside resorts, where directions were given as to the mode of proceeding. One necessary proviso was that the salt water should come in contact with the nasal cavity, thus helping to unblock both the nose and the throat. The salt helped to flush out the back of the throat, drawing out any bacteria and thoroughly cleansing the mouth. Once the gargling was over, a marked improvement in the malady was quickly perceived.

The Hay Fever Preventative (1882)

It is estimated that one in four people in twenty-first century Britain suffers from the seasonal allergy hay fever when the body reacts unfavourably to clouds of fresh pollen released by plants into the summer air. Since around 1819, when the world began to understand the triggers of this affliction, medical professors and sufferers alike have bandied various remedies, including bloodletting, vomiting, iced baths and the consumption of opium. Though treatments were many, relief was minimal. It therefore came as a delight to sufferers in 1882 when the German physicist Professor Hermann von Helmholtz (1821–1894) published a remedy, which he claimed was infallible. His method was to apply up each nostril a solution of the anti-inflammatory drug known as quinine. It was administered by means of a small pipette while lying with the chin held in the air, and the relief afforded lasted a considerable period.

This was followed by a further preventative discovered by two researchers independently of one another. They were Dr Blakely and Mr Hannay. Their method was to prevent the hay pollen entering the nose at all by pinching it with a large spring-clip,

similar to those used to hang up washing, which was to remain in place all summer long. The latter gentleman also advised plugging the ducts of the eyes by means of small, dumb-bell-shaped pieces of glass that were only to be removed once the season had ended.

Interestingly, hay fever was almost unheard of in nineteenth-century Scotland, although common in the south of England. This curious observation elicited the explanation that the more insensitive membrane of the Scot's nose was inherited from a long line of snuff-taking ancestors.

The Remedy for Asthma (1882)

Newspapers in Queensland and New South Wales began printing glowing testimonials in praise of a new remedy for asthmatic and bronchial affections, in the shape of a species of the indigenous Euphorbia plant, known scientifically as *Euphorbia pilulifera*. It was said that an ounce of the leaves placed in two quarts of water, and allowed to simmer until the quantity was reduced by one half, afforded a medicine which, taken a wine-glassful at a time, two or three times a day, would relieve the most obstinate cases of asthma, as well as ordinary coughs. The leaves of the plant were gathered and dried and were found to keep for a considerable period of time. The remedy is still used today.

Herbs for Digestion (1895)

Bailahuén was the common name for the leaves and stems of *Haplopappus baylahuen*, a species of aster plant that grew in Chile. The shrub was introduced into England as a stimulant for weak digestion. Three leaves were placed in a cup of boiled water, which was drunk hot without sugar after every meal. This digestive tonic was said to alleviate a variety of stomach complaints as well as curing liver diseases, relieving cold and flu symptoms, and even boosting one's libido!

In tropical Africa was a bush known as the *Kinkelibah*, or *Combretum glutinosum*, which grew about 10 feet high. By 1895 it attracted much attention in medical circles, for it was reputedly the only good remedy for hematuric bilious fever, a digestive disorder that was fatal to Europeans in Western Africa. An infusion of the leaves was made comprising one weight of leaves to 60 weights of water, and a dose of 250 grams was administered every ten minutes.

Though the tea was primarily taken as a preventative of this deadly fever, especially during the rainy season, it was also said to cure a variety of general stomach complaints.

Preventing Scurvy (1880 and 1882)

According to a report of the Board of Trade, it appeared that outbreaks of scurvy – the dreaded disease that so often plagued sailors at sea – had been increasing in the British Navy since 1873. It was therefore crucial to find a remedy as quickly as possible. Since the eighteenth century, daily doses of lime juice had been a popular preventative, but the board concluded that this wasn't an efficient remedy, and too much reliance was being placed upon it. Instead, they recommended that naval food supplies ought to include a fair proportion of fresh and preserved meats, along with more fresh fruit and vegetables.

Between 1878 and 1879 the famous arctic explorer Friherr Nils Adolf Erik Nordenskiöld (1832–1901) led a successful expedition along the northernmost coast of Eurasia in search of the Northeast Passage. He made history, becoming the first man to navigate the Arctic Ocean between Europe and Asia. Among the seafaring dangers to which his crew were subjected, none was more dreaded than scurvy, though the sailors on board Friherr Nordenskiöld's ship, the *Vega*, needn't have been concerned, for during the voyage the ship's naturalist discovered a preventative in the form of a peculiar little Arctic berry, produced by a plant that was said to enjoy a brief existence amid the snow and ice during the short glacial summer. The plant yielded its berries in great abundance, and the fruit, rich in vitamin C, was in high demand among some of the natives of the coasts where it was found. Except that it was rather more acidic, its flavour wasn't unlike that of the ordinary raspberry.

When used on board the *Vega*, the berries were prepared by first being dried, then preserved in reindeer milk, and afterwards allowed to freeze so they would keep for a long time. As proof of their efficacy, it was reported that there wasn't a single case of scurvy during the entire voyage, even though there were nearly thirty men on board.

The End of Seasickness (1875)

Victorian landlubbers often liked to sing along to a good tune about 'a life on the ocean wave', and to praise the sounding of the sea when standing on the shore; yet when one was afloat, it was quite often a different tune they were singing to. Those who suffered the doleful complaint known as sea or motion sickness were undoubtedly delighted when a French physician discovered a successful method of treatment. It involved the administration of a medicinal syrup, known as chloral hydrate, in small doses – no more than two teaspoonfuls before the vessel set sail. The patient was then required to lie down, and, weather permitting, remain on deck.

As the drug was a mild sedative, it generally induced sleep, so the patient passed into a semi-conscious dreamy state, quite free of any nausea for the remainder of the journey. During long voyages, doses were taken twice daily until the patient became accustomed to the motion of the vessel.

Unfortunately, chloral hydrate was potentially lethal if taken in large quantities, so the British physician Dr John Hughes Bennett (1812–1875) proposed an alternative remedy. He had deduced that seasickness was actually a consequence of the liver, rather than the stomach, being 'mauled about' by the ever-changing position of the ship. The liver, a solid organ, stood less chance of accommodating itself to the violent motion, and it discharged bile into the stomach, which induced vomiting. Dr Bennett therefore concluded that the liver and stomach should be soothed prior to undertaking the voyage.

'Do not go on board with a full stomach,' he advised would-be travellers. 'Instead, take a good meal three or four hours before embarking; and one or two hours after the meal, take a cup of strong black coffee as a stimulant, and by way of fortifying the liver.'

On embarking, the stomach would then be empty, while the body had been sustained by the meal. The passenger was then advised to rest by lying in the recumbent position.

Of course, today's medical experts attest that motion sickness has less to do with the stomach or liver, and more to do with the mind. While the nerves in the inner ear are telling the brain that the body is moving, the eyes are relaying visual information suggesting the body is stationary, and this conflicting information causes the brain to become confused, resulting in the sensation of nausea.

Reindeer Lifebelts (1887)

As part of his studies, a Norwegian engineer, Herr W. C. Möller, found that reindeer hair and skin had remarkable buoyancy. For instance, a reindeer skin, weighing less than 2 kg and rolled up with the hair outwards, would support the same weight as an ordinary cork lifebelt for ten days, while also possessing the additional property of keeping the body warm. This was due to the tubular structure of the reindeer hairs, the insides of which were hollow to provide both insulation and buoyancy.

According to his findings, a suit of reindeer skin would save a man from drowning, and Herr Möller expected such a dress to be supplied to all seafaring men over the coming years. He also proposed that boats and sledges should be constructed of the hide.

How Not to Drown (1881)

In 1881 an American journal published a step-by-step account, illustrating how a person in danger of drowning, such as a sailor thrown overboard, may prevent himself from sinking. It was already a well-known fact that if the hands and arms were submerged, and the lungs were kept filled with air, the body would, according to the laws of nature, float. Unfortunately, however, the majority of people thus endangered became panic-stricken, and, in throwing their arms wildly above their heads, almost immediately sank. It was therefore recommended that the following demonstration was shown to Victorian children as part of their scientific education.

The first diagram depicts a short-necked, square-shouldered bottle, representing a human figure, with a brass-headed nail securely fastened on each side by means of a rubber band. The bottle was ballasted with sand so that it just floated when the

nails, or arms, were turned downwards. After this has been satisfactorily demonstrated, the nails were turned upwards, as in the second figure, and at once the bottle would either be forced under water, or tipped over so that the water entered the mouth, at which point it would speedily sink.

The Treatment for Electric Shocks (1895)

With electrical installations on the rise all across the country, the risk of receiving an accidental shock became a real threat, particularly to engineers who were regularly exposed to electric wires. With this in mind, Messrs Alabaster, Gatehouse & Co., proprietors of the *Electrical Review* magazine, issued a series of hints and tips for the use of anyone who frequented establishments where there was a high danger of electrocution.

'In many cases death is only apparent,' the magazine explained, 'and every effort should be made to resuscitate the victim by the method of artificial respiration now applied to drowned persons, or those who have been shot in the brain.'

As these shocking accidents happened every now and again, the general public were encouraged to familiarise themselves with the instructions given in *Electrical Review*, based on the researches of eminent authorities.

People were advised that whenever a victim was found still grasping the electric wire that gave him the shock, he wasn't to be seized, as there was danger of the rescuer being electrocuted as well. Before taking hold of him, even by his clothes, the rescuer was to don a pair of rubber gloves, or otherwise insulate his body by covering his hands with a thick layer of dry rags.

A doctor was to be sent for at once, but pending his arrival, artificial respiration should proceed. This was to be done by rolling the victim on to his back and loosening his clothes. A suitable item, such as a rolled up coat, was to be placed under his shoulders so as to prop up the spine and allow the head to hang backwards. The operator then knelt behind the victim's head, grasped his arms by the elbows, and drew them well over the head, so as to bring them almost together above it, and held them there for two or three seconds. Once this was enacted the arms were drawn down to the sides and front of the chest, and the rescuer applied firm compressions by throwing his own weight upon the arms. After two or three seconds the arms were again carried above the head, and the operation repeated at the rate of sixteen times a minute.

In addition to the foregoing treatment, if there was an assistant at hand, the tongue of the victim was to be gripped with the aid of a cloth, and drawn out forcibly from the mouth during the act of respiration.

These efforts were repeated vigorously until either the victim's full and normal breathing was restored, or it was certain that life was extinct. It was stated that one couldn't feel sure of this until the treatment had been applied for at least an hour. Furthermore, the rescuer was advised to block any attempt by bystanders to pour stimulants, such as brandy, down the throat of the victim,

for nothing was to be passed through the lips until a medical man had arrived at the scene.

Sheltering from a Lightning Storm (1895)

According to interesting experiments made in Germany, varieties of trees that contained starch were more likely to be struck by lightning than any other. The species deemed to be most at risk were the oak, poplar, plane, elm, ash and willow, as all these were found to contain a high amount of starch; while the lime, walnut, beech and birch were thought to be the least likely types of tree to be struck. A health warning was thus issued, advising people not to shelter under any type of starchy tree in a thunderstorm, and only to seek cover underneath a non-starchy one.

The Removal of Pain (1887)

In 1883 the German chemist Professor Ludwig Knorr (1859–1921) discovered how to manufacture the world's first anti-inflammatory drug, known as antipyrine, which became a common cure for fever.

Following further investigations into the use of the drug, it was found by the French Academy of Sciences that the removal of pain was achieved by hypodermic injections of antipyrine to the affected area. Experiments showed that the injections were followed by a disagreeable feeling of tension which lasted a few seconds, but when it passed, the pain, whatever its cause, abated at once. This was indeed a remarkable medical breakthrough, and though antipyrine is still used as a painkiller and antipyretic in many countries, a more commonly available drug of the same classification is ibuprofen, developed by Boots the Chemist in the 1960s.

The Ozone Anaesthetic (1882)

As surgical procedures became more advanced, Victorian medical professionals started searching for reliable kinds of anaesthetic. It became necessary to keep the patient subdued for as long as possible in order to allow the surgeon to perform increasingly complex operations. In the early part of the nineteenth century, there was no such thing as anaesthetic. If the invalid was lucky, they may have been administered a few swigs of alcohol to steady their nerves before surgery commenced. By 1847 some surgeons were knocking their patients out with chloroform, but as this occasionally resulted in death, a safer alternative was required.

In the 1880s some interesting experiments to test the powers of ozone as an anaesthetic were made by the German pharmacologist Dr Karl Binz (1832–1913). The ozone was manufactured in a laboratory by the discharge of electricity into the air, and when the correct quantity was inhaled it caused the doctor's test subjects to enter a drowsy state. A deep sleep generally ensued after seven to twenty minutes, and was usually preceded by a feeling of greater ease in breathing.

The effect of the ozonised air on small animals was clear. At first they became restless, then their breathing slowed, and finally they became lethargic. The initial restless behaviour was the same observed in wild animals when thunder, or rather, electricity, was in the air.

Overall the experiments were deemed interesting by the medical boards of the day, though the use of ozone wasn't recommended as an anaesthetic, as nitrous oxide, or laughing gas, had already been considered a suitable enough chemical for the purpose of preparing patients for surgery.

Local Anaesthetic (1885)

Victorian surgeons had long sought an anaesthetic which, when applied externally to a given part of the body, would render it completely void of feeling for a certain length of time, without the need to send the patient to sleep. According to a report from Germany, this was discovered completely by chance by a medical student.

The substance in question was hydrochlorate of cocaine. After accidentally splashing some of the chemical in his eye, the student was surprised to find that it caused the surface of his eyeball to become insensitive to the touch. Further trials served to confirm this remarkable observation, and an eminent oculist performed cataract surgery on the eye of a patient without causing her any pain whatsoever. This was achieved by applying a few drops of hydrochlorate of cocaine onto the surface of her eye.

Additional experiments conducted by Professor Joseph Grasset (1849–1918), the Montpellier-born neurologist, also demonstrated that when injected underneath the skin, the anaesthetic permitted painless operations on other parts of the body without producing sleep or general insensibility.

It is interesting to note that had it not been for a total lack of health and safety regulations, this early local anaesthetic may never have been discovered. Had the medical student been working in the twenty-first century, he would have been required to wear a pair of safety goggles in his laboratory.

Molten Lead in the Eye (1885)

There was once the mysterious case of a French workman, employed in the forges of France, who accidentally got a jet of red-hot molten lead lodged in his eye. The curious thing was, the metal caused no pain or injury whatsoever.

The incident was investigated by Dr Perrier, who ascertained that the immunity to pain was because the lead had entered into what was known as a 'spheroidal state' due to the presence of moisture on the surface of the eyeball. This scientific state occurred when a liquid came quickly into contact with a highly heated surface. The liquid became spherical, and rolled around en masse, but without actually coming into contact with the heated surface. This phenomenon was caused by a mixture of the repulsive force of heat and a 'cushion' of vapour, which was swiftly formed between the two surfaces as the moisture evaporated.

Dr Perrier found that the temperature of the lead was higher than 171° C, the point at which he believed the spheroidal state occurred, and hence the moisture from the workman's eye was vaporised, forming an invisible cushion around the lead, preventing it from making contact with the flesh.

'The phenomenon,' the doctor explained, 'is a case similar to that of a person plunging his moist arm into a vat of molten lead with impunity.'

It wasn't recorded how many Victorian labourers decided to test the doctor's theory; however, it need hardly be added that twenty-first-century workmen ought to resist the temptation of trying this for themselves.

Removing Motes from the Eyes (1885)

Victorians generally agreed that there were few things more aggravating than a small object – be it a fly or an eyelash – becoming stuck in the eye. It was an American physician named Dr C. D. Agnew who offered his own solution to this problem in 1885.

Firstly, a splinter of wood was to be obtained and whittled into the shape of a large needle. The pointed end was then inserted into a small bundle of cotton, which was wound around the stick and secured in place. Once ready, the patient was to lay his head on the breast of a friend, who would draw the upper eyelid up with the forefinger of his left hand, and press the lower lid down with the middle finger. Then, with his right hand, he would lightly sweep the surface of the eyeball with the end of the cotton probe.

Modern doctors, however, advise rinsing the eye thoroughly with lukewarm water in order to safely remove foreign bodies.

The Eye Electromagnet (1892)

An ingenious new way of removing iron splinters from the eye was dreamed up by Mr Snell of Sheffield in about 1881. This was particularly useful for labourers at the local steelworks, who often found that tiny pieces of metal became accidentally lodged in their eyes during the working day. A projecting collar of soft iron attached to a magnetic probe was gently waved over a patient's eyeball, and the iron splints that had become embedded inside were attracted to the magnetic pull and thereby freed, without any need to make contact with the eye.

The Medical Magnetic Probe (1887)

Sir William Henry Preece FRS (1834–1913) was a prominent electrical engineer from Wales. He was a family man who lived in a large house run by a team of domestic servants.

One day, one of his daughters was attending to her embroidery when the needle slipped, penetrating deep beneath the flesh of her hand, where it splintered into three pieces. Without much trouble, a surgeon was able to extract two pieces of the needle, but the third defied localisation. Even the 'induction balance' metal detector, invented by the scientist Professor David Edward Hughes (1831–1900), failed in its task.

In the end, the girl's father took the opportunity to test a theory based on the properties of electromagnetism. A delicate magnetised needle was suspended from a single fibre of cocoon silk, and when the injured hand was brought near, the point of the needle was drawn to a particular spot on her palm. An incision was made at the point where the needle was indicating, and the missing fragment was duly found and extracted.

Solar Surgery (1885)

There were numerous reported cases throughout the era of ordinary household articles, like fishbowls, glass paperweights and the lenses of Victorian stereoscopes, spontaneously setting fire to nearby articles such as tablecloths or pieces of paper, particularly on sunny days. The Victorians understood that this phenomenon was due to the sun's rays becoming concentrated as they travelled through the glass prisms.

When the late president of the United States, James Abram Garfield (1831–1881), was shot twice in the back on 2 July 1881, the medical team who tried to save his life were unable to locate the final bullet, which they believed had become lodged near his liver, though it was impossible to see. Inspired by the phenomenon of focussing light into a single, powerful beam, an enthusiastic inventor persuaded the lead physician that the concentration of a powerful light directed into the president's wound would be bright enough to reveal the hidden bullet. The physician agreed, but insisted on using a test subject first before he would allow the inventor anywhere near the dying president.

To assess his theory, the inventor used an electric light, which was focussed by an elliptical hand-mirror on to the bare back of a substitute for President Garfield; but, as soon as the lamp's main current was switched on, the man screamed in pain. Upon examination, it was found that a 2-inch patch on his skin had been terribly burnt.

Over the next couple of months doctors continued in vain to attempt to locate the missing bullet. Even Professor Alexander Graham Bell, the inventor of the telephone, stepped in to help by adapting the induction balance of Professor Hughes. This metal detector served to determine the locality of the bullet to a certain degree of closeness, but the president's condition slowly deteriorated, and he died on 19 September 1881.

The technique of concentrating the sun's rays using glass prisms was refined over the centuries, and is currently being used by concentrated solar power systems to generate renewable energy at solar power plants, where a large area of sunlight is focussed on to central solar cells. The United States is currently one of the global leaders in this field of technology, and a recent study by Greenpeace International suggests that by the year 2050, CSP could account for as much as one quarter of the world's energy needs.

How President Garfield May Have Been Saved (1887)

Following the failings of the late president's medical team, the French electrical expert Monsieur Gustave Trouvé (1839–1902) began a series of scientific experiments, and by 1887 he had discovered a technique that he believed would have saved the president's life. Based on Professor Bell's modified metal detector, Monsieur Trouvé devised an electrical device in the form of a fine steel probe, which was inserted into a patient's body within the area previously indicated by the induction balance as containing a bullet.

The probe was in circuit with a battery, a telephone and a plate of metal, as shown in the figure overleaf, where P was the probe, B the battery, T the telephone and M the metal plate, connected together by wires. When the metal plate was laid over the surface of the body, it would indicate a general area where the bullet was lodged. The probe could then be thrust inside the body to begin searching for the location of the bullet. As soon as it made contact with it, the circuit was complete and the telephone would ring, alerting the surgeon to a successful discovery.

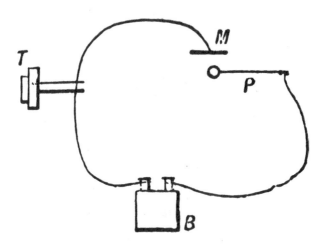

Though it was too late for President Garfield, Trouvé hoped this principle would prove serviceable in military surgery.

Music Therapy to Treat Illness (1892)

Reverend Frederick Kill Harford (*c.* 1832–1906) was an accomplished musician who founded the Guild of St Cecilia in Westminster Abbey in 1891 in order to apply soft, sedative music as a remedy to sickness. The reverend firmly believed in the healing power of music, so he sent musicians from the guild to visit various invalids lying in London hospitals. Their stimulating melodies, he believed, would aid speedy recoveries, and where a visit wasn't convenient, the choir would perform for the patients over the telephone. It was also proposed that music halls were to be erected within the hospitals so that beautiful symphonies would be audible to the patients day and night.

To begin with, the scheme met with distinguished approval. The guild was offered much encouragement from the principal reformers of the Victorian era, including Miss Florence Nightingale (1820–1910), who shared the belief that music helped to soothe the mind, alleviate pain and induce sleep. However, the Guild of St Cecelia soon disbanded after being publically criticised by music and medical professionals alike. A lack of funds also hindered the guild's success.

Despite the failure, over the years medical opinion on the benefits of music therapy has changed, and music has since been found to positively affect parts of the brain and reduce the heart rate. This form of alternative therapy is now regularly used to treat children and adults who suffer from behavioural, emotional or neurological disorders, as well as stroke patients and people with heart disease.

The Cure for Poisoning (1875)

The life of a Victorian was undoubtedly precarious, not least because many were being slowly poisoned. What with unwholesome food and adulterated drink, it was a wonder that any Victorian made it to old age. Frequent were the cases of upset stomachs, or perhaps something worse, arising from the ingestion of a toxic substance, and in 1875 the public were advised about a novel method of treating someone suspected to have been poisoned.

'Fly to the mustard pot,' was the advice. 'It may save one's life!'

A tablespoonful of ordinary mustard mixed in a wineglassful of water seldom failed to produce sickness, swiftly emptying the stomach of the offending article. Food writers of the day agreed that mustard was one of the safest and swiftest of emetics, and this, they believed, was a fact that everyone should be aware of.

Mountain Sickness (1893)

In 1880 the London-born mountaineer Mr Edward Whymper (1840–1911) became the first man in history to reach the summit of Chimborazo, the inactive volcano in the Andes, known to be the highest mountain in Ecuador. Twelve years later he published an

account of his journey, entitled *Travels among the Great Andes of the Equator*, in which he made a special study of the illness that attacked mountaineers at great altitudes. Notwithstanding the ordinary perils of climbing mountains, the debilitating condition of altitude sickness rendered the ascent of the highest mountains dangerous to certain people, particularly those with a weak constitution.

In 1885 another British mountaineer, Mr Clinton Thomas Dent (1850–1912), published a paper on the subject of climbing to the summit of Mount Everest in the Himalayas, a feat which, at that point in history, wouldn't be achieved for another sixty-eight years. Mr Dent went so far as to say that only persons of strong vitality and full blood ought to attempt the highest peaks. Despite this assertion, one delicate man in Mr Whymper's climbing party, who was far from robust, was the only climber to escape the affliction. It was, however, noticed that the all climbers lost their appetite, and as soon as they refrained from eating they recovered from the oppression and giddiness of the sickness.

The cause of the disease was later explained by the natural scientist Professor Robert Holford Macdowall Bosanquet FRS (1841–1912), who showed that mountain sickness was due to a deficiency of oxygen in the rarefied air of high altitudes, and in consequence the blood couldn't carry enough oxygen around the body in order to sustain physical and mental activities.

It was concluded that the best remedy for mountain sickness wasn't an artificial supply of oxygen, as had previously been proposed, but a period of preliminary training whereby physical exercise was undertaken while the body was partially starved in order to prepare it for a lack of sustenance.

Health on Mountains (1895)

In spite of these findings, by 1895 it had been determined that mountaintops were, in fact, the healthiest places on Earth to live. This was due in part to the absence of microorganisms in the air. It was reported that the meteorological observers of Ben Nevis enjoyed remarkably good health and freedom from colds or chest affections while on the summit of the mountain. After three months in the observatory they were allowed a holiday, and on descending to the valleys they were struck down with influenza. This was caused by germs in the lower atmosphere, which seldom attained the summit.

The Breathing Exercise (1893)

A German physician, Dr P. Niemeyer, devised a breathing exercise that was said to restore one's health to its full potential. He advised his patients to set aside two or three quiet periods in their day in which to sit comfortably for a few minutes and concentrate on nothing but their breathing.

The technique was known as *atherngymnastic*, which translated into English as 'air exercise', and in each sitting the patient was to take fifty or sixty breaths. The inhalation was made slowly, deliberately, pleasurably, and with the fullest attention and intention, through the nose. In this way the air was forced into the body's smallest air passages, and the blood became thoroughly oxygenated.

The practice was strongly recommended by German doctors, especially for brain-workers and persons of sedentary lifestyles, who were apt to form habits of incomplete breathing, thus stinting their bodies of oxygen. After a few weeks of performing the exercise, patients noticed a general overall improvement in their health.

The Curative Helmet (1893)

The Scottish philosopher Mr Thomas Carlyle (1795–1881) had suffered from severe indigestion since he was very young and noted that the jolting of an omnibus helped to relieve his symptoms. This prompted an investigation into the health benefits of using public transport, and it transpired that the vibrations of a train remedied certain nervous affections, such as Parkinson's disease.

Acting on this discovery, Professor Jean-Martin Charcot (1825–1893), of the Salpêtrière Hospital, Paris, constructed an armchair which oscillated by means of electromagnetism, shaking the sitter in the same manner as a train would. The vibrations made the patient feel better and following the treatment would be able to enjoy a good night's rest.

The success of the armchair prompted one of Professor Charcot's most brilliant pupils, Dr Georges Gillis de la Tourette

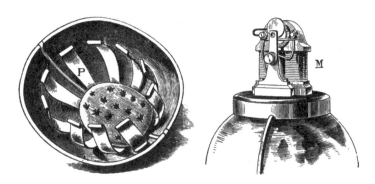

(1857–1904), to design a vibrating helmet in order to treat neuralgia, headache, hysteria and sleeplessness. The interior of the headgear is shown in the first image and the electro-magnet hammer for causing the vibrations in the second. The steel plates, P, were flexible and designed to keep the helmet firmly on the head. On top of the helmet by way of a crest was mounted a small electric motor, M, the armature of which, on being excited by an electric current, made 600 revolutions a minute, producing the vibration of the helmet. The helmet began to massage the wearer's head, and after a few minutes a feeling of lassitude was experienced, which more often than not sent the patient into a deep, mesmeric sleep.

On 8 December 1893 one of Dr Tourette's female patients, who was at that time an inmate at Salpêtrière Hospital, turned up at his study and shot him three times in the head. She claimed she had acted in revenge, as some days earlier the doctor had 'hypnotised' her 'against her will', perhaps by treating her with the helmet. He survived the attack and continued using his vibrating contraptions on his patients, allegedly with great success.

The curative helmet was said to have proved exceedingly beneficial to sufferers from a variety of neurasthenic complaints. It even successfully treated cases of hemicrania, a headache disorder for which no cure has ever been found.

Science and Sorrow (1895)

It was well known that sorrow and grief exerted a negative influence on the functions of the body. All too frequent were the cases of people who had been suffering from some kind of depression, or mental disorder, being committed to one of the many lunatic asylums that littered the Victorian landscape. 'Treatment' for their conditions ranged from solitary confinement to a turn in the electric chair, and few patients were ever released.

However, by the 1890s medical perceptions had begun to change, and psychologists started to examine the nature of depression. In fact, it was a lady doctor from New York, Dr Louise Fiske Bryson, who was one of the first to explain that sorrow was a disease and should be treated as such.

The internal organs of dogs believed to have died of homesickness, or other forms of depression, showed a deterioration similar to that caused by starvation or infectious diseases. Dr Bryson therefore considered that the disease of sorrow should be left, like a fever, to run its course, and that all attempts to banish it and cheer the patient were futile.

'Yet, as with any disease, depression should be treated,' she explained, 'though mental illnesses must be treated in a special way.'

The good doctor recommended quiet drives in the country, or gentle walks with Mother Nature in the woods or by the seashore. Though the patient should be kept occupied, they shouldn't be overtasked either in mind or body. The bright, sweet society of children was preferable to that of adults, and the presence of a familiar newspaper or magazine was often a comfort where the most tender and sympathetic friend was troublesome. Mourning wear was, in her opinion, useful for a time – a year at most – because it secured consideration for the sufferer, but if continued too long it became a burden and a source of gloom.

House Nerves (1895)

'House nerves' was an American name for a type of nervousness and low spirits, common with broody women who lived sedentary indoor lives. Such women, it was observed, were prone to self-analysis, and if left untreated would become anxious about their affairs and suspicious of other people. They imagined that evil was likely to befall their husbands or children while they

were away from home; they conjured up imaginary dangers and in the end would become so timid they would even fear the weather outside, never daring to travel anywhere.

According to an American researcher, the remedy for this condition wasn't a doctor or drugs, but exercise in the open air with bright, pleasant company. Those suffering from such melancholia were to take long walks in the sunshine with a friend or two, banishing each gloomy and anxious thought by force of will. If that didn't work, they were advised to supplant the negative thoughts by instead concentrating the mind on an impending domestic chore, which no doubt cheered up every discerning housewife.

Trepanning for Idiocy (1890)

Microcephaly, or insufficient growth of the skull, was a devastating disease that attracted much ridicule in the nineteenth century, with some sufferers even touted to freak shows owing to their unusual, shrunken appearance. Physicians who studied the condition in infants believed that if left untreated it triggered 'idiocy' by arresting the development of the brain.

Though there was no known cure for the disease, an interesting operation was successfully performed by Professor Odilon Marc Lannelongue (1840–1911) in l'Hôpital des Enfants, Paris. A girl of four years, born of healthy parents, displayed unmistakable signs of idiocy: she could neither walk nor speak and took no interest in anything. Professor Lannelongue, after mature consideration, removed a slip of her skull, about 11 centimetres long, from the left wall, and a month later the wound had healed, the child could walk, had begun to speak and showed the usual animation.

Encouraged by his success, the professor continued to perform this controversial operation, and hoped there was scope to develop the treatment in the future. No official cure for microcephaly, however, has ever been discovered.

The Witchcraft Disease (1881)

The extraordinary exhilarating power of laughing gas was familiar to the Victorians, and in 1881 a similar property was discovered in a liquid mixture of phosphate of soda and the essence of ergot of rye, the former being a tangy beverage, the latter a fungal disease infecting crops.

While treating a female patient with the ergot of rye for a painful affection of the knee, her physician, Dr Luton, of the French city of Rheims, discovered that by adding a little of the phosphate of soda to the medicine, it sent the patient into uncontrollable fits of laughter, which evidently sprang from the merriest ideas. No effect was observed until forty-five minutes after the dose was taken, and once the intoxication died away, the patient continued in the best of humour for quite some time.

Experiments were then made on a number of persons, but it was found that females were most susceptible to the influence of the potion. In the case of some men, only giddiness and a slight headache was the result.

Ergot poisoning, also known as ergotism, has plighted mankind for centuries, as a result of consuming bread made from an infected batch of rye. The disease was particularly rife in the Middle Ages, when it was known by the name Saint Anthony's Fire, and in the 1970s it was suggested by an American professor of science that the hysterical symptoms of females could explain why so many women from the past were accused

of being witches. Perhaps, then, the cackling, concocting old connivers who were so feared and persecuted in centuries gone by weren't under the influence of Satan after all, and were simply the unfortunate victims of a toxic little fungus.

7

FOOD AND DRINK

Vibration and Taste (1887)

Any inhibitions the Victorians may have had about their diet were forgotten by the end of the century when a variety of new and unusual dishes came into vogue. Intrepid explorers were returning home with stories about the exotic foods consumed by the natives of foreign lands, and because meal times were important social gatherings for many families, a great deal of time and preparation went into ensuring that dishes were interesting and flavoursome.

Professor John Berry Haycraft (1857–1923) was a London-born physiologist and medical researcher. In a delivered paper to the Royal Society of Edinburgh, he put forth the theory that, just as

certain compounds containing elements of the same chemical groups had similar colours, so too they had similar tastes. This, he believed, was due to the vibration of the 'radical', or chemical compound, common to the group. For example, he explained that the carbon compounds mannite, grape sugar, glycerine and glycol all tasted sweet because they possessed a common radical (CH_2OH) which was responsible for providing the sweetness.

Professor Haycroft's contemporaries also considered the hypothesis that the sensation of taste was caused by vibrations, transmitted to the brain by the nerves in the taste buds, which became excited by the different flavours.

These theories were later proved to be correct. Compounds which contain two hydroxyl (OH) groups are commonly known as glycols, from the Greek word *glycys*, meaning sweet. Sodium ions make food taste salty, amino acids produce a savoury taste and sourness is caused by the presence of hydronium ions.

A person can have up to 10,000 taste buds in the tongue, mouth and throat, each bud containing as many as 100 taste receptor cells, which respond to the different tastes in food, that is to say, sweet, salty, sour, bitter or savoury. The cells then transmit this information to the brain via nerves.

Earth Soup (1880)

While the middle classes in Victorian England were delighting their taste buds with roast pheasant, plum pudding and mulled wine, explorers returning from Japan were sharing bizarre stories about semi-civilised tribes of men who ate earth. Nobody could say for certain why these tribesmen should do such a thing, but an array of possible explanations for the unusual practice was offered.

The famous explorer Herr Alexander von Humboldt (1769–1859) was believed to have attributed this dietary habit to a desire to fill the stomach, thus allaying the pangs of hunger. However, this explanation seemed unlikely, for the Ainos people of Yesso, the northern island of Japan, had plenty of flesh and bread to eat, yet they still persisted in regaling themselves with clay from the earth. Another theory, proffered by Dr Fuchs, was that the unctuous sensation of the clay in the mouth was agreeable, while other writers traced the custom to times of want, when ordinary food was scarce.

Following analysis of the edible earth by an American researcher named Dr Love, of New York, the clay was found to contain silica, alumina and lime, as well as rust, magnesia, potash, soda, sulphuric and phosphoric acids, and traces of water and volatile matter. Nothing nutritious was present, but some of these ingredients were believed to be medicinal, thus justifying a notion that the earth was eaten for its restorative qualities.

The Ainos consumed the clay in the form of a thick soup, boiled with lily-roots in a small quantity of water, then strained. The volatile matter found by Dr Love was thought to be the remains of some aromatic herb mixed accidentally or purposely with the clay.

It was interesting to note that the clay was harvested in the north of Japan, in a valley known as Tsie-toi-nai, which literally translated into English as 'eat-earth-valley'.

Edible Peat Bogs (1875)

Every now and again the Victorians suffered bad harvests and cattle plagues, which greatly affected the price of food. This was a concern for many of the poorer families who had little money to live on, but by 1875 the public were comforted to know that there was a prospect of Britain becoming unaffected by such spates, thus enjoying a golden age in which there was no more dear meat. Astonishingly, the source of this nineteenth-century superfood, which wasn't a crop or livestock, was found in the peat-fields of Scotland.

A decade or so earlier the Duke of Sutherland, George Granville William Sutherland Leveson-Gower (1828–1892), had introduced a pugmill on his Highland estates at Forsinard, close to his family seat at Dunrobin Castle, for the purpose of compressing the peat that had been excavated from the local peat bogs, and so rendering it fit for fuel. The duke's peat works operated successfully for several years, and by the mid-1870s the manager of the factory asserted with unquestionable truth that peat contained all the elements from which the human body was built up. After much study, he was confident that these elements could be separated from what was worthless, and the nutrition could be presented in a palatable form. He even began offering to visitors a dish prepared from raw peat, which was described as being rather tasty, and which perhaps possessed all the nutritive value he claimed for it.

The New Potato (1884)

At a meeting of the Linnean Society of London, the world's oldest biological fellowship, Mr J. G. Baker drew attention to the discovery of a new kind of potato, indigenous to the moister parts of Chile. Under cultivation this new plant, *Solanum maglia*, yielded 600 potatoes in one year, the tuber-bearing stems reaching 7 feet long. Furthermore, as it was more suited to a moist climate like Britain than the common potato, which originated from drier regions of South America, Mr Baker proposed that the new variety should be introduced without haste. He knew that the ordinary potato was prone to disease, and was of the opinion that the best way to prevent this was to grow the type of potato best adapted to the climate.

Other suitable varieties were also found, such as the *Solanum commersoni*, which was tried in France, and the *Solanum jamesii*, which was tested in America, although the tuber roots of this class were only edible before the plant matured.

Black Potatoes (1881)

By 1881 a lady farmer claimed to have produced a black variety of the potato, black to the very core, and, though presenting a strange appearance on the table, they were actually described as being tasty and pleasant to eat.

Around fifteen years earlier a dark sort of potato, known as the 'black heart', was cultivated in some of the north-eastern parts of Scotland, including the Shetland Islands, but these were not quite so ebony in looks, nor were they said to be as good to taste.

Sugar from Corn (1880)

In 1880 it was reported that a remarkable development had been made in the Western States of America, where grain resources

were plentiful. Farmers had discovered that glucose could be manufactured from their leftover corn. Many factories were erected for working this new industry, and one in Chicago was so big it was capable of converting 20,000 bushels into sugar every day. One bushel of corn yielded 30 lbs of glucose, or 3 gallons of syrup, the sugar costing one penny per lb, while the corn sold at one shilling and eight pence a bushel.

The English hoped that local farmers would consider the possibility of utilising a portion of the immense grain supplies of Britain and Europe for the same purpose.

Today this type of sugar is known as glucose syrup and is derived from maize. The syrup is a main ingredient in the manufacture of confectionary.

Sweet-Flag Candy (1882)

The recipe for a good digestive candy, found to be particularly nutritious for children and dyspeptics, was formulated in America using the roots of a tall, wetland plant known as sweet-flag. The roots were washed and finely sliced, then placed in a pan with enough cold water to cover them. Next, the pan was slowly heated over a stove or fire until the water boiled. The roots were treated four or five times in this way, and after each time the water was poured away.

Then, to each two cupfuls of the boiled roots, a cupful and a half of white sugar was added, before the mixture was covered with water and allowed to simmer slowly on the stove until the water had boiled away. The candy was then emptied out on to buttered plates and stirred frequently until dry. The result was a delicious, healthy snack that was even capable of curing minor ailments such as sore throats.

Meat-Bread (1880)

A new type of prepared food, known as meat-bread, was the practical outcome of the observed fact that the leavening, or fermentation, of ordinary bread caused the digestion of meat. A beefsteak cut into small pieces and mixed with flour and yeast was found by the chemist Monsieur Auguste Scheurer-Kestner (1833–1899) to disappear entirely during the process of fermentation. When he began his experiments he used raw, finely minced meat, three parts of which he mixed with five parts of flour and five parts of yeast. Sufficient water was then added to make the dough, which in due time began to ferment. After two or three hours the meat had been completely digested and absorbed into the bread. The meaty dough was then baked in the ordinary manner.

However, when thus prepared the bread had a disagreeable, sour taste, and it was therefore recommended to first boil the meat for an hour in the same quantity of water necessary to afterwards moisten the flour. Before cooking, the meat was carefully removed of fat, and wasn't to be too salty, as salt tended to spoil the bread.

Meat-bread was said to form an excellent and nutritious food for invalids, and as it kept for a long time it was hoped it would prove serviceable to sailors or travellers.

The Kola Nut (1882, 1887 and 1892)

The *Sterculia acuminate* was a flowering plant that grew in West Africa. For centuries the plant's edible nuts, known as kola nuts, were gathered by the natives so they could use them to flavour their water, which was often unsavoury. The nuts were also chewed to help stave off hunger and were even thought to cure diseases of the liver.

Western travellers surmised that the nut contained caffeine; in fact, analyses by two German chemists showed that it contained more caffeine than coffee did. The nut also comprised the sweet substance, glucose, which wasn't present in cocoa. Furthermore, unlike cocoa beans, kola nuts contained no fatty matter. This being the case, they were considered a worthy constituent for brewing a delicious and healthy beverage, and it was expected by eager Victorians that the nuts would soon occupy a prominent place in Western culture alongside cocoa and coffee.

By 1887 a new use of the little-known nut was discovered when kola chocolate was produced, cocoa beans having been replaced by the nut. Its nutritional qualities were plentiful, and the chocolate was particularly beneficial to invalids, children and those in need of a tonic.

In June 1891 four cyclists covered the distance between Paris and Clermont-Ferrand – nearly 400 kilometres – in seventeen hours. The speed of the winner, an eighteen-year-old Englishman, completed on average 22.802 kilometres an hour, but he was greatly exhausted by his effort. The second was a Frenchman of twenty-eight, who accomplished 22.055 kilometres an hour quite comfortably and without fatigue. The first supported his energies with alcohol, champagne and bouillon; the second with bouillon, tea and kola chocolate. The other two competitors, who managed 21.957 and 19.79 kilometres an hour, took bouillon, coffee and wine, but no kola chocolate; a fact considered worthy of note by amateur Victorian cyclists.

The popularity of kola chocolate began to spread across Europe, and in 1935 a German company, *Hildebrand, Kakao und Schokoladenfabrik GmbH*, launched Scho-Ka-Kola, the so-called sports chocolate for the 1936 Summer Olympics. The brand, which contained kola nut powder, was issued during the Second

World War as part of the rations for the Luftwaffe and is still available to purchase in Germany.

Exploding Fruit (1895)

The illustration depicts a new type of dried fruit from Indonesia, which had the curious property of exploding when placed in water.

The fruit was nearly an inch long and shaped like a cigar. After floating on the water for a few moments, it suddenly burst open with a violent force and scattered its bullet-like seeds in all directions. The water moistened a glue-like gum on the outside of the seeds, making them adhere to whatever they struck.

This explosive fruit grew on a plant called the Justicia, but it wasn't unique. There were other fruits and nuts that possessed the same peculiar method of scattering their seeds, notably the *Hura crepitans*, which was said to be capable of hurling its seeds 100 metres into the air following the explosion. The blast was so loud that the plant was often referred to as the Dynamite tree.

Edible Flowers (1890)

The *Calligonum* was a type of flowering shrub that grew across Asia. The flowers were, according to the botanical director for Northern India, mixed with flour and eaten with a sprinkling of salt by the poorer inhabitants of the region. A little 'ghee' – a type of clarified butter – was added as a luxury by those who could afford the expense.

The flowers were swept off the ground and kept overnight in a closed vessel of earthenware, where they could be kept for a long time without deteriorating in quality or losing their flavour. They are still used in Asian cooking and are sometimes used to prepare the traditional yoghurt condiment known as *raita.*

Fresh Eggs (1875 and 1884)

Among the minor troubles of nineteenth-century city life was the difficulty of procuring a regular supply of fresh eggs. The Victorians agreed that an egg was generally considered fresh when it had been laid one or two days ago in summer and two to six days in winter. The shell being porous, the water inside was prone to evaporate over time, leaving a cavity of air, the size of which

indicated the age of the egg. Over time the yolk of the egg sank, too, as could be easily seen by holding it towards a candle or the sun, and when shaken a slight shock was felt if the egg wasn't fresh.

To determine the precise age of eggs, chefs were instructed to dissolve about 4 ounces of common salt in a quart of water, and then immerse the egg. If it was one day old, it would descend to the bottom of the vessel, but if three days, it would float in the liquid. If aged more than five days, it would rise to the surface, projecting above the water more and more as it became full of air with increased age.

It was also stated that eggs could be preserved for a long time by rubbing the shell with tallow wax or oil, in order to fill all the pores and so exclude the air.

The Luminous Egg (1895)

Sir James Dewar FRS (1842–1923) was a famous Scottish chemist, perhaps best known for inventing the Thermos flask in 1892. Three years later he made a novel discovery by exposing an ordinary egg to light and then cooling it with liquefied air to a temperature of -180° C. Remarkably, thus treated, the egg began to shine like a globe of blue light.

A feather was also rendered luminous in a dark room by the same treatment; so were cotton wool, paper, leather, linen, sponge and white dianthus flowers. Celluloid, paraffin and rubber, after being excited by a magnesium light then cooled to the same low temperature, emitted a greenish or bluish light. Milk was found to be more phosphorescent than water, the white of egg more than yolk, and in general white substances more than coloured.

Another distinguished worker in the field of low temperature was the Swiss scientist Herr Raoul-Pierre Pictet (1846–1929) who allegedly found a remedy for indigestion. He observed that animals confined in a cell refrigerated with liquid air became ravenously hungry, and, as the researcher was afflicted with chronic indigestion, he tried the cold air bath himself. On coming out he felt the pangs of hunger and after ten doses of the remedy found his dyspepsia was completely cured. He therefore declared his intention of fitting up refrigerated chambers in hospitals, or other places of treatment, to cure indigestion.

Transporting Frozen Fish (1882)

In 1809 the French discovered that perishable food, such as meat and fish, could be kept a long time by cooking it inside sealed glass jars. This quickly became popular with travellers and naval or military men, and as the century progressed, tinned food became an essential item on the family's shopping list.

Though this convenient source of food didn't go off for a long time, tinned meat wasn't quite as tasty as it was when fresh. Tinned salmon, for instance, was by no means as palatable as the fresh variety, so the Victorians were interested to learn that in September 1881 a shipload of this freshly caught delicacy had set sail from Hudson Bay in Canada, and arrived in London some time later without any deterioration of quality.

The revolutionary vessel was the steam-yacht *Diana*, belonging to the Hudson Bay Company. She had been fitted up with a state-of-the-art dry-air refrigerator, making her one of the world's first commercially successful refrigerated ships in history, paving the way for the refrigerated meat industry to set sail.

After decades of trial and error, a method was at last discovered for transforming ships into floating refrigerators. *Diana*'s hold was made airtight, capable of containing, when full, some 35 tons of fish, kept at a temperature of 10° below freezing. The fish were caught in Hudson Bay, near the Fur Trading Factory of the Hudson Bay Company, at the rate of 3 tons daily, and placed in the cold-air chamber on arriving at the vessel. On opening the hold, after the ship had reached the West India Docks in London, the salmon was found in as good condition as when taken out of the water.

It was hoped that the success of this trial-trip would open up a new trade between Billingsgate fish market and North America, as well as other parts of the globe.

The Perfect Bouillabaisse (1875)

Most Victorians had heard of bouillabaisse, that most perfect of fish soups, whose praises were sung by the late satirist Mr William Makepeace Thackeray (1811–1863), but few in England could claim the pleasure of a personal acquaintance with it. To enjoy it at its best, one had to travel to Marseilles, the French coastal town from where the recipe originated, but in 1875 a Victorian chef offered housewives a series of tips in order to make their own bouillabaisse at home.

The soup, or stew, was a hotchpotch of every sort of fish that could be netted; nothing too large, nothing too small was placed in the boiling cauldron, the larger fish having first been cut into pieces. Then, to make the perfect bouillabaisse, the cook was to crown the mess with bay, sharpen it with lemon, stimulate it with tomatoes, fortify it with white wine and olive oil, tickle it with garlic, sprinkle it with saffron, and behold, bouillabaisse! It was said that as soon as it was first tasted, one would be inclined to taste again.

Rag Sugar (1880)

Though the Victorians were great consumers of natural resources, they were also active recyclers, keen to reuse as much waste as possible. Nowhere was this more inventively demonstrated than in Germany, where a manufactory was established that every day turned out 1,000 lbs of pure glucose, made entirely from old, unwanted linen.

As peculiar as this sounded, linen was actually formed from vegetable fibrin and when treated with sulphuric acid was converted into dextrin, a type of carbohydrate. This was washed with limewater then treated with more acid, at which point it began to crystallise into glucose.

The process was said to be economical, and the sugar was found to be chemically the same as that of the grape. It was hoped, therefore, the product would be put to good use in the food industry. Unfortunately, however, public opposition to the manufactory eventually forced it to close down.

Old-Boots Jelly and Old-Shirt Coffee (1875)

The Victorians were well acquainted with horrifying tales of lost travellers who tried in desperation to allay the pangs of hunger by gnawing on their old boots and shoes as they wandered hopelessly through some foreign wilderness. Curious to learn whether or not this 'food' proved in any way nourishing, scientists began testing these articles of clothing. By 1875 it was proved that out of the cast-off coverings for one's feet, a tempting jelly could be extracted.

To create this strange dish, the articles of footwear were thoroughly cleaned then boiled in soda under a pressure of two atmospheres. After a while a layer of gelatine would rise to the surface, which was removed and dried. From this, the delicious jelly was easily concocted.

By a similar method, it was found that a clever imitation of coffee could be had from old shirts, sugar for sweetening it being manufactured from the linen cuffs and collars.

Dairy Products and Good Bacteria (1895)

The nineteenth century was the age when mankind became aware of the dangers of germs. Louis Pasteur was actively promoting the germ theory of disease, which affirmed that sickness was often spread by bacteria, and as a result parents became cautious not to expose their children to anything that may have been contaminated, even going so far as to burn the wallpaper of a bedroom in which a poorly member of the family had been confined.

It came as a surprise to many, therefore, when a team of American farmers declared that certain strains of bacteria promised to be useful in making butter. The cream was first warmed to a temperature of 70° C and inoculated with bacteria from sour milk. This preliminary heating tended to kill the germs that caused disease, leaving behind the 'good' bacteria, which ripened the cream and produced a butter of excellent flavour.

In Berlin, a researcher named Dr A. Bernstein discovered a method for making milk transparent. This was due to the presence of a certain type of bacterium, which rapidly turned sterilised milk transparent. More importantly, it peptonised it – in other words, made it easily digestible.

Firstly, two types of milk were required: a fresh batch, and a portion in which the bacteria was growing. The former was inoculated with the latter, and as the two intermingled the action spread from the surface downwards, the milk growing clear as the proteids it contained were converted into peptone. Milk in this state was then prepared as an article of food by mixing fresh skim milk with it and keeping the mixture at a temperature favourable to the bacteria until the whole became transparent. It was then boiled to sterilise it, and the result was a slightly reddish and acidic liquor. The drink had a pleasant aroma, and was said to be both nourishing and digestible.

Such experiments served to show that microorganisms, which had hitherto been regarded as inimical to the life of man, were now essential to his very existence and in the hands of science were being turned more and more to his advantage.

Thunder and Milk (1892)

Professor Tolomei was a nineteenth-century Italian physicist who discovered through experimentation that milk curdled during a thunderstorm. This, he inferred, was due to the electrically charged ozone in the atmosphere, which reacted with the milk and generated lactic acid, curdling the batch.

Subsequent studies by Professor Aaron L. Treadwell, of the Wesleyan University, Connecticut, confirmed that ozone did indeed curdle freshly expressed milk, but it failed to affect the drink after it had been sterilised and kept in a sealed container, away from contact with the air. Dairymen, too, deduced from their experiences that if milk was kept cold, it didn't sour in bad weather.

Modern-day scientists can offer no conclusive proof to back up this alleged phenomenon.

Koumiss (1885)

Koumiss was the name of an ancient fermented drink from Central Asia, traditionally made from mare's milk. It was particularly suitable for those who were lactose intolerant, and during the late nineteenth century it became a popular remedy for all sorts of ailments, from anaemia to TB. Indeed, demand for this marvellous drink was so high that special health resorts were set up around Europe and Russia, where people could go to relax and drink copious amounts of *koumiss* while enjoying various kinds of entertainment.

For those who found it an inconvenience to travel to these healtheries, a recipe was published in 1885, enabling housewives to make the refreshing drink in the comfort of their own kitchens.

To two pints of fresh milk were added two tablespoons of white sugar, which had first been dissolved in a little water. A small quantity of compressed yeast was added before the mixture was bottled, corked and shaken thoroughly. After leaving them to stand at room temperature for six hours, the bottles were placed in an ice bucket and left to cool overnight. The following morning, a refreshing and healthy drink of *koumiss* would be waiting.

Paraguay Tea (1875 and 1880)

Since the seventeenth century the British have been importing tea leaves from China, and by the middle of the eighteenth century the infusion was so popular that it became accepted as the nation's favourite beverage. The precise origin of the drink, however, had seemingly become lost to history, but in about 1875 the Victorians learned that the tea-plant wasn't introduced into China until about the fourth century AD. Furthermore, it wasn't used as a beverage in the Celestial Empire until the ninth century, when the government recommended the use of the infusion of tea leaves as a corrective to the bad quality of the drinking water.

By 1880 a new type of tea, known as Mate or Paraguay tea, had been introduced to the British Isles. Though new to the Victorians, the South American Indians had used the leaves for millennia, and its consumption throughout that continent was estimated to reach an incredible 50 million lbs per annum. The leaves came from a type of shrub known as the yerba mate, and the infusion was said to have a slightly bitter, but pleasant, taste. When brewed, the tea wasn't drunk from cups, but sucked up through a tube furnished at the lower end with a perforated bulb to strain the leaves.

The drink's restorative power was described as marvellous. It acted as a tonic stimulant, for it possessed the same active principles as tea or coffee, in addition to essential vitamins and minerals. However, it has since been deemed a potential carcinogenic as studies in the 2000s have identified a possible link between hot Paraguay tea and cancer.

Holly and Wild Strawberry Tea (1890 and 1892)

Long before the New World was discovered, the Creeks and Cherokee Indians of Georgia and Florida used to brew a 'black drink' from the freshly roasted leaves of a species of holly called *Ilex cassine*, which grew abundantly along the coast of the southern States of America, from James River to the Rio Grande.

According to a study by the United States Department of Agriculture, the leaves and twigs were found to contain caffeine, and the infusion had salutary properties, such as vitamins A and C, as well as antioxidants, which were wanting in ordinary tea. It was therefore proposed to cultivate the plant on the maritime belt mentioned above, of which some 40,000 acres were available for the purpose.

Germany, meanwhile, found a new industry in the collection of the young leaves of the wild strawberry, which, when carefully dried, formed an excellent substitute for Chinese tea. Young bramble and woodruff leaves were occasionally added to improve the flavour. Assam tea was found to be richest in theine, or caffeine, and the best teas of all came from Darjeeling, in West Bengal. This particular beverage became celebrated for its distinctive aroma and taste.

Roasted Fig and Lupin Coffee (1875 and 1880)

Coffee was first introduced to Europe from Africa in the sixteenth century and very quickly coffeehouses were established in large numbers. Over the decades the drink became a popular social beverage, but due to the high price of coffee beans, some countries began searching for cheaper alternatives.

In Austria roasted figs were sold as a substitute for coffee. They possessed a sweetish-bitter taste, like Victorian caramel, and sometimes had a sour twang, possibly owing to the type of fruit used.

Another lesser-known substitute was found in the seeds, or beans, of the yellow lupin, a popular garden flower. When roasted they not only tasted but smelt like coffee. A mixture of one part of lupin seeds and two parts of rye yielded a palatable draught, and one which was quite as nourishing and refreshing

as real coffee. Furthermore, these seeds, which were known to be high in protein and fibre, were found to possess a range of health benefits, including aiding digestion, reducing blood pressure and suppressing the appetite.

Spurious Coffee (1875 and 1892)

In America, imitation coffee beans were manufactured on a large scale and yielded enormous profits. In fact, it was estimated that by 1892 20 per cent of all the coffee sold in the United States was artificial. These economical substitutes were made of rye flour, glucose and water, and were intended to pass as genuine beans after being mixed with the real berry to acquire the aroma.

Spurious coffee was also manufactured in Germany, but this was curbed by Imperial decree, forbidding the constructions of the machines for making it, these having been advertised so widely as to attract the notice of the government. Artificial almonds for mixing with the genuine ones were also manufactured in Holland by a similar process.

The production of spurious coffee in America was eventually legislated against, though some of the manufacturers continued with their trade, advertising their products as 'coffee substitutes' rather than genuine coffee so as not to violate any laws against adulteration.

As the green colour of the coffee-berry was taken as a sign of its goodness, many coffee-manufacturing companies adopted the unwholesome practice of dyeing the berry with a copper dye. A Victorian dietician therefore recommended that, before roasting, the berries should be washed in hot water and dried in a clean cloth. A little acid was poured into the water in which the berries had been washed, and then the polished blade of a knife was placed into it. If copper was present, the knife would come out with a thin red coating on it.

On the Continent the poorer classes used a very cheap coffee made of burnt acorns. These were bitter to taste, and in roasting secreted a hot, pungent oil. Coffee so made wasn't pleasant, and the tannin it contained was injurious to the stomach. Adulteration of coffee reached such an extent that carrots, swedes, a type of earth called bolus, burnt bread, sand and even brick-dust were used in its manufacture.

An Act of Parliament restricting food adulteration was passed in 1860. This, and subsequent amendments to the Act, went some way towards protecting the mass of consumers, but for the poor there was still a need for simple methods to distinguish the wholesome and nutritious from the unwholesome and spurious food.

Colour and Beverages (1882 and 1895)

In addition to hot beverages, fizzy drinks were also growing in popularity across Europe and America, a method of producing carbonated water having been discovered in 1767 by the noted chemist, theologian and writer Mr Joseph Priestley FRS (1733–1804).

By the late nineteenth century it had become common in Germany to aerate certain soft beverages with oxygen rather than carbon dioxide. Oxygen gas was a medicine of considerable value in cases of diabetes, anaemia and diseases of the respiratory organs. With the promise of health benefits, these new drinks were mass-produced and sold in bottles, like lemonade.

As the popularity of soft drinks – not to mention alcoholic ones – continued to spread, the Victorians conducted some interesting experiments into the effect of the colour of glass bottles on liquids contained therein. It was proved that liquors contained in colourless bottles, exposed for some time to the light, acquired an unpleasant taste, even if they were of superior quality before the treatment. On the other hand, liquors in brown and green bottles remained unchanged, even when exposed to strong sunlight.

The experiments seemed to prove that the changes in quality were due to the chemical action of light. In consequence it was recommended that red, orange, yellow, green or opaque bottles were to be selected for the preservation of liquors, avoiding white, blue and violet glass at all costs, lest some harmful ailment befell the unsuspecting consumer.

8

SOCIETY'S HIDDEN DANGERS

Graphite Tea (1875)

The Victorians went about their business blissfully unaware that all around them unseen jeopardies were lurking. From organ-crushing corsets to exposed electrical wires, the Western world was full of perils.

Food adulteration was a major health hazard that many Victorians, particularly those among the lower classes, had to contend with. Eager to manufacture their wares as cheaply as possible, disreputable millers would whiten their flour with plaster of Paris, butchers would fill their pies with diseased meat and tea dealers would adulterate their leaves with lead. In order to make tea leaves visually appealing, an artificial glazing was added to both green and black varieties. In the case of green tea this was generally a mixture of turmeric, calcium sulphate and a type of chemical pigment known as Prussian blue, while a coating of graphite, the same substance commonly found in drawing pencils, was added to black tea.

Tea prepared for the English market was notoriously subjected to these adulterations, and this arose entirely from the Victorians' own fancy, not from any desire on the part of the Chinese to pursue such practices. The adulteration was easily discovered, however, by treating the tea with cold water then straining through muslin and allowing the fine graphite powder to subside.

Poisonous Pans (1880)

At a conference held at the Royal Dublin Society, one of the philanthropists, Dr Reynolds, drew attention to the fact that poisonous frying pans were being manufactured and sold in Dublin. They were made of ordinary iron, but instead of the usual tin coating, a poisonous alloy of lead was used instead. Dr Reynolds discerned that Dublin tea dealers had been presenting a number of these utensils as free gifts to their most valued customers, and one of his friends had nearly lost her life by eating food that had been cooked in one such pan.

'In some cases a small dose of lead may do no harm,' the doctor told the society, 'but there are acidic foods which may, in combination with the lead, produce the symptoms of cholera, attended by death.'

To distinguish a dangerous utensil from a safe one, Dr Reynolds advised boiling a little nitric acid diluted with pure water in the suspected pan, then diluting the liquid further before pouring the solution into a clean vessel. On adding to it a little potassium, the presence of lead was indicated by the formation of a yellow substance.

Narcotic Nutmegs (1880)

There were few households in the kingdom in which nutmegs weren't used to prepare family meals. So popular was the spice – particularly when making soups, sauces and cakes – that it came as a shock to cooks and housewives across the nation when a public health warning was issued, stating that nutmegs possessed noxious properties. Though a little sprinkling was harmless, it was discovered that excessive use of the condiment was attended by serious consequences.

The Victorians were well aware that their forbears consumed copious amounts of nutmeg tea, and there was once the case of an elderly lady whose nurse incautiously supplied her with this drink, which was still favoured by the older generation. Unfortunately, however, the nurse was unaware of the dangers and made the brew from one and a half nutmegs, which consequently threw the patient into a profound stupor for

several hours. The symptoms were similar to those produced by taking opium, but eventually the narcotic effects subsided and the old lady returned to her normal health.

Cases were also reported of trances and delirium resulting from the consumption of just two or three drachms of nutmeg. When added to wine, it brought on a feeling of ecstasy, which lasted several days, and people who suffered from insomnia began sprinkling it in a glass of lemonade before bedtime.

Dangerous Mussels (1882 and 1890)

Mussels have featured on mankind's menu for thousands of years and were among the Victorians' favourite types of shellfish. When healthy and properly prepared they were tasty and nutritious, but when they lived in water which was tainted with sewage, they were apt to become poisonous.

On 30 June 1890 an entire family was wiped out after eating a batch of unhealthy mussels. Mrs O'Connor and her four daughters lived at Seapoint, a few miles from Dublin City. Earlier that day the girls had gone fishing in a saltwater pond that lay on the landward side of the railway embankment, where they gathered a quantity of mussels for their tea. Almost immediately after their meal all five of them were seized by illness, and by the time Mr O'Connor returned home from work, his wife and daughters were barely alive. Despite immediate medical attention, they all perished one by one. The youngest child was just five years old.

It later transpired that the pond had been contaminated with sewage, perhaps having become infected from the railway. From this it was deduced that when the muscular tissues of vertebrate and invertebrate animals underwent putrefaction, certain poisonous chemicals were formed. Furthermore, as mussels were filter feeders, they drew in water through their shell; thus, when their watery environment was tainted with sewage, the septic matter ended up inside the creature.

A simple method of ascertaining whether or not water was free of organic pollution was to cork up a small bottle full of it, after putting in a lump of sugar. If, on letting it stand in the light for two or three days, no milky cloud became visible, and the water retained its clearness, it was considered free from sewage.

The Purity Tests (1885 and 1887)

Today's shoppers take it for granted that a bottle of olive oil, bought at a local supermarket, contains exactly what's on the label – olive oil – and it probably wouldn't cross their minds that the contents may be contaminated. For Victorians, however, things were very different. 'Olive oil' sold in Florence flasks was largely adulterated by cottonseed oil, the manufacturers having added this objectionable ingredient to dilute the product and save money. With a view to protecting consumers, the following test for detecting contamination was proposed.

One sixth of an ounce of nitrate protoxide of mercury – a type of salt – was dissolved in a test-tube with one fifth of an ounce of nitric acid. A sample of the olive oil to be tested was then poured on to this solution until the test-tube was two thirds full. The tube was then corked, the two fluids shaken together for five or six seconds, and the change of colour noted. If cottonseed oil was present, the liquid turned dark brown, almost black.

Similar problems were encountered with condiments, and it wasn't uncommon for sand grains to be found mixed with pepper. By following this simple test, purchasers were able to pick the pure pepper for their table.

An ounce of chloroform was first obtained at one's local chemist's shop, and poured into a test-tube until it was half full. To this was added about half a teaspoonful of pepper. The test-tube was corked and shaken a couple of times. Real pepper would float on the top of the chloroform, while the sand, if present, would sink to the bottom. In this way the buyer could judge the quantity of pepper before purchasing it.

Tinned food, too, was potentially lethal; in the early nineteenth century, cans were sealed with a corrosive chemical known as chloride of zinc. In 1885, following a spate of poisoning from eating tinned tomatoes, a doctor from New York made careful inquiries into the toxicology of canned goods, and lay down a series of rules for the guidance of those purchasing these items. These included rejecting every can that showed rust around the lid, and also every can that didn't bear the name of the wholesale dealer, or the name of the town where it was manufactured. When the manufacturer was ashamed to have his name on the goods, it was highly likely that the contents were deficient.

It was later discovered that a solution of lactic acid and glycerine made a harmless soldering mixture for tin cans, and had none of the poisonous properties of chloride of zinc.

Sanitary Handwriting (1892)

Today the Victorians are admired for their attention to detail, and their artistic disposition often manifested itself in beautiful handwriting, each word so carefully penned with the utmost care and deliberation. However, by 1892 the world had become such a precarious place that even the simple act of writing a letter had been declared potentially harmful to one's health. So concerned were certain authorities that they announced their desire to ban the teaching of slanted handwriting.

Austria's Supreme Council of Hygiene had been studying the relative advantages of upright compared to slanting characters in handwriting, and concluded that an upright hand should

be taught in schools instead, because it was healthier for the penman. The slanting style, though beautiful, was believed to cause the body and neck to twist unnecessarily, resulting in a permanent spinal curvature.

The Electrified Sitting Room (1884)

Just when one thought it was safe to sit down, it was unexpectedly discovered in a New York sitting room that the entire room had been electrified, and several ladies experienced an intense shock upon their posteriors when attempting to make use of the couch. In fact, it was discovered that nothing in the room was safe to touch, for everything had become charged with electricity.

Investigation showed that the belts of a small motor, which had been installed near the room to generate power for the home, also generated an unusually high amount of static electricity by rubbing on the pulley, and this had communicated itself along the carpet to the couch and various other items of furniture.

Lightning and Electric Light Wires (1884)

During a musical festival in the Drill Hall at Minneapolis, in the United States, a terrible thunderstorm erupted in the skies above, and the building was struck by lightning, which, attracted by the metal flagstaff over the entrance, caused serious damage. The electricity traversed an iron bolt in some timberwork and escaped to earth by some bare electric light wires which entered the building and led to the electric lamps within. These were shattered, causing a great deal of damage and also injuring some of the people inside.

This explosive incident proved conclusively that naked electric light or telephone wires were a source of danger unless proper care was taken by the electricians in erecting them; otherwise they had the potential to act as lightning-rods, inviting a dangerous electrical discharge by providing for it an avenue of least resistance to the ground. It was concluded that in future such wires should run into buildings at suitable points, a good distance away from spires, flagstaffs or other prominent parts of the building likely to attract lightning.

In another incident, a workman of the electric light company, while engaged in splicing the wires during the same thunderstorm, was rendered unconscious, and on coming to felt an intense pain in his right foot. On examining himself he found that his leg had been struck by lightning below the knee. His clothing had been torn to shreds, his boot split open from toe to heel and his foot blistered as if it had been burned.

The Safe Limelight (1884)

Before the introduction of the bright electric arc lamp, theatres and concert halls around Britain relied on 'limelight' for their stage lighting. This was achieved by heating cylinders of quicklime to over 2,500° C, thereby producing a brilliant white flame, the light from which was directed onto the performers. Due to the high temperatures involved, this was a risky business, and numerous were the headlines announcing the latest theatrical tragedy.

'THE FATAL EXPLOSION AT DRURY LANE THEATRE', the *Pall Mall Gazette* proclaimed on 17 June 1884.

'DESTRUCTION OF EDINBURGH THEATRE BY FIRE', the *York Herald* declared some years earlier, on 13 February 1875, while the *Derby Daily Telegraph* stated, on 25 February 1884: 'ALARMING EXPLOSION AT AN ENTERTAINMENT. ONE KILLED AND NINE INJURED.'

These catastrophes were caused by the explosion of the gas that heated the quicklime, thus prompting Mr Richard Anthony Proctor (1837–1888), a well-known astronomer and public lecturer, to devise a plan for rendering limelight safe from explosion.

In the ordinary unsafe arrangement, the reservoirs containing pressurised oxygen and hydrogen shared a solitary jet, from which the mingled gases issued, and were then ignited to heat the quicklime. Mr Proctor's improvement consisted in having the jet made double, so that each gas was released separately. By this reckoning there was no danger of one gas diffusing into the other, making the whole operation safer to perform.

The White Darkroom (1884)

The low red light employed by photographers to develop their plates was thought to be significantly injurious to the eyes. In an

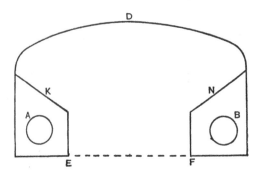

effort to protect one's vision, the London-born photographer Mr William Elliot Debenham (1839–1924) introduced a new method, outlined in the sketch. He had developed a non-actinic white light, composed of complimentary red and green rays, and he employed a lantern consisting of two lamps, A B, with glass faces at K and N. The glass at K was of a deep yellowish-green tint, while that at N was of a red colour, with a superposed pane of pale yellowish-green. The light from these lamps fell on to the curved reflecting surface, D, which was of a deep yellow colour, and was reflected down through the opening, E F, which was covered by a sheet of translucent white tissue paper. The light, after passing through this paper, was nearly white, but had so little actinic effect that a highly sensitive photographic plate, placed at reading distance below it for a quarter of an hour, showed scarcely a trace of an image. When a yellow fabric was substituted at E F, an hour's exposure failed to produce more than the slightest mark on the plate, while giving sufficient light for the photographer to work by.

Deadly Paints (1880 and 1887)

Though the dangers of lead poisoning have been known for centuries – a Greek physician from the first century AD having noted that lead makes the mind 'give way' – the manufacture of lead-based products was widespread throughout the nineteenth century.

There was a popular impression in Victorian times that those who inhabited freshly painted rooms were in danger of succumbing to lead-poisoning, owing to the high levels of this toxic metal in paint.

However, according to Dr Clement Biddle, an American scientist, this notion was quite unfounded. He based his conclusion on the result of an experiment, in which a number of sheets of paper, saturated with white lead paint, were enclosed in a box along with a dish of pure distilled water. The water was left thus exposed to the vapour of the paint for three days, and then analysed, but no trace of lead precipitate was found in it. He therefore deemed that lead-based paints were quite harmless to human health.

Later, in 1887, a curious case reported from America showed that care ought to be exercised when using paints that emitted hydrocarbon vapours in enclosed spaces. Some workmen, who had been painting a large iron tube with a mixture of benzine and asphalt as a protection against rust, were found to become strangely exhilarated and wildly excited, some even descending into a state of absolute stupor. Suspecting the cause, the superintendent had the men carried out of the building. The open air revived them, but disagreeable after effects soon began to take hold.

Lead in the Brain (1887)

In 1887 numerous cases of sudden death were alleged to have taken place at a lead factory in the East End of London, and upon investigation these were attributed to lead poisoning. In one case lead sulphate was extracted from the liver of one victim during a post mortem, and in another the same substance was found in the brain. It was calculated that the whole of the brain contained 117.1 milligrams of lead sulphate, an amount 780 times over the threshold limit value, or the level at which the chemical is today considered to be 'safe'.

The full extent of the risk of exposure to lead wasn't fully understood until the latter part of the twentieth century, when it was conclusively proved that lead is an extremely toxic substance, causing damage to the nervous and reproductive systems, as well as bones and internal organs.

The Stars and Firedamp (1882)

By the 1880s it had been observed that the stars seemed to twinkle most brightly just before a fall of the barometer, which indicated

a decrease in air pressure. This observation prompted Meneer Somzée, a well-known Belgian mining engineer, to suggest the employment of a night watchman to gaze into the heavens in the hope of providing warning to miners in collieries, for a fall in the barometer was usually attended by a greater discharge of deadly gas from the seams. Firedamp was an explosive underground gas that would cause the deaths of hundreds, if not thousands, of miners across the world before the end of the century. Somzée's plan was to establish observatories connected by telegraph to the mining districts, and to advise the coal masters of the brightness of the stars. This information was automatically relayed by an apparatus known as the photophone, the Victorians' answer to fibre-optic technology, in which a ray of light was used to send an electric signal along a wire and was picked up at the other end.

Recycling Refuse (1892)

The disposal of waste was becoming something of a headache as the Victorian era drew to a close. Rivers ran thick with sewage, garbage was piled high in the streets and special dumping barges were constructed to dispose of toxic waste in the earth's oceans, which were quickly becoming polluted. With a view to reducing the amount of waste society was generating, while also saving money, a new method of utilising the contents of the dustcart was trialled at Chelsea in 1892.

The cart was tipped into a sorting machine, and the contents underwent a sifting action: the paper, straw, rags, tin, etc., all being separated into different compartments ready for reuse, and all the offensive material that couldn't be recycled was ground up with the cinders. These ashes found a sale among brick makers, and by mixing them with pitch, or mortar, they could be pressed into briquettes for fuel. The recycled paper was reduced to pulp, and the straw was employed in making straw boards.

The Sewage Treatment Process (1885)

During the height of the Industrial Revolution, towns and cities across Britain began to expand. This resulted in overcrowding, and consequently there was much concern regarding sanitary arrangements. Taking their lead from London, many local authorities began constructing extensive sewerage systems to clear the waste products away from the streets and houses of the towns. Many of these fed directly into the country's waterways, which ultimately flushed the raw sewage into the sea. Owing to the serious water pollution that resulted, not to mention the outbreaks of cholera and other waterborne diseases, the Victorians began devising ways in which to sanitise the nation's sewage.

In the 1880s a pharmaceutical chemist named Dr John Clough Thresh (1851–1932) formulated a new process for treating the sewage in Buxton, Derbyshire. His method utilised the famous natural mineral waters of the town, which were derived from the lower coal formation about 2 miles below the ground. Victorian experts had noted that the spring water from Buxton contained 1.2 grains of iron per gallon, held in solution by carbonic acid. On exposure to the air, the carbonic acid escaped, and the iron, upon taking up more oxygen, subsided in the state of ferric hydroxide, taking with it many of the organic impurities in the water. This was the reason why Buxton's mineral water was so celebrated for its purity, and thus Dr Thresh surmised that if the sewage was treated with the water, the impurities in the waste would combine with the iron and subside with it.

Before treatment, the town's sewage was said to contain 11.74 parts per million of free ammonia and 1.6 parts per million of albuminoid ammonia, a type of water pollution. After Thresh's new treatment, these figures were reduced to 4.00 and 0.30 respectively.

In 2003 it was announced that the 142-year-old sewage works in Buxton would face a £11 million overhaul to introduce membrane technology, the process of filtering treated water through microscopic holes in a plastic membrane, which greatly improves the purity of water.

Flooding the Streets with Seawater (1887 and 1890)

During the Victorian era, the roads of busy towns and cities were often covered with sludge, waste and horse manure, and disease was rife. Though labourers were employed to sweep the streets, it was often the responsibility of householders to ensure the pavement outside his or her door was kept clean, though this duty was frequently neglected. Sick and tired of having to deal with filthy, rat-infested streets, the aldermen of Bournemouth devised an ingenious plan for cleansing the coastal town of its grime. They began flooding the streets with seawater, flushing not only the roads and pavements but also the polluted sewers, and washing the waste into the sea. For this purpose water mains and hydrants were rigged up, and it was anticipated that in thirty years' time, when the debt for the works had been paid off, the cost for water wouldn't exceed 3*d* per 1,000 gallons.

Experiments had shown that once the seawater had dried, the remaining salt formed a kind of barrier on the streets, helping to keep them clean until the next flooding. According to one authority, using saltwater two or three times a week was said to be just as effectual as using fresh water every day. Moreover, studies had shown that regular exposure to saltwater posed no threat whatsoever to the health of the townsfolk.

It wasn't long before the Americans latched on to this ingenious street-cleaning plan, and by 1890 the residents of Ocean Grove, on the Atlantic coast of the United States, began pumping seawater into a special reservoir that had been constructed 40 feet in the air. 40,000 gallons of seawater were supplied to the reservoir each day, and every so often a plug would be opened in order to flush the drains and water the filthy streets.

Preventing Ships from Sinking (1882)

Every year in the nineteenth century dozens of vessels were lost at sea. This was a great concern, particularly for the families of sailors. In 1881 alone a total of twenty ships were wrecked at sea, resulting in the death of more than 550 people. The following year Victorians listened with interest when a new safety procedure was announced, which promised to prevent the loss of ships. The annexed diagram explains the method, which was devised by Mr R. G. Sayers, and consisted of the use of airbags.

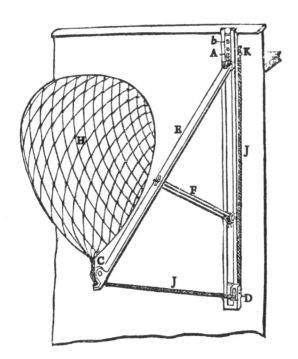

Supposing a vessel sprang a leak, or was otherwise in a foundering condition, each of the flexible airbags, H, was inflated with the greatest of speed; the wing, E, and stay, F, of the supporting apparatus being meanwhile fixed to the side of the ship in the position shown. The bar, *b*, was then lowered into the grooves provided for it in the fixed bar, A, and was fastened to the ship's side by two or more bolts. The airbag was attached to the end of the rope, J, having first been passed through a hole in the vessel's side and over the pulleys, K, D and C. Thus secured, the airbag would serve to keep the vessel afloat. The wing, E, and stay, F, acted as fenders, helping to keep the bag from swaying against the ship during a heavy sea or strong gale.

It was estimated that the whole process could be completed in eighteen minutes from the time of the accident, and public hopes were high that Mr Sayers' plan would one day prove serviceable out on the ocean waves.

Alleviating Thirst at Sea (1875)

The burning sensation of thirst on land was bad enough, but thirst at sea, with water everywhere, yet not a drop to drink, was described by sailors as being ten times worse. In 1875 members of the public were horrified to read in the papers about the sinking of the British sailing ship *Cospatrick*, which caught fire off the coast of New Zealand on 17 November 1874, carrying 472 passengers and crew. Only a handful of people managed to scramble into the lifeboats, and by the time they were rescued ten days later, just five of the men were still alive. Two of them perished soon afterwards, and the three survivors later related how their agonising thirst had driven them to drink the blood of their dead comrades to stay alive.

Nobody knew what horrors the Fates had in store, so for the benefit of the public, the Board of Trade Examiners published an examination question that was posed to candidates applying to become mates in the merchant service.

'What would you do in order to allay thirst, with nothing but seawater at hand?'

The answer was: 'Keep the clothes, especially the shirt, soaked with seawater.'

Drinking salt water to allay thirst drove the sufferer mad, but an external application of it gave at least some relief, for it kept the skin hydrated. The Board expressed their disappointment that this simple yet scientific remedy was known to few who tempted the treacherous main. They felt that if more people were made aware of this simple fact, perhaps more lives could be saved.

Exploding Coat Buttons (1892)

Though items of clothing were alleged to save lives at sea, on dry land they were proving something of a hazard. In 1892 an alarmed citizen named Professor Boys was the first to draw the public's attention to the fact that exploding buttons were being manufactured on a large scale by firms ignorant to the laws of chemistry. A lady of his acquaintance, while standing near a fire, suddenly found herself enveloped in smoke. Her dress had gone up in flames, and the ignition was traced to a spot where a large fancy button had been affixed. The button had disappeared, and Professor Boys, having managed to obtain a similar fastening, performed various experiments upon it. The button vanished in a puff of smoke and flame as soon as it was exposed to heat. He promptly issued a warning to all fashion-conscious ladies, advising them to purchase their buttons from trustworthy manufacturers.

Thanks to his caution, the production of flammable buttons eventually fell into decline as the manufacture and wholesale of more reputable brands began to increase.

Detonating Diamonds (1880)

Exploding buttons weren't the only items of clothing proving deadly to one's health. In 1880 the case of the detonating diamond cufflink was investigated by Professor Joseph Leidy (1823–1891), a distinguished palaeontologist and mineralogist from Philadelphia, USA. It appeared that a gentleman, wearing a diamond mounted in the solitaire of his cuff, was leaning his head on his hand upon a windowsill in the sun, when the diamond suddenly exploded with such force as to drive a portion of the gem into his hand and forehead. On examination, the fractured surface of the cufflink was found to exhibit a thin cavity such as was occasionally seen in quartz crystals. A conspicuous particle of coal was also exposed.

Professor Leidy believed that the explosion was due to the sudden expansion of some volatile liquid, such as liquid hydrocarbon, that had been contained in the cavity. He presumed it was excavated along with the diamond and the trace of coal, and had been ignited by the heat of the sun.

Firearms for Children (1881)

In an era long before health and safety dictated the dos and don'ts of everyday life, most Victorian mothers wouldn't have thought twice about buying their children loaded toy pistols to play with. These 'harmless' playthings, however, came under scrutiny in the 1880s, when some people began to perceive them as intolerable nuisances that had been allowed to exist in the possession of delinquents for far too long.

On 4 July 1881 an alarming number of accidents befell young boys who attended Independence Day festivities at Baltimore, Maryland. Jubilant, patriotic youths began firing their toy pistols at random, and no fewer than sixteen deaths resulted. In several instances the boys suffered lockjaw as a result of injuries sustained by the hand that fired the gun.

The toys were made of cast-iron and had 2-inch-long barrels containing a highly explosive substance known as amorse. The trigger was crudely made, and there was a risk of accidental discharge when the hinged barrel was returned to its place after the insertion of the cartridge. This happened every so often, inflicting ugly wounds upon the palm of the user, and bruises resulted from fragments of the bullets discharging with considerable violence.

As a good deal of this kind of amusement was in vogue on Guy Fawkes Day, the Queen's Birthday and other holidays, parents in Britain and America were advised to prohibit their children from playing with these toys.

'Parents have no more right to send their boys into the streets with toy pistols than they have to turn them loose with small pox,' the *New York Herald* admonished, following the tragedy on Independence Day.

There was no doubt in people's minds that the inventiveness of youth would speedily find another, and hopefully safer, outlet for the exuberance of their spirits.

The Death of a City (1875)

'Mushroom Cities' was a term used to describe cities that sprang up one day and were deserted the next. One such example was the American city of Pithole, Pennsylvania. Within one month from the completion of the first house, erected in 1865, this city had a telegraph office and a hotel, costing the owners $80,000. In a month more there was a daily paper established and in the next a theatre. In another month came another theatre, and then an academy of music. Within six months there were seventy-four hotels and boarding houses, and in the seventh month the city had reached its highest prosperity. It had at that time between 15,000 and 20,000 inhabitants, elaborate waterworks, a city hall and an expensive government.

Then the Fates played a cruel trick, and diverted the oil business on which Pithole depended into another channel. At once the hotels, theatres and the telegraph office were closed, the daily paper incontinently died, and almost everyone packed up their trunks and moved out. By 1875 only nine families remained, demonstrating how precarious and unpredictable life in the ever-changing nineteenth century really was.

9

MAKE DO AND MEND

Wearing Newspapers (1875)

The innovative Victorians were always searching for new ways to improve their quality of life. From generating cleaner energy and recycling waste to trying out new gardening and interior design techniques, almost every aspect of daily life was scrutinised as the people sought to construct a perfect society.

Without the luxury of central heating or electric blankets, winter nights were often long and cold. In the days when diseases were harder to cure, it was essential to keep warm, thereby reducing the risk of contracting a potentially fatal illness such as pneumonia. In 1875 health officials recommended the adoption of a simple plan to ward away illness and declared that those who followed their advice would never suffer a cold night again.

They recommended that before covering up for the night, two or three large newspapers were to be spread over the entire body and the blankets thrown over the top. The result was a warm and comfortable night, without any perceptible increase in the weight of the bedding. The method was therefore found particularly suitable for those who disliked the sensation of heavy or too many bed sheets.

Similarly, before taking a cold ride on a boat or coach, or a long walk against the wind, if a newspaper was spread over the chest before buttoning up the overcoat, no chill was felt. No other method for keeping warm was found to be as cheap or effective as this.

Drying Wet Boots (1875)

In order to avoid catching a cold, it was essential to keep one's feet as warm as possible. This was often difficult to achieve, especially in wet weather, when one's boots were liable to become saturated with rainwater. Mothers would advise their children and husbands never to go outside in wet boots, but without radiators to lean them against, keeping footwear dry in the autumn and winter was a troublesome task.

Fortunately, in 1875 a new way of drying wet boots was advised. As soon as they were removed from the feet, they were filled to the brim with dry oats. This particular grain was appropriately porous for the task and would rapidly absorb the least vestige of damp from the wet leather. Furthermore, as it soaked up the moisture, the oats would swell and fill each boot with a tightly fitting filling, helping the leather to retain its shape.

The following morning, the oats were shaken out and hung in a bag near the fire to dry, ready for use on the next wet night.

Soot-Water for Roses (1880)

Ash and soot was produced in abundance during the nineteenth century, as families relied on coal to keep the home fires burning. The majority of this waste was thrown out with the rest of the household rubbish, but in the 1880s a new use for unwanted soot was discovered. It was observed that a rapid growth of garden roses was promoted by the use of soot-water, and the application had the advantage of costing nothing. Some soot was collected from a chimney or stove, put into an old pitcher, and then hot water was poured upon the contents. When cold, the mixture was used for watering the plants every few days.

Weeding with Salt (1885)

Every gardener knows how difficult it is to permanently remove weeds from the garden path once they have taken root. However, the Victorians discovered that salt is one of the best weed-removal remedies around, and they issued instructions on the best way of applying it.

The salt was to be boiled in water – one pound of salt to the gallon – and the mixture was poured boiling hot out of a watering can. This, it was said, would keep weeds and worms away for two or three years. Subsequent applications could be made a little weaker.

Care was taken that none of the liquid fell on to the garden, for salt would remain in the soil for a long time, preventing not only the weeds from growing, but any type of plant at all. This remedy was therefore only suitable for paths and patios.

Banana Carpets and Cotton-Plant Bags (1882 and 1890)

In the nineteenth century a few innovative merchants began shipping affordable bananas from the Caribbean to fruit dealers in Britain and America. As time went on, this novel fruit started to become popular with Western consumers, and banana farms were established in tropical regions, ready to transport the produce all over the world.

In 1890 a German consular recommended the utilisation of the castoff fibres of the banana plant for industrial purposes. These were hitherto unwanted by the European market and would otherwise have been discarded. The leaf of the plant was found to contain an exceptionally tough fibre, which was used by the indigenous natives of Central America for making carpets, hammocks, strings and other useful things. The consular proposed that strong paper, coffee-bags and powerful ropes ought to be manufactured from the fibre, which was readily available.

In a similar way, the stalks of the cotton-plant had previously been considered useless after the cotton had been gathered, but by the 1880s it was pointed out that the fibres would be suitable for the manufacture of strong bagging. The cotton plantation labourers began making bags from the cotton stalks and using them to transport the cotton in.

Meanwhile, in France, a chemist named Monsieur Bertrand introduced a process for cleaning cotton waste of its oil and utilising the product for printers' ink.

Grape Seed Oil (1884)

In Italy, the abundant oil from the surplus grape seed – a by-product of the winemaking industry – was made use of for illumination purposes. As extracted at Modena, in Northern Italy, 33 lbs of grape seed yielded about 13 quarts of golden yellow oil, which was used as fuel in oil lamps. The seeds of the black grape yielded more oil than the white varieties, and those of young vines were found more prolific than older ones.

Since then, the oil of the grape seed has been clinically proven to increase 'good cholesterol' levels, and is now commonly used as an ingredient in cookery.

Gas from Castor Oil (1881)

At the gas-works of Jeypore, India, illuminating gas was manufactured from castor oil. To extract the fuel, the seeds of the castor plant were crushed to free them from their shells; then they were ground to a paste, heated in a pan and packed into horsehair bags. Upon being pressed, oil was exuded, and this was manufactured into gas by a chemical process known as destructive distillation. 82 lbs, or 1 maund, of castor oil produced 750 cubic feet of gas, capable of generating a light equivalent to 26 ½ candlepower. The total cost of the oil was about £1 per maund.

The Jeypore gas-works used to supply their gas to customers in portable reservoirs, in much the same way as Monsieur Camille Alphonse Faure (1840–1898), the French electrical engineer, proposed to retail stored-up electricity for electric lamps. The gas was compressed to three atmospheres of pressure in a wrought-iron holder and delivered to the residence of the consumer, where the holder was then connected to the pipes supplying the house.

Cheap, Clean Gas (1882)

A method for producing cheap gas was discovered by Mr Dowson by 1882, and it was expected to be widely used for domestic heating, or for driving gas-engines, in the coming years. It was made by passing a mixture of steam and air into red-hot anthracite coal, a type of fuel possessing few impurities. The process produced a combination of carbonic oxide and hydrogen, which, after being purified from sulphuretted hydrogen and dust, was ready for use.

Unlike other types of fuel, this gas was free from tar and ammonia, and was therefore clean in preparation. It didn't burn with a smoky flame, and thus produced no soot. Moreover, it didn't require so great a draught to burn as ordinary coal-gas.

The cost of Dowson's gas was just 3*d* per 1,000 cubic feet, or under 1*s* for the equivalent power of 1,000 cubic feet of ordinary coal-gas, as about four times the volume of anthracite gas was necessary to give equal power with coal-gas.

Fuel from Straw and Hay (1881)

An American farmer issued an appeal to inventors for a machine that would compress straw and hay into bricks, which could then be used as fuel for ordinary stoves. Though he had found a method for doing this by hand, the labour involved was great, and he believed an automatic machine, which would do the job quickly and cheaply, would revolutionise the Western economy.

Over the years he had observed that immense quantities of unwanted straw were allowed to rot in fields all over the country. Thousands of tons were burned every year, merely to get them

out of the way, and while this waste went on, fuel was scarce and over-priced. He argued that if machines could be devised to turn out straw-bricks at a moderate cost, American farmers would be prepared to patronise them and save the country thousands of dollars every year.

Electricity from Sugar (1885)

One day in 1885, Signor Salvatore Mazza, an Italian electrician, was crushing a quantity of sugar in a copper mortar with a wooden pestle when he noticed sparks of electricity about an inch long. He believed the sparks, which were sometimes blue and sometimes reddish-yellow, had been generated by the breaking down of the sugar, and though Signor Mazza saw his experiment repeated successfully with an iron pestle and a copper mortar, his contemporaries put down the development of electricity to friction and nothing more.

This electrical phenomenon was largely forgotten about until 2007, when the electrical company, Sony, announced the development of a biological battery that generated its power from sugar, nature's energy store. Two years later, researchers at Brigham Young University in Utah published their theory that clean energy could potentially be generated from a mixture of sugar and weed killer. In 2012 it was publicised that a proposed 23-megawatt co-generating electrical plant at the Andrews Sugar Factory, in Barbados, could potentially generate enough electricity to power 75,000 Barbadian homes. Meanwhile, scientists in Virginia have been busy developing a sugar-powered battery for use in smartphones. This remarkable battery, which was unveiled to the press in 2014, is said to be ten times more powerful than conventional lithium batteries and could be released for sale in just a few years' time.

The Molecular Electric Light (1880)

The Victorians' quest for a source of clean, renewable energy was progressing apace by the 1880s, and this was when scientists began searching for an effective way to generate light. It was generally believed by physicists of the day that molecules of gas, when confined in a vessel, flew hither and thither, striking against each other and the sides of the vessel in the wildest confusion; however, Sir William Crookes FRS proved that if a great part of the gas was pumped away, the remaining molecules were far less liable to knock against each other. Then, when under the influence of electricity, they would be forced to move in straight lines.

If the negative pole of an electric battery was made concave and sealed inside the vacuum, the molecules electrified negatively by contact with this pole would fly across the vacuum at right angles to the surface of the pole, and their path was rendered visible as soon as they struck against another piece of metal, which was also contained within the vacuum. In short, the gas was turned into light.

The figure herewith illustrates this heating and lighting action. A glass vacuum bulb mounted on a stand had a negative pole,

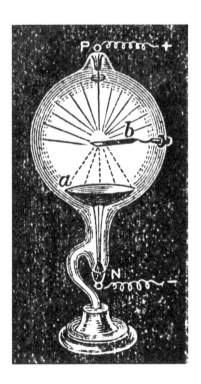

N, in the form of a metal cup, *a*, sealed into its lower end, and a positive pole, P, shaped like a button, sealed into its upper part. The electrified molecules bounced off the cup, *a*, and met at a focal point in the centre of the bulb, as shown by dotted lines. Here a piece of platinum or platinum-iridium, *b*, was held, and in a few moments was seen to glow with insufferable brilliancy until it melted with the intense heat.

Crookes applied this phenomenon to the production of a vacuum light equivalent to 33 candlepower, which could be maintained at a cost of about 1*d* per hour.

Recycling Sewage (1890)

In 1889 the Wimbledon Sewage Farm developed a new process for recycling raw sewage. It consisted in blending amine salts with the waste. The salts comprised fifty grains of limestone with three grains of herring brine, which were then added to every gallon of sewage. The lime was decomposed by the brine, yielding a soluble gas, which the discoverer, Mr Hugo Wollheim, called aminol. This gaseous reagent was a powerful disinfectant, destroying all microbes capable of producing disease.

The disinfecting mixture was mingled with the sewage as it issued from the sewers, and the putrid odour was replaced by the briny smell of the reagent. The sewage and salt mixture was allowed to flow into settling-tanks, where the solids subsided and the remaining sludge, free from germs, was run off. This was collected, pressed and formed into blocks, which were sold to farmers as solid fertiliser.

Fish and Bat Fertiliser (1882 and 1887)

The manufacture of guano, or manure, from the heads, bones, skin and other fish waste was a growing industry in Norway during the late nineteenth century. Formerly the custom was to dispose of this offal, but in the 1880s it was left to dry on the hills before putrefaction set in, then it was cut into small pieces, baked in a kiln and ground into powder by millstones. This fish-flour was said to contain a large percentage of fertilising materials, and was consequently in high demand by the Scandinavian farmers, who claimed it performed wonders on their agricultural land.

Factories for this new industry began springing up in Finnmark and Lofoden, on the coast of the Norwegian Sea, where codfish and herring were plentiful.

In Australia, meanwhile, the guano produced by thousands of bats was known to exist in vast quantities in certain caves of Victoria and New South Wales. Samples taken were found to be so sufficiently rich in nitrogen and phosphoric acid that the manure made an exceptional fertiliser. When treated with water, the guano yielded a dark brown liquor that was sprinkled on farmland.

Texans, too, boasted the discovery of bat-infested caves in Uvalde County, which were so deeply paved with rich guano that steps were taken to utilise the produce in the interest of American agriculture. One cave, termed the Cibolo Cavern, was about 400 feet in length, and the deposit of guano was in some places over 30 feet deep! A factory was erected in the district for the treatment of the fertiliser.

Street Dust (1880)

The dust of the street may have been worthless to many Victorians, but, nevertheless, one man of science detected something valuable even there. Signor Parnetti, a Florentine experimentalist, began analysing the dust, not only of his native town but also of Paris, and found to his satisfaction that the debris of the Parisian carriageways uniformly yielded 35 per cent of iron abraded from horseshoes, while that of the pavements returned a regular average of 30 per cent of glue from the soles of people's boots. The sweepings resulted in a healthy profit for Signor Parnetti's labours.

The Value of Sweepings (1884)

An American gentleman estimated that the value of the sweepings of the floor of a goldsmith's workshop, if left to accumulate for a decade, were worth about £30 per square foot. A small tub, used

in one workshop as a receptacle for the dust from one polishing lathe, yielded £10 worth of gold per annum.

Of course, the labourers who worked in such places often employed a variety of tricks in order to secure as much of the dust as possible. It was said that the men sometimes oiled their hair before going to work, then ran their dusty fingers through it during the day. The gold dust that adhered to their heads was washed out as soon as they returned home. In just a few weeks one man carried away, on the moistened tip of his finger, £6 worth of gold filings. That would have been the equivalent of around £545 in today's money, based on the retail price index.

Curious Paper (1882, 1884 and 1890)

As technology developed and the century progressed, the list of vegetable matter from which paper could be manufactured increased year on year. This was good news for the Victorians, since the greater the number of available materials, the lower the price of paper, and the better and cheaper the literature of the day.

Straw of all kinds, including wheat, rice and flax, were brought into service, and attempts were also made to utilise the fibres of leaves as well as relatively unpromising material like the refuse of the sugar-cane. Perhaps the most satisfactory results came from various grasses, notably diss grass and esparto, both of which were grown largely in North Africa. A quantity of a new type of grass – the elephant grass of British Burma – was sent to England, and, after being boiled in caustic soda and bleached, was made into paper.

In Germany, some 'natural address cards' were introduced from Cameroon on the western coast of Africa. They consisted of the dried leaves of the silver poplar, which were written upon with ease. An outstandingly pretty visiting card was the result.

In 1884 the Norwegian diplomat Consul Fredrik Herman Gade (1871–1943), of modern-day Oslo, submitted a recommendation to the United States Government for a new material for papermaking. This was the white moss that grew widely across Norway and Sweden, and when it died it accumulated in the woods. A factory was duly erected in Sweden, in a district where millions of pounds of the dead moss could be harvested, and paper of various thicknesses was manufactured. Moss cardboard was as hard as wood, could be easily painted and polished, and had the advantage of not warping or cracking. It was therefore proposed that this new environmentally friendly material be used for making window frames and other items of household furniture.

In Massachusetts, it was found that a new kind of strong aromatic paper could be manufactured from the bark of the cedar tree, which grew abundantly in New Bedford. The sheets were found serviceable for putting on the floor underneath carpets, and the odour proved effective at keeping spiders and insects away.

Fireproof Ink and Incombustible Paper (1882)

In 1882 a German chemist discovered a recipe for fireproof ink and paper, neither of which could be damaged in a blaze. A fluent ink for writing with an ordinary pen could be made from five parts of a chemical known as platinum chloride mixed with fifteen parts of lavender oil, fifteen parts of Chinese ink and one part of gum Arabic, all dissolved in sixty-four parts of water.

The incombustible paper was prepared by mixing ninety-five parts of asbestos with five parts of woody fibre, then beating the mixture into a pulp with borax and glue-water.

When the ink was written with on fireproof paper, the burning of the paper rendered the writing transparent, and the paper remained intact. Then, even though the ink had faded, the writing was made legible again by reheating the paper.

To create a fireproof ink suitable for use by industrial printers, ten parts by weight of dry platinum chloride was used, and this was mixed with twenty-five parts of the lavender oil, thirty parts of varnish, and a small quantity of a carbon-based pigment known as lamp-black. The action of fire on this ink reduced the platinum salt to its metallic state, leaving behind a permanent, brownish-black stain.

Pigments for painting could also be rendered fireproof by mixing with the ordinary metallic paints the chloride of platinum and painters' varnish, together with some watercolours to enhance the colour.

Waterproof Paper (1881)

Germany was one of Europe's leading countries when it came to experimental papermaking, and in 1881 the Germans declared their discovery of a method for making paper waterproof.

To a weak solution of ordinary glue a little acetic acid was added. A second solution was made by dissolving a small quantity of bichromate of potash in distilled water. These two liquids were mixed well together, then the sheets of paper were drawn through the chemical. They were hung up, and once dry the paper was completely waterproof.

Invisible Writing (1892)

Sympathetic, or invisible inks were well known in the Victorian era, but in 1892 Professor M. Bruylauts, a Belgian chemistry professor at the University of Louvain, discovered it was possible to convey a secret letter without using any ink at all.

The professor laid out several sheets of notepaper, one on top of the other, and began writing on the uppermost with a sharp pencil. Once he had finished, he selected one of the bottom sheets on which no marks of the writing were visible. On exposing this sheet to the vapour of iodine for a few minutes, the paper took on a yellowish tint, and the 'writing' began to develop in a violet-brown colour. On moistening the paper, it turned blue, and the letters appeared in violet lines. Sulphurous acid made the writing disappear again.

This phenomenon was due to the fact that notepaper contained starch, which, after being subjected to the pressure of a pencil, turned blue in the toxic iodine fumes.

Petroleum Soap (1881)

The relatively low price of petroleum, as compared with that of other fatty oils, led to its use in the manufacture of soap. However, the main difficulty to be overcome in using this chemical was its conversion into a solid, but this was accomplished by an inventor named Mr Bastet, of Brooklyn, New York, by mixing it with a proportion of vegetable oil and alkalising the mixture in a special manner.

Petroleum soap became something of a hit with the Victorian public. Farmers began treating their granaries with the soap in order to rid their grain of beetles and other pests, and a Victorian dog lover, who stated categorically that dogs were 'probably the next object, after woman, that shared the affection of mankind', recommended that mangy pets be bathed in petroleum soap for a speedy recovery.

Petroleum-based chemicals are still widely used today to manufacture soap and detergents, though they can often have a drying effect on the skin.

Sheep Wool Soap (1887)

While most ordinary bars of soap were made from lard and lye during Victorian times, in 1887 a new type of cleanser made entirely from the grease from a sheep's fleece was utilised to produce an economical bar. This unconventional ingredient was

first discovered by a gentleman named Monsieur Robart, who communicated the details of his process to the French National Society of Agriculture.

Though he insisted his soap was useful for killing fleas and other insects, thereby proving beneficial to one's personal hygiene, it wasn't until the 1930s that this kind of soap was introduced to Britain. Mr Fred Mitchell, a chemist from Bradford in the West Riding of Yorkshire, couldn't help but notice how soft and smooth the hands of the local sheep shearers were. How he came to learn this snippet of information was never disclosed, but after experimenting with lanolin, the natural substance found in sheep's wool, Mr Mitchell concocted a secret soap recipe, which is still being used to make toiletries to this day.

Nature's Soap (1890 and 1895)

'Wyoming Soap' was a naturally occurring mineral that was discovered in the Blue Ridge, about 35 miles west of a small town named Sundance, in Wyoming Territory. It was found in sinkholes and in the neighbouring springs, and was already wet and soap-like when excavated.

The mineral was a yellowish-grey colour, had a clayey odour and a saline taste. Its chemical constitution was found to be rather complex, for it was made up of seven different oxides, namely those of silicon, iron, aluminium, manganese, calcium, magnesium and sodium, combined with water and sulphuric acid. The ranchers and cowboys of the vicinity used to employ the soap for removing grease.

In California, a number of labourers were put to work to gather a saponaceous material, or natural soap, from the banks of Owen's Lake. It was formed from a solution of borax and soda in the water, which combined with the oil from the myriads of dead flies that fell into the lake. The soap gathered like scum on the surface and was nearly an inch thick.

The Old Sponge Ornament (1875 and 1882)

Many Victorians adopted a 'make do and mend' attitude, particularly if their families were large and budgets were tight, and countless households were keen to reuse as much as they could.

For those who struggled to afford decorations for their homes, it was found that a pretty and original ornament could be made out of an old, unwanted sponge. Having dipped it in warm water, half the fluid was squeezed out, and into the holes were inserted the seeds of millet, barley, cress, purslane, red clover, ornamental grasses, and so on, according to taste. The whole was then placed in a vase, or hung in a sunny window. If sprinkled with water every morning, it would soon grow green with vegetation, and once the seeds had germinated, the sponge would yield a variety of harmonious colours to brighten up any room.

Another way of sprucing up one's home without spending lots of money on expensive materials was to mix equal proportions of turpentine, linseed oil and vinegar; the result was an exceptional polish for furniture.

Poetic Signboards for British Streets (1875)

Large and attractive signboards were a prominent feature of nineteenth-century shops in China, and to the Victorians the words upon them were a strange mixture of the flowery literature of the land and the advertising instinct of commercially minded merchants.

'The Shop of Heaven-Sent Luck', 'The Tea Shop of Celestial Principles', 'Flowers Rise to the Milky Way' and 'The Mutton Shop of Morning Twilight' were just a selection of the signs spotted on the streets of Peking, though why anybody felt the need for such a substantial meal at that particularly early hour wasn't made clear. In these signs, however, it was clear that the Chinese could combine the soul of a poet with a keen eye for business, and when such efforts were contrasted with 'The Noted Eel Pie House of London', the Victorians feared that other cultures must have regarded the West as utter barbarians in comparison. It was therefore proposed to apply the same principle to British shops, to inject a little vivacity onto the streets, though the propriety of the English prevented this wild notion from ever truly catching on.

The Gas Pipe Telephone (1893)

In 1876 Professor Alexander Graham Bell patented an electrical machine that would go on to become a commodity in more or less every household across the land. This, of course, was the telephone, but before this revolutionary invention became commonplace, a French investigator, Monsieur M. G. Mareschal, began conducting his own experiments into telecommunication. At the end of the century he made the curious discovery that simply by connecting his local gas and water mains through a galvanometer, a current of electricity was detected. Intrigued, he began to see whether or not these pipes would also serve as telephone lines.

He duly purchased two telephones, one for his house and the other for a friend's, and instead of using ordinary telephone wires he connected them together using the existing gas pipes. The result was astounding: not only was he able to converse with his friend quite clearly, he could also discern music coming from several other houses en route. Moreover, he was able to overhear Morse signals on a neighbouring telegraph wire.

'Tapping the wire' was an offence in America, where it

was sometimes carried out for fraudulent purposes. This new discovery caused quite a concern for the authorities, for if the gas and water pipes of a house could lend themselves so easily to the practice, it would have been difficult to find and apprehend the culprits.

Sound Mills (1884)

In Croatia, Professor Vinko Dvorák (1848–1922), of the University of Agram, made a most remarkable breakthrough when he discovered it was possible to generate clean and free energy from sound waves, and he succeeded in devising miniature 'mills' that were driven purely by this means. His research was based on an older discovery made in 1868 that a tuning fork in vibration had the power of attracting light objects, such as playing cards, that were freely pivoted or suspended in the air. The discoverer, Dr Frederick Guthrie (1833–1886), explained that the attraction was due to a difference of air pressure, set up by the sound waves issuing from the fork.

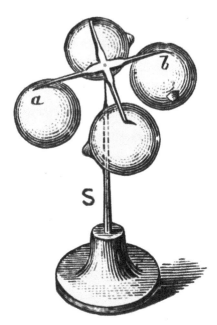

One of Dr Dvorák's sound mills is shown in the first diagram, opposite. It consisted of a cluster of four glass balls, suspended from cross-arms, *a b*, each ball having a small nipple, pierced with a hole, blown into one side of the glass. The framework was pivoted on a needlepoint which rose from a stem or support, S, as shown. When this little mill was presented to the open mouth of a resonance box, on which was mounted a vibrating tuning fork, the balls began to turn slowly round.

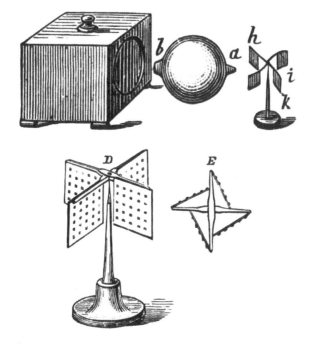

The second diagram, above, represents a resonance box. Another sort of mill with four vanes, *h i k*, in place of the glass balls, is also illustrated. These vanes are represented on a larger scale in the third diagram, where at D and E are shown light cardboard flags pierced with a number of needle-holes. The whirl of the flags was promoted by placing a brass ball, *a b*, with open nipples, between the resonator and the mill, as shown in the second diagram. This hollow ball concentrated the wind on the flags; the puff it made was quite sensible to the bare hand, and was even powerful enough to blow out a lighted match.

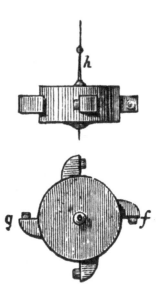

Another form of mill or turbine is shown in the final diagram, above. It consisted of a hollow box of paper, with projecting ears, $f g$, open to the outside. The box was suspended by a silk thread, h, before the open mouth of the resonator and began to turn like the balls when the note of the tuning fork was loud enough.

It was expected that science and technology of the future would offer cheap, renewable energy based on the same principle to every household in the land.

Magnetic Railways (1890)

For eons science has recognised that when a piece of iron is attracted to a magnet it adheres to the poles as if attached by some invisible glue. During the Victorian era this magnetic adhesion was applied directly to the iron wheels of a railway carriage, in order to provide a better grip of the rail, thus helping the vehicle to ascend a steep incline. A dynamo and engine on the locomotive were caused to generate a current, which magnetised the rear driving wheels.

These experiments were carried out on the Trackville line, in America, at a point that rose 185 feet per mile. By attracting the rails, it was stated that the train completed the ascent in twenty-eight minutes, whereas without the aid of magnetism it would have taken nearly an hour.

It was hoped that the experiments would be pursued, as the device, if properly applied, would also be useful when travelling up wet inclines.

Since the 1890s magnetic railway technology has slowly advanced, with patents for magnet-propelled trains granted to inventors in the early 1900s. Throughout the twentieth century developers continued working on magnetic levitation, or 'Maglev' railways, whereby the wheels were completely replaced by magnets, thus propelling the vehicles at high speeds across specially modified tracks. Japan, Germany, the United States and the United Kingdom have all introduced these magnetic vehicles to their cities, although at present only a handful of commercial lines remain in operation.

The Cure for Steamed or Frosty Glass (1884)

The Victorians used to swear by a very simple remedy for preventing their windows becoming steamed up in hot weather or frosted over during the winter. An application of a thin coat of glycerine applied on both sides of a windowpane would prevent it from becoming obscured by steam or frost. In fact, it was advised that glycerine, the colourless chemical often used as a sweetener in food, could be used in this way to prevent condensation gathering on almost any article in the home.

Cutting Glass with Scissors (1880)

Only a few people in the nineteenth century knew of a simple trick that made it not only possible, but also easy, to cut panes of glass to almost any shape using an ordinary pair of scissors. Three things, however, were necessary for success: firstly, the glass was to be placed under water; secondly, it was to be held level while the scissors were applied; and finally, it was better to perform the cutting by cropping small pieces at the corners and along the edges, thus reducing the form gradually to that required. If an attempt was made to cut the glass at once to the proper shape, as one would cut a piece of cardboard, the glass would most likely fracture. When the operation was successful, the glass would break away from the scissors in small pieces in a straight line with the blades.

Horseshoe Knives and Swords (1887)

It was believed that a Chinaman discovered the curious fact that castoff horseshoes made exceptionally good cutlers' steel, suitable for the manufacture of knives and swords. Having been constantly hammered by the blacksmith, the wrought iron of the shoes subsequently acquired the hardness of steel. It was also supposed that the heat from the horse's hoof attributed to the hardness of the metal.

There are still various boutique manufacturers in America, the UK and perhaps elsewhere in the world that produce original items of cutlery from old horseshoes.

The Bulletproof Blanket (1885)

The Victorians were intrigued to learn that the Indians of Mexico had developed a special type of blanket that could be transformed into a shield fit for warfare. This multi-faceted material was hand-woven and fuelled until thick and waterproof, and it was found to be so strong that it was even able to deflect bullets, either by causing them to glance, or by swaying to the blow, effectively 'catching' the projectile in the fibres.

The advancing Western world, however, had to wait another eighty years before this kind of technology was introduced. A high strength fabric called poly-paraphenylene terephthalamide, otherwise known as 'Kevlar', was developed in 1965, and was strong enough for use as body armour. In 2011 it was announced that bulletproof blankets made from this fabric would be issued to the CO19 unit of the British Police Force, and would be capable of stopping the bullets from a machine gun. More recently, in 2014, certain schools in America began adopting the bulletproof blanket in order to protect their pupils from mass shootings.

Nature's Barometer (1884)

The natives of the Chiloé Islands, off the coast of Chile, made use of a curious natural barometer to tell when bad weather was coming. In the 1880s it attracted the attention of the captain of an Italian corvette, who dubbed the barometer the *barometro arancano*. It was made from the shell of a king crab belonging to the *anomura* species and was hung outside dwelling houses. The shell was nearly white in dry weather but exhibited small red spots on the approach of moisture. During the rainy season it became completely red.

Meanwhile, in England, the renowned physicist Sir Charles Vernon Boys (1855–1944) drew the public's attention to his discovery that the human ear was a natural barometer. He, and doubtless many others, experienced a peculiar sensation of pressure on the ear when a train entered a tunnel or when rapidly descending a mine. He calculated that his own ear was sensible in this way to a tiny fraction of an inch of pressure compared with the barometer, but, of course, the atmospheric change had to be a sudden one in order to be felt. He theorised that somewhere in the midst of mankind's history the ear was once finely tuned to detect a coming change in weather, but over the millennia this ability, like the magnetic sense, has been lost.

Finding the South (1892)

A simple method for finding south without the aid of a compass was taught to soldiers and officers who served in the British Army during Queen Victoria's reign. They were told to hold a watch horizontally in their hand with the hour hand pointing to the centre of the sun. South would then lie midway between the position of the hour hand and twelve o'clock on the dial. If it was before noon they were to count forward; after noon, backwards. Thus, if the hour hand pointed to three o'clock, the south would be in the direction of the 1.30 p.m. line. If the hour hand was at 10 a.m., south would be indicated at eleven o'clock.

The Way to Montreal (1885)

In 1885 the Canadians were preparing to survey a new route from England to their capital, Montreal, via Hudson Bay. The existing traffic was carried either by way of New York from Liverpool, or by the Dominion Line and other steamers, which plied to places such as Halifax in Nova Scotia. The new route, from Liverpool, would permit of steamers proceeding through Hudson Straits into the Great Bay – the vast inland sea of North America, which was easily accessible from the ocean. On the western side of the Great Bay stood Fort Churchill, which was only 2,900 miles from Liverpool. Once at Churchill, the merchandise on the steamers could be conveyed quickly to Montreal, more rapidly than ever.

Though there was much promise offered for merchants and immigrants alike by the introduction of this new route, the great disadvantage was that the sea so far north was only navigable for about three months in the year due to the arctic conditions. This, however, wasn't too much of a stumbling block, and since the nineteenth century cargo and passenger ships have been able to make regular trips directly between Liverpool and Montreal. Today the journey is calculated to be 2,812 nautical miles and takes between eight to ten days depending on the speed of the vessel.

Canada's only arctic seaport, the Port of Churchill at Hudson

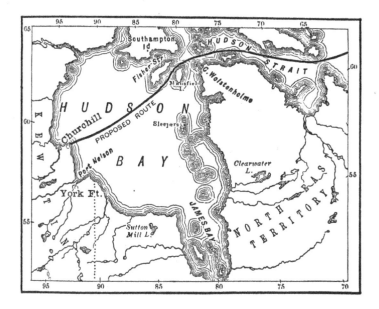

Bay, is still widely used for the exportation of grain, mining goods and timber, to countries all across Europe, Russia and the Middle East. Cargo ships import building materials, fertiliser and fuel, to be distributed to the rest of the country and also the United States via the Hudson Bay Railway. The shipping season at Churchill runs from mid July to early November due to the climate.

The Co-operative Society of Tasmania (1892)

Throughout the nineteenth century, suggestions for co-operation in various social and business schemes were debated. In 1844 the Rochdale Pioneers Society was established, selling unadulterated food and provisions at fair prices, and was operated on the principle that a share of the profits was distributed accordingly to their members. This was known as the 'divi', or 'dividend'.

During the 1860s and '70s this business model began to take off, with the establishment of other co-operative societies, including the Co-operative Insurance Company and the Co-operative Bank.

By 1891 another, and perhaps more ambitious effort, was being made in Tasmania with every prospect of success. This was the Co-operative Timber Company Limited, which was to be entirely managed and worked by shareholders in the concern.

The plant for sawmills was purchased by the company to fell, cut up and convey valuable timber by steam power from the acquired territory to the mill. The novel feature in this enterprise was the employment of the shareholders in the business of clearing and farming. There were no directors of the company; a manager had been employed to sail to Port Sorell on the north-west coast of the island with each contingent of shareholders, each of whom had been instructed to purchase at least ten shares for £100, but weren't permitted to have more than thirty in the venture. Nearly the whole of the millwork was to be carried out by these men, and as gentleman in the Colonies often undertook this kind of work, there was no loss of social status. Thus, by machinery and co-operative labour, the savings were hoped to be great. Each shareholder was to be paid no less than six shillings a day for his work, and when the working expenses had also been satisfied, a balance would be available for dividends.

The cost of living was reputedly very small; there were many 'healthful amusements' on the island, and the climate was considered perfect. The utopian scheme was thus promoted across London, with attractive advertisements headed 'What to do with our boys', suggesting parents should buy their sons shares in the company and send them away to Tasmania. As a result many young gentlemen of superior standing cast their lot and embarked on what they hoped would be prosperous new lives across the sea.

Unfortunately, however, the founder of the society, Mr Roland Ladelle, ended up in court in August 1895, following a financial dispute with the company that provided the machinery for the timber plant. In the end the Tasmanian Co-operative Timber Company Limited was ordered to be wound up and liquidated.

10

BEWILDERING PHENOMENA

The Spectre of the Brocken (1881 and 1884)

By the late nineteenth century modern science was offering answers to life's most perplexing mysteries, yet there were still many things between heaven and earth that the Victorians could barely explain. The fact that the world had refused to give up all its secrets held great appeal. Many people wanted to believe in the fairy tales their grandparents once told them, despite the learned men insisting that such fantasies no longer held a place in the modern, scientific age.

Magazines, newspapers and local gossips relished sharing tales of the unexplained. Eyewitness accounts of strange occurrences kept the public enthralled, and the unusual observations of Professor John Tyndall (1820–1893), a prominent Irish physicist, attracted much attention and curiosity. On opening the door of his cottage in the Alps on the evening of 27 September 1883, he noticed his own shadow, thrown by a small lamp on the wall behind him, was projected on to the fog outside. It was abnormally large and distinct, and around his shadowy head there was a luminous halo, devoid of colour. He couldn't explain the cause of this heavenly vision.

Earlier, in October 1880, a resident in Putney, near Wimbledon Common, observed a similar spectacle in his own back garden one dark and misty night. Having occasion to go outside at about half past ten, he was greeted by a thick, white fog, upon which was cast a gigantic shadow of himself, projected by the lighted candle he carried in his hand. The shadow was at least 12 feet high and oddly distorted.

Such cases, though baffling to the Victorians, were far from unique. Tales of the shadowy 'Spectre of the Brocken' have haunted travellers and explorers of this German mountain, and other summits around the world, since at least 1780.

'He only appears on rare occasions,' the legend told, 'and we have met him more than once on the top of the mountain. Like a royal visitor, he is very polite, and adopts the exact costume of those favoured individuals before whom he appears, donning his cap for headgear-wearing tourists, and invariably returning salutes punctiliously in kind.'

This particular phenomenon, however, had a natural explanation. On a sunshiny day when the mountaintop was clear, and there was a bank of fog lying under the precipice, a spectator standing on the edge could see his own shadow, enormously magnified, on the fog, often with a rainbow-coloured halo round the head.

The great scientist Mr Michael Faraday (1791–1867) was accustomed to amuse himself by producing the same phenomenon in his own home by means of dense vapours, and indeed, Professor Tyndall began a series of experiments in an attempt to recreate the illusion he witnessed in 1883. He eventually succeeded by heating spirits of turpentine and petroleum inside a copper boiler, from which steam billowed into the cold night air to form an artificial fog, and using the illumination of a lamp behind his head he was able to reproduce the Brocken spectre.

The Curious Halo (1885)

On 6 June 1884, at about half past one in the afternoon, a gentleman observed the halo, illustrated overleaf, while fishing on an Irish lough. The day was fine and the sky free from clouds, except for a few vapours on the northern horizon. The brilliant halo, *a b*, surrounded the sun, *f*, and left the spectator in awe. The space, *g h*, was filled with a leaden blue vapour, and the halo displayed all the colours of the spectrum, the red being closest to the sun.

Scientists have since declared that a halo around a luminous solar body is an optical phenomenon caused by tiny ice crystals

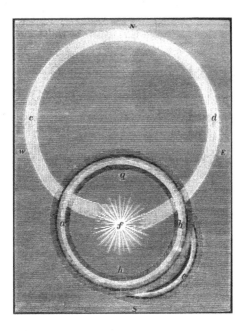

in the atmosphere, which refract the light as it passes through them, producing a rainbow.

The White Rainbow (1884)

On the morning of 28 November 1883, the famed astronomer Monsieur Marie Alfred Cornu witnessed the rare phenomenon of a *cercle d'Ulloa*, or a white rainbow, at Courtenay in France. The sun rose in the mist, and was most pale in hue. A thick frost covered the ground, and the light fog formed a thin veil through which the white sky was visible, free of clouds at the zenith, but clouded at the south-east. Opposite the sun a great white arc, or rainbow without colour, was pictured on the fog.

Though the sighting mystified the Victorians, white rainbows sometimes occur when sunlight is refracted through the tiny droplets of moisture in fog, rather than rain, and are more commonly known as fogbows. The particles of water are so small that the colours of the spectrum are weak and almost seem completely white.

The Sun Pillar (1892)

Since the days of Moses, the book of Exodus in the Old Testament has told of a legendary 'pillar of fire' that once lit up the Eastern night sky and guided the people of Israel safely through the wilderness. On 5 March 1892, Miss Annie Ley, a rector's daughter

from Ashby Parva in Leicestershire, witnessed exactly the same phenomenon in her own back garden. This miraculous sun pillar manifested itself as a vertical beam of light that rose from the rim of the sun as it was setting, as represented in the figure. The disc was partially hidden behind a cloud but the column of light was extraordinarily brilliant as it reached up into the darkening heavens. The effect lasted some minutes after the sun sank out of sight and then gradually faded out.

The cause of this spectacle wasn't fully understood by meteorologists at the time, although it has since been explained as being a reflection of the sun's light from tiny ice crystals in the atmosphere.

The Green Ray (1887 and 1890)

New technology of the nineteenth century had fired the imagination of young and old alike, and perhaps none were more inspired than the French novelist Monsieur Jules Verne who wrote dozens of science fiction and adventure stories.

In 1882 he published a romantic tale in which he described the phenomenon known as *le rayon vert*. This was a beautiful flash of emerald green light in the sky, sometimes seen by sailors when the sun was on the point of sinking below the sea, or sometimes behind a mountain. Five years after *The Green Ray* was published, a French observer claimed to have witnessed the same phenomenon several times over the Red Sea during October, both at the rising and the setting of the sun.

There was much discussion among Victorian scientists as to the cause of the phenomenon. Professor Schönke considered it an effect of refraction; as the vanishing light was refracted by the atmosphere, the more refrangible rays – that is to say, the blue and green end of the spectrum – were displayed uppermost. Professor Charles Michie Smith (1854–1922), however, dissented from this view, and regarded the phenomenon as an effect of absorption by the atmosphere, akin to the green sun that was once witnessed in southern India, in September 1883. A moist atmosphere, with dust particles in it, was sufficient to cause the appearance; the green sun of 1883 being, it was thought, an effect of the volcanic dust disseminated by the eruption of Krakatoa.

Though there was dispute within astronomical circles, the one thing that could be agreed on was that there was plenty of room for further observation on the matter, and today scientists have been able to confirm that this beautiful green spectacle is caused when the sunlight is refracted and scattered through the atmosphere – in other words, it is the same scientific phenomenon that causes the light to appear red at sunset.

Ball Lightning (1884, 1887 and 1892)

On 17 August 1886 a terrible and unusual thunderstorm struck the City of London. A curious bolt of lightning flashed overhead, discharging spherical fireballs, like burning objects, which flew across the sky in all directions.

Nobody knew how or why this extraordinary phenomenon, known as ball or globe lightning, was caused, but sightings have been recorded over hundreds of years. During the nineteenth century alone hundreds of well-attested instances were observed and chronicled across the globe. The mysterious balls of fire usually appeared during thunderstorms, or when the atmosphere was highly charged with electricity, and the apparent size of each globe of light varied from an inch to several feet in diameter.

What became of these balls after their sudden appearance, nobody knew. Sometimes they burst with a loud explosion, which occasionally proved destructive, or else they whizzed across the sky and vanished without a sound.

Reported sightings most frequently occurred during the summer months, and August 1884 was no exception, when enormous globes of fire were witnessed rolling down the slopes of Mount Lochnagar in Scotland during a violent thunderstorm.

Owing to its rarity, no photographs of the lightning had ever been taken, but the illustration overleaf is believed to show evidence of a case that happened on 17 July 1891, at about quarter past ten in the evening. If genuine, this is the first ever photograph of ball lightning, and for more than a century it

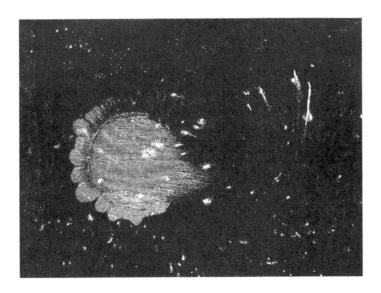

remained the only known example in existence, until Chinese scientists succeeded in capturing the phenomenon on film during a lightning storm in 2012.

The sighting in 1891 was witnessed by an ironmonger, Mr Henry J. Dunn, from the window of his residence at 130 Westmoreland Road, Newcastle-on-Tyne, which overlooked the valley of the Tyne. A thunderstorm was raging over the town and the great ball of fire suddenly appeared over the river, moving as fast as a man could run. It was estimated to measure about 2 feet in diameter, and when it came opposite the house it stopped and vanished. Before it did so Mr Dunn called to his son William to expose a plate in his camera, and the cap was removed for an instant. The result was this picture, which was engraved for publication in 1892.

The peculiar streaks and patches on the photograph were not, it was asserted, due to imperfect development; in fact, similar luminosities had already been observed on photographs of lightning. The principal blotch of light was certainly of interest to scientists of the age, and over the centuries further sightings have continued to shake the nerves of witnesses and rattle the brains of many leading experts, who thus far have been unable to offer a definitive explanation for the phenomenon.

Artificial Ball Lightning (1884)

Monsieur Gaston Planté (1834–1889) was a well-known French physicist, who, in 1884, offered the best explanation of globe lightning to date, as he claimed to have produced an excellent imitation in the form of a miniature artificial fireball.

The figure illustrates his apparatus, which simply consisted of two damp surfaces formed of pads of filter paper moistened with distilled water and brought very close together. These pads were connected with a Planté secondary battery of 16,000 cells, giving an initial electromotive force of 40,000 volts. On making contact, a small ball of fire, shown by the white spot, appeared between the pads and ran from one side to the other between the two surfaces. In the experiment the pads took the place of charged clouds and the ground, Monsieur Planté conceiving that globe lightning was produced when a column of charged air or vapour came in very close contact with the earth.

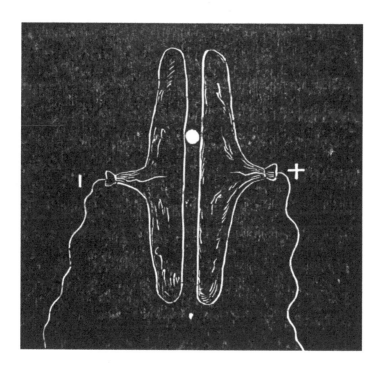

St Elmo's Fire on Ben Nevis (1890)

St Elmo's Fire is the name of a natural discharge of plasma from points on the surface of the earth, such as the masts and rigging of ships, particularly when the atmosphere is highly charged. Though traditionally witnessed at sea, it has been frequently observed to dance on the tips of chimneys, burst from the foliage of pine trees and illuminate the crests of mountains with a beautiful green, blue or violet flame.

One starry night in 1890 this ghostly discharge was spotted on the anemometers above the roof of the meteorological observatory on the top of Ben Nevis. As the spectator was standing on the roof, his hair, hat, pencil and so forth also began to glow with the auroral fire. He raised his walking stick aloft and saw that the end of that, too, was pointed with a bright blue flame. Beyond a slight tingling sensation in his head and hands, the gentleman suffered no injury.

There was a feeble hissing heard during this display, and the stormy character of the weather, with squally winds and clouds of snowdrift, was said to heighten the peculiar effect.

THE MAYFLOWER AT NEW PLYMOUTH

The Barking Sand of Hawaii (1890 and 1892)

The sonorous sand that covered the Jebel Nagous, or Bell Mountain, on the Gulf of Suez, was a legendary phenomenon that held everyone who heard of it in awe. When disturbed by the wind, or the steps of a traveller, the sand would emit a deep symphonic chorus, resembling the bass of an organ.

Intrigued by this curious mountain, an American scientist, Mr Henry Carrington Bolton (1843–1903), paid a visit to the site to experience the musical wonder for himself and later discovered that the sounds of the Sinai Desert were by no means unique. He had also heard tales of the so-called 'barking sand of Hawaii', so he travelled to the island in order to investigate. There he found a tract of sand on the south coast of the island, which took the form of dunes about 100 feet high.

The sand was calcareous and apparently contained a mixture of broken coral and shells. When the grains were dislodged from the side of a dune by Mr Bolton's feet, they slid down the slope with a deep bass tone that could be heard over 100 feet away. The noise was likened to the hum of a buzz saw in a planing mill, and the note was similar to that emitted by Jebel Nagous.

When two quantities of the sand were separated in a bag and forcibly brought together, the shock was accompanied by a strange hooting noise. The drier the sand, the louder the sound, and a bag of sand preserved its sonorous property for a considerable period of time.

The natives of the island attributed the music to the restless spirits of the dead who, according to an old custom, were buried beneath these dunes. Mr Bolton, however, being a man of science, believed the phenomenon was due to films or cushions of air, capable of vibration, surrounding the dry grains of the sand.

A geologist named Mr Cecil Carus-Wilson (*c.* 1857–1934) had long given his attention to this particular phenomenon, and his theory was that the grains, in rubbing against each other, produced tiny crepitations that amounted to an audible note. To prove this he conducted many experiments and not only succeeded in embracing the quality of the note obtainable from specimens of well-known musical sands, but he also elicited a note from sands not naturally thought to be sonorous, by carefully cleaning and sifting each grain one by one, so as to create smooth, rounded surfaces, and a certain uniformity of size.

The polished interior of a porcelain or china cup was found favourable to the production of the note, the sand being placed inside and struck. Different types of sand invariably produced different notes, and Mr Wilson's ambition was to devise an entire musical scale of porcelain pots, with which to create a musical sand instrument.

The Painter of Callao (1892)

The curse of the *pintor* or 'painter' of Callao often struck this Peruvian bay between December and April each year. Sailors taking their vessels out to sea were stunned to find that a sinister influence would begin to 'paint' their ships, which had previously been coated in white lead. Furthermore, whenever the unseen artist paid a visit, the sea would turn a brilliant red, as if he had cleaned his invisible brushes in the ocean. This was clearly toxic, for the bodies of many fish and other marine life could soon be found floating on the surface.

This mysterious occurrence, however, had a worldly explanation. According to investigations by a scientist named Señor Raimondi, it was caused by natural excretions of sulphuretted hydrogen gas, which reacted with white lead and changed its colour. The gas was produced by rotting vegetable mud that was washed into the sea by the River Rimac during the winter and spring months. The red colouring of the Pacific was due to a species of infusoria – minute aquatic creatures, which were attracted by the decaying matter and smothered the existing marine life.

The Southern Cross Pearl (1887)

During a fishing trip in the gold rush town of Roebourne, Western Australia, an Irishman discovered a remarkable cluster of pearls that became known as the 'Southern Cross Pearl'. When he opened the shell, the fisherman, who was a Roman Catholic, was filled with awe and amazement by what he beheld. In front of him was a unique group of nine pearls, of the finest quality, which formed the shape of a Latin cross. Seven pearls composed the shaft, which was 1.5 inches long. From the second pearl down sprang the two arms of the cross. These were made from a single pearl situated on either side. Nothing of its kind had ever been discovered before, and it was thought that this specimen was unique.

Sceptics of the era pointed out the Chinese were well known for producing artificial pearl deposits on wire frames, so thorough examinations of the curio to detect any artificial means of joining the individual pearls together were carefully undertaken. The cross withstood the most rigorous tests and was eventually pronounced on the highest scientific testimony to be bona fide.

In 1886 it was exhibited at London's Colonial and Indian Exhibition before being unveiled at the great Paris Exhibition of 1889, where it received great accolade. The American mineralogist George Frederick Kunz (1856–1932) offered to purchase the cross for the princely sum of £10,000 and present it as a gift to Pope Leo XIII. Whether or not the exchange ever happened was shrouded in secrecy, but over the years the mystical cross, hailed by Roman Catholics as the 'eighth wonder of the world', passed from one guardian to another, and its current whereabouts remain a mystery. Some claim it lies in a secret vault in the depths of the Vatican, where it remains anonymous to the world, but nobody really knows for sure.

Hot Ice (1881)

In Shakespeare's *A Midsummer Night's Dream*, Theseus, Duke of Athens, expresses his astonishment at Bottom's bill of the play, by exclaiming, 'Merry and tragical! Tedious and brief! That is hot ice, and wondrous strange snow. How shall we find the concord of this discord?'

As paradoxical as it seemed, nineteenth-century science claimed to have found the concord of hot ice in 1880, almost 300 years after William Shakespeare penned his famous comedy. The scientific experiments of Professor Thomas Carnelley (1854–1890), of Firth College, Sheffield, led him to conclude that in order to convert a solid into a liquid it must be subjected to at least a certain pressure. Unless it experienced this pressure, or a greater one, no amount of heat would melt the solid; it would simply vaporise without melting.

It followed that by reducing the ordinary atmospheric pressure, ice would remain in its solid state at temperatures far above the usual melting point, and Professor Carnelly thus succeeded in obtaining blocks of ice that were so hot it was difficult to touch them without burning one's fingers! Indeed, he found that when the atmospheric pressure was maintained below a specific point, it was impossible for the ice to be melted, no matter how high the temperature was raised.

The River Flame (1885)

Near Bothwell Bridge on the River Clyde, in Glasgow, a single flame was spotted dancing above the surface of the flowing water in 1885. This wasn't the first time the strange phenomenon had been observed, for a local rumour held that the flame had been seen before at exactly the same spot. Townsfolk on the shore were able to extinguish it by throwing stones at it, but the flame immediately reappeared again.

Though the spectacle was never explained, one theory was that there was an escape of gas from some coal-workings deep below the surface of the river. The gas had caught fire, probably by accident, and had somehow found a release through the riverbed.

The Burning Lake (1882)

There was once a large lake in Russia that accidentally caught fire, and the effect was catastrophic. The entire lagoon went up in flames, and the heat was said to be intolerable within a distance of 1,000 yards from the edge of the fire. So bad was the disaster that the trees and buildings within 3 miles of the scene became coated with a thick layer of soot.

The catastrophe came about because the lake was formed from a fountain of naphtha, which spewed forth from a crack in the earth's crust. Over time this lake of oil grew to be 4 miles long by over a mile wide and 2 feet deep. The quantity of burning naphtha was estimated at 41 million cubic feet, including the fountain, and it was feared that the flames would explode the subterranean sources. Even the earth saturated with oil began to burn but mercifully no explosion occurred.

The entire lake, illuminated by fire, was said to have been a sight to behold, especially after the sun had gone down.

The Layered Lake (1895)

In 1895 Russian explorers claimed to have found a unique lake on the island of Kildin, in the North Sea. It was separated from the sea by a narrow strip of land, and, most curiously, contained both fresh and salt water, which existed independently of each other. The latter was found under the surface, in which codfish, jellyfish, crustaceans and other sea-life flourished. The surface water was fresh and was replenished by the brooks and rainwater that fell in the district, supporting an array of freshwater organisms.

The bottom of Lake Mogilnoye, as it became known, consisted of mud and decaying matter, emitting an odour of sulphur, and the uniqueness of this curious body of water is such that it remains the only dual-watered lake in the world.

Luminous Liquid (1884)

Lieutenant Diek, of the Russian Army, was said to have discovered a mysterious new luminous powder that came in three colours: green, yellow and violet, the latter emitting the most powerful light. When mixed with water in a glass vessel, an illuminating liquid was produced, which the lieutenant believed may one day prove useful in mining and military operations. The light lasted for eight hours, after which time fresh powder was required.

Flowers of Ink (1895)

The Victorians appreciated the beauty of crystals of snow when viewed under the microscope, and in the 1890s they were surprised to learn that similar crystals were also formed in ink, which, unlike those of water, didn't melt. The specimens were prepared for examination by letting a drop of ink fall on a plate of glass, spreading it out a little and letting it dry. A microscope capable of magnifying from fifty to 200 times revealed the crystals on the bluish-black background of the ink, and their appearance will be gathered from the accompanying figure.

When the ink was allowed to dry slowly, the crystals became larger than when they were dried over a flame, but a slight acceleration of the drying process gave a great variety of shape. Some observers compared their likeness to flowers in full bloom, and while they appeared to be formed of a magnetic oxide of iron, the exact composition of the crystals was never accurately determined.

Crystals in Books (1895)

Some contemporary readers of Victorian literature were left stunned with curiosity upon finding, concealed within the pages of books, collections of pretty dendritic crystals resembling the organic growths observed inside the semi-precious gemstones known as moss-agates. These oddities, however, were rare, and most members of the public were unaware that such things even existed.

According to a researcher called Mr A. T. Tait, who made an exhaustive study of these arborescent crystals, they were seldom or never found in books older than 1835 or younger than 1882. This led him to conclude that a couple of decades, as a rule, were required for their development. He attributed their growth to a chemical reaction set up by the accidental deposition of minute particles of copper upon the paper, either during printing or manufacture, so differences in local processes probably accounted for their presence or absence. In American and European books he wasn't able to find any crystals at all.

Magnetised Watches (1884)

Since the introduction of the electric light, a great many good Victorian watches had begun to go haywire. If the wearer ventured too close to the poles of a dynamo machine, their watches were ruined as timekeepers. Professor George Forbes FRS, the celebrated electrician, owned a gold chronometer watch, which formerly kept excellent time, but became so far destroyed that it lost several minutes a day, and it wasn't uncommon for watches to lose up to twenty minutes in the hour.

Professor Forbes investigated the cause of the losing rate, and found it was due to the bar of the lever and some iron screws in the works becoming magnetised. His chronometer was cured by

removing the balance, spring and screws, and substituting others of non-magnetic metal, the new balance being of platinum-iridium and the spring of gold. Non-magnetic brass was used for the screws.

As an alternative remedy, the American electrician Sir Hiram Stevens Maxim (1840–1916) devised the machine here illustrated for removing every trace of magnetism from a watch without taking the inner workings out of the case. The watch was firmly clamped at C, and the handle, H, turned for a minute, when every trace of magnetism was found to have disappeared.

The principle on which the demagnetiser worked was to rotate a powerful bar electromagnet, M, on a vertical spindle on a level with the watch, which was gradually withdrawn from the magnet, while at the same time revolving round in front of it. Turning the handle, H, effected these movements. The wires, W W, conveyed an electric current to the magnet to magnetise it. In this way, the demagnetism was achieved.

Volcanoes and the Telephone (1884)

On Monday 27 August 1883 Mount Krakatoa exploded during one of the most violent volcanic eruptions known to man. During this fatal event a curious observation was made by one Mr A. C. M. Weaver of the Oriental Telephone Company at Singapore; he discovered that it was impossible to talk over telephone lines in that country, which was 500 miles distant from the scene. On raising the instruments to the ears a perfect roar, resembling the crash of a waterfall, was all that could be heard, and by shouting at the top of one's voice, the clerk at the other end of the line heard the caller, but of the whole speech not a single sentence was understood.

The staggering eruption produced the loudest volcanic blast ever recorded, which was heard up to 3,000 miles away. The detonation destroyed most of the Indonesian island, killing over 36,000 people and plummeting the earth into a chilly volcanic winter for the next five years. In short, it was no wonder that telephone users experienced technical faults that day, and the peculiar sounds were explained by a disturbance in the earth's magnetic field, caused by the explosion and reacting on the telephone lines.

The Human Telephone (1884)

Monsieur Dunand was a French investigator who found that a 'condenser', that is to say, an apparatus made by separating two or more sheets of tinfoil by an insulating material such as paraffin paper, would receive telephone currents and transmit speech, especially if the condenser was charged by another source of electricity before the telephone currents entered it.

Using this discovery as a starting point, an engineer named Meneer J. W. Giltay, of Delft, in the Netherlands, theorised that if two people standing a little apart made a condenser – the bodies being, as it were, the tinfoil, and the air the insulator – it was entirely possible to create a human telephone. Astonishingly, in about 1884 this gentleman claimed to have succeeded in causing two individuals – particularly their hands – to act as a working telephone. He used an Ader microphone to transmit the sounds, and the two willing volunteers acted as the receiver.

The microphone, which was a type that enabled sounds to be received by a larger surface area rather than a smaller earpiece, had an induction coil used in connection with it, the primary wire of the coil being in circuit with the carbons of the microphone and a battery. The secondary wire of the coil was in circuit with a battery of nine Leclanché cells, which charged up the two men, referred to as man A and man B. When music and speech were sent into the Ader microphone, they were heard by man B when man A put his gloved hand over B's ear. Singing and whistling was heard best, but Meneer Giltay believed that speech would be received well with an induction coil of greater power.

He concluded that, had the two persons simply laid their heads together, they would have mutually heard the sounds being transmitted, provided that their hair was dry and non-conducting.

Autographism (1890)

Dr Ernest Mesnet (1825–1898), of Paris, drew attention to a curious phenomenon that was first observed in about 1880 by Monsieur Georges Dujardin-Beaumetz (1833–1895), who brought before the Société Médicale des Hôpitaux a female patient afflicted by the condition. It appeared that if a moist pencil was lightly drawn over the skin of some persons, their flesh rose into a weal, which followed all the traces of the pencil, so that handwriting or a drawing appeared in relief. The colour of the mark was whiter than the rest of the skin, which was usually a rosy blush. The relief was quite visible from a distance of 10 to 20 yards and sometimes remained on the skin for several hours.

In the 1870s a French artillery officer reported a case of autographism, as the phenomenon became known, in a bay horse belonging to the Versailles garrison. If a piece of straw was plucked from its litter and drawn lightly over its flank, the flesh rose almost immediately and showed its course. The soldiers often amused themselves in doing so, but the animal seemed to be unaware of the experiment and was in other respects as well and efficient as the rest of the horses.

The cause of the phenomenon was unknown in Victorian times, but according to Dr Mesnet, human subjects who suffered this condition were easily hypnotised.

Today it is estimated that up to 5 per cent of the world's population suffer from this mild skin disease, which is also known as dermatographism. It is caused by weak membranes in the skin cells, which break under the slightest pressure and release histamine, the substance that causes the inflammation. Though the sufferers experience no pain – just a little irritation sometimes – autographism can be treated with antihistamines.

The Magic Mirror of Japan (1885)

The ancient belief that the mirror is an object of magic, a doorway into a parallel world, was as strong as ever during Victorian times. Indeed, in 1871 Mr Lewis Carroll (1832–1898) published his famous novel *Through the Looking-Glass, and What Alice Found There*, which told of a fantastical universe that lay hidden beyond the glass.

This fascination extended all the way to Japan, the country in which was said to exist real-life magic mirrors. They were made of highly polished metal, and when peered into, observers saw only themselves. However, when a bright light was shone on the mirror and reflected on to a white screen, the reflection revealed,

in a quasi-magical kind of way, the presence of figures and mottoes that were otherwise completely invisible.

The workings of this mysterious looking glass were based upon an ancient Chinese art, dating from around 100 BC, in which one side of a solid bronze mirror was highly polished and a three-dimensional design cast upon the other. The same relief on the reverse of the mirror appeared in the reflection.

Various theories claimed to account for the science behind the magic, but the most plausible explanation was that the reflected figures were down to a difference of density in the metal, caused by intense polishing on the flat side of the mirror, even though the entire surface appeared to the naked eye to be equally smooth and bright. The varying thickness of the bronze metal reflected the light at different angles, thereby projecting the corresponding design on to the screen.

In an effort to prove the theory, Dr Muraoka, of Tokyo, reportedly took half a crown and rubbed down one surface of the coin until it was completely flat. He then shone a strong light on to the smooth side. Its reflection on a white paper screen revealed the outline of the figure on the reverse side of the coin.

Crystal Vision (1892)

'Crystal gazing', or 'crystal vision', was the name given by psychologists to the phenomenon of seeing pictures in water, mirrors, crystals and other clear bodies, which once played an important part in the witchcraft of olden times. This sensation was akin to the old illusion of seeing 'faces in the fire', and some people claimed to be possessed of a highly developed form of the gift. At the Congress of Experimental Psychologists, which took place in August 1892 at University College, London, numerous examples of such experiences were cited.

One lady, who had experimented with her faculty of crystal gazing for many years, once saw and read in the crystals an announcement of the death of one of her closest friends. Later, on opening that day's copy of *The Times* newspaper and scouring the pages for the birth, marriage and death announcements, she read confirmation of the passing of her friend. The lady insisted she hadn't looked in the paper earlier that day, but sceptics argued that her eyesight had simply conveyed the information to her brain without her mind being aware of it.

From this it was concluded that humans sometimes gleaned information from the outside world without knowing they had done so, and the collected information often trickled into the conscious mind at some point in the future, perhaps in a daydream. Over the years there were many reported cases of people dreaming about the exact place where a lost possession was lying and finding it there the next day, even though they had already searched the same place, or nearby, without consciously seeing it.

Some hypnotised subjects were also known to see scenes from stories which had been read to them. At a séance conducted by the congress, Dr John Milne Bramwell (1852–1925), of Goole, Yorkshire, performed interesting experiments on four young subjects – two men and two women – who had consented to appear before the meeting to aid the furtherance of science. One of the men was put into a mesmeric sleep and told the story of Robinson Crusoe discovering the footprint in the sand. On being awoken from the sleep he stated that he hadn't heard or seen anything during the process, yet when a crystal ball was put into his hands he saw inside it a picture of Crusoe alarmed at the footprint and described it in his own words. The story of Vivien beguiling Merlin, which was less well known, and had probably never been heard by him before, was also read to him. On awakening from the trance, he, without knowing he had been told the story, saw it enacted in the glass and gave a crude but faithful account of the scene.

As a good deal of misconception existed with regard to the safety of such experiments, Dr Bramwell asserted that he had ensured the wellbeing of the subjects throughout, and that the four of them woke up perfectly bright and happy, in full possession of all their faculties. Furthermore, as they were travelling home to Yorkshire by boat, he had instructed them under hypnosis not to be seasick. None of them were so afflicted, for just as hypnotism was said to cure pain and drunkenness, it was also a remedy for psychological conditions.

The Colour of Music (1882)

It was widely accepted that certain people had the curious ability of associating different colours with different musical notes, and in 1882 the subject was investigated by two Swiss savants, Herren Bleuler and Lehman, of Zurich. Their findings showed that, as a rule, higher notes were visualised by lighter colours, and lower notes by darker ones. Chords were attended by corresponding colour combinations. A skilled musician examined by the pair stated that he perceived a distinct colour with each key. For C major, that colour was grey; for G flat major, it was a reddish-brown; A major, blue; A minor, lead; F sharp major, yellow, and so on, right across the musical scale.

The results of the investigation revealed that the colours weren't fixed, and that the same piece of music played by different instruments appeared to the gifted in different colours, depending on the type of instrument. The authors also found that some minds perceived colours on hearing consonants, vowels, diphthongs, words and sentences. Others perceived sounds on seeing light and colours, so the reverse phenomenon also existed. A quiet gas-flame suggested the sound 'We', and when the light flickered the sound changed to 'L'.

The peculiar faculty was said to be in a high degree hereditary.

Phantoms of the Opera (1890)

There was once an accomplished lady musician who had the remarkable ability of seeing images in the air whenever certain musical instruments were played. The sound of the oboe caused her to visualise a white obelisk, which became more acute the higher the pitch of the note. Sometimes, if the notes were of an intense and yearning character, the figure moved rapidly towards her, point first, as if it was about to strike. The sound of the violoncello, the high notes of the bassoon, trumpet and trombone, and the low notes of the clarinet and viola, conjured the image of a flat undulating ribbon of strong white fibres. Whenever the violins of an orchestra began playing after the wind instruments had been prominent, she sometimes saw a shower of glistening white dust. These phantoms were usually seen floating in the air halfway between her and the players.

Investigations into such sensory phenomena carried on well into the twentieth century, but were ultimately wound down owing to the fact that psychologists found it difficult to measure the individual experiences of the test subjects. Many people still experience this unique condition today, which is known as synaesthesia, and described as an inexplicable union of the human senses.

Ghostly Apparitions (1892)

In 1889 a thorough, statistical enquiry was made into the nature and frequency of 'sensory hallucinations' experienced by persons of otherwise sound mind, and the results were sent to the Congress of Experimental Psychologists. It was concluded that this order of mental phenomena had given rise to the popular belief in ghosts.

According to the study, these strange visions sometimes appeared at night, sometimes in broad daylight. The figures were often surrounded by a glow or halo, but occasionally they appeared as solid and lifelike as any living person. Moreover, now and again more than one person saw the same figure at the same time, meaning that the apparition apparently existed outside the observer, and wasn't merely visible in the mind's eye.

Though the telling of ghost stories was a popular pastime for all the family, who would gather around a crackling fire on a dark, winter night, there were countless tales of otherworldly happenings that were rarely shared with the outside world, so the congress issued a national appeal for those who were acquainted with such instances to communicate the facts of their experiences publically, in the hope of furthering the field of psychology. A few people answered the invitation, and some of the most striking cases relayed were documented in the record books.

On the night of 17 November 1890, Mr Samuel Walker Anderson, a native of Mirfield, Yorkshire, but then living in Australia, woke up and distinctly saw his elderly aunt, Mrs Sarah Elizabeth Pickard, standing near the foot of the bed. She was dressed in an ordinary black dress, such as he had seen her wearing many times before. She looked much older and stouter than the last time he had seen her three years earlier, and she moved her lips as if to say 'Goodbye.' It was then she began to fade away before his very eyes.

There was a lighted lamp in the room, and Mr Anderson was fully awake at the time. He hadn't been anxious about his aunt beforehand, but on seeing the vision he began to fear she was dead and took a note of the time, which was just before midnight. Later that week, the mail brought news of her death, which had occurred at 11 a.m. on 17 November 1890.

Reverend Matthew Frost (1855–1905), who resided in Bowers Gifford, Essex, stated that on the first Thursday of April 1887, while partaking of tea with his wife, he distinctly heard a rap at the window.

'Why, there's my grandmother!' he exclaimed, glancing outside.

The reverend went to the door but there was nobody there.

He walked around the perimeter of the house, for he felt sure his grandmother was about, but couldn't see a soul. The following Saturday he received news that his grandmother, who lived in Yorkshire, died about half an hour before he had heard the raps.

Not all the hallucinations recorded by the congress referred to apparitions of people known to the witnesses. Some were unrecognised, some incompletely developed, some of a religious or angelic character, and some were even monstrous. Others were figures of animals, balls of lights and inanimate objects, while other sensations, such as touches, audible voices or bumps in the night, were also experienced.

Sceptical scientists were quick to point out that only a tiny proportion of reported sightings related to people seeing or 'speaking' to a loved one only to discover they had very recently died, and without irrefutable evidence, modern-minded Victorians remained largely unmoved by these spooky tales, regarding them as nothing more than fireside entertainment. The occult had no place in this new era of enlightenment, and ghostly beliefs were left to remain in the shadows of the past.

INDEX

Absolute Unit of Time 7
Absorbing Studies 148
Affection of Dogs 119
Age of the Earth 31
All Things Great and Small 65
Alleviating Thirst at Sea 224
Aquarium and the Wicked Fish 108
Argon, The Discovery of 33
Asthma, The Remedy for 167
Atlantis Discovered 64
Autographism 274
Ball Lightning 261

Ball Lightning, Artificial 263
Balloon Trip to the Pole 62
Banana Carpets and Cotton-Plant Bags 232
Barking Sand of Hawaii 264
Black Gold 54
Black Potatoes 194
Brain of Laura Bridgman 142
Brains of Men and Women 141
Breathing Exercise 184
Breeding and Killing Microbes 156
Boot-Polishing Plant 73
Bulletproof Blanket 250
Burning Lake 269

Calculating Boy 143
Carrier Falcons 116
Catarrh, The Cure for 165
Cave Villages of Mexico 130
Cheap, Clean Gas 233
Chinese Garden Plants 78
Cold-Curing Tree 84
Colour and Beverages 208
Colour Music 151
Colour of Music 278
Colour of the Sun is Really Blue 28

Colour of Water 40
Co-operative Society of Tasmania 253
Crystal Vision 277
Crystals in Books 271
Cultivating Water-Lilies 79
Curative Helmet 184
Curious Halo 257
Curious Paper 239
Cutting Glass with Scissors 249

Dairy Products and Good Bacteria 203
Danger of Mental Excitement 144
Dangerous Mussels 212
Deadly Coca Plant 71
Deadly Paints 218
Death of a City 227
Death of the Solar System 29
Decimal Time 8
Detonating Diamonds 226
Devil's Corkscrew 92
Dinosaur-Eating Bird 90
Disappearing Little Toe 137
Doctor's Carrier Pigeon 117
Dog Battalion 118
Dog that Could Read 120
Dreams, A Study of 145
Drying Wet Boots 230
Dyeing Flowers 77

Earth Soup 192
Earth's Tail 10
Earthquakes, The Astonishing Study of 47
Edible Ferns 75
Edible Flowers 199
Edible Peat Bogs 193
Elderly Falcon 115
Electric Plant 72
Electrical Earthquakes 48
Electrical Insects 98

Electrical Test of Death 152
Electricity from Sugar 235
Electrified Sitting Room 215
Electromagnetic Photography 21
Exploding Coat Buttons 225
Exploding Fruit 198
Exploration of Mount Roraima 50
Extraordinary Swimming Feat 139
Eye Electromagnet 177

Fairy Rings 68
Fern Perfume 76
Finding the Poles 58
Finding the South 252
Firearms for Children 226
Fireproof Ink and Incombustible Paper 240
Fish and Bat Fertiliser 237
Fish-Eating Plant 69
Fish-Killing Mosquito 97
Fish Leather 107
Fish that Breathed Air 110
Fish that Lived Underground 110
Floating Reed Island 42
Flooding the Streets with Seawater 222
Flowers of Ink 270
Flying Shellfish 103
Fossil Mammal from the European Chalk 93
Fountain Tree 83
Four-Legged Bird 111
Fresh Eggs 199
Fuel from Straw and Hay 234

Gas from Castor Oil 233
Gas Pipe Telephone 245
Ghostly Apparitions 280
Giant Crystals 56
Giant Cypress and the Fairy Horse 86
Gibbon from Borneo 124
Glass Cliff 49
Global Warming 33
Glowing Mushroom 67
Grape Seed Oil 232
Graphite Tea 210
Gravity and the Hidden Energy of Ether 19
Greatest Waterfall on Earth 43
Green Moon 14
Green Ray 260

Handy Marks of Handicraft 153
Hay Fever Preventative 165
Health on Mountains 183
Hearing Plants Grow 81

Helium, The Discovery of 35
Herbs for Digestion 167
Hiddenite 56
Hittite Inscriptions 132
Holly and Wild Strawberry Tea 206
Homicidal Houseplants 82
Honest Men 149
Honey-Bearing Ant 96
Horse that Knew the Days of the Week 121
Horseshoe Knives and Swords 250
Hot Ice 268
House-Building Shrimp 104
House Nerves 187
How Not to Drown 171
How President Garfield May Have Been Saved 179
How the Sun Grew Hot 27
How to Detect Earth-Tremors 49
How to Treat a Weak Heart 159
Human Foot 136
Human Telephone 274
Hydrophobia, The Cure for 158

Ink Plant 72
Inoculating for Disease 158
Insect Repellent 163
Insects and the Electric Light 98
Inspiration, The Explanation of 146
Invisible Writing 241
Island of Salt 43

Judging by Appearances 149
Jupiter and Venus 17

Kangaroo-Lion 95
Kola Nut 197
Koumiss 204

Land of the Giants 126
Laughing Plant of Arabia 70
Layered Lake 269
Lead in the Brain 219
Leech Barometer 95
Light as a Motive Power 23
Lightning and Electric Light Wires 216
Liquid Air 37
Liquid Diamonds 38
Liquid Sky 38
Local Anaesthetic 175
Longevity, The Secret of 152
Lost Dwarfs of the Atlas Mountains 134
Luminous Coral and the Electric Light in Aquaria 109
Luminous Egg 200

Luminous Liquid 270
Luray Cavern 53

Magic Mirror of Japan 275
Magnetic Railways 248
Magnetised Watches 272
Malaria Inhaler 161
Malaria Screens 162
Mammoth Caves 52
Mankind's Lost Magnetic Sense 138
Mars and Its Martians 15
Masrium 55
Measuring Irregular Solids 57
Meat-Bread 196
Medical Magnetic Probe 177
Mimicking Caterpillar 100
Molecular Electric Light 235
Molecular Music 35
Molten Lead in the Eye 176
Monster of the Deep 105
Mont Blanc Observatory 12
Mountain Sickness 182
Mud Volcano 47
Music Therapy to Treat Illness 180
Musical Gases 36
Muzzled Fish 106

Nampa Figurine 128
Nansen Polar Expedition 60
Narcotic Nutmegs 211
Nature's Barometer 251
Nature's Soap 243
Neanderthal Bone Cave 127
New Ostrich 112
New Potato 194
Nosebleeds, The Cure for 165

Old-Boots Jelly and Old-Shirt Coffee 202
Old Hats, New Fashions 134
Old Sponge Ornament 244
Oldest Tree on Earth 88
Ozone Anaesthetic 174

Painter of Callao 266
Paraguay Tea 205
Perfect Bouillabaisse 201
Petroleum Soap 242
Phantoms of the Opera 279
Photographing Meteorites 11
Pictures in Dead Eyes 154
Poetic Signboards for British Streets 244
Poisoning, The Cure for 181
Poisonous Pans 211
Postman Cat 118
Pressure of the Sea 39

Preventing Scurvy 168
Preventing Ships from Sinking 223
Projecting Microscopic Views 156
Purity Tests 213

Rag Sugar 202
Railway that Cured Malaria 161
Rain Bird 110
Rearing Puppies in Coloured Light 119
Recycling Refuse 220
Recycling Sewage 237
Red Water 67
Reindeer Lifebelts 170
Removal of Pain 174
Removing Motes from the Eyes 177
Rings of Saturn 19
River Flame 268
Roasted Fig and Lupin Coffee 206

Safe Limelight 216
Sanitary Handwriting 214
Seasickness, The End of 169
Seaweed and Vegetable Leather 73
Sewage Treatment Process 221
Science and Sorrow 185
Sheep Wool Soap 242
Shell with Eyes 102
Sheltering from a Lightning Storm 174
Shifting Latitudes 10
Silurian Scorpion 89
Singing Snake 101
Sketching the Arctic 63
Solar Surgery 178
Soot-Water for Roses 231
Sorcery of the Electrical Telegraph 114
Sound Mills 246
Southern Cross Pearl 267
Spectre of the Brocken 256
Speed of Tidal Waves 42
Spurious Coffee 207
Squaring the Circle 58
St Elmo's Fire on Ben Nevis 264
Stars and Firedamp 219
Steamed or Frosty Glass, The Cure for 249
Street Dust 238
Stupendous Statue 135
Sugar from Corn 194
Suicidal Wasp 97
Sun Pillar 259
Sunshine Fire Extinguisher 25
Sweet-Flag Candy 195
Sword-Swallowing Fish 107

Temperature of the Solar Surface 25
Thunder and Milk 204

Thunderstorms and Sunspots 27
Titanotherium Robustum 91
Tombs of the People of the Sea 129
Transporting Frozen Fish 201
Travelling Plants 70
Treatment for Electric Shocks 172
Tree of Hippocrates 87
Trepanning for Idiocy 188
Trout that Wore Cologne 106
Twenty-Four O'Clock 9

Underground City 131
Underwater Atmosphere 38

Valerian Dressing 164
Value of Sweepings 238
Vegetable Barometer 75
Vegetable Pearls 74
Vegetables Rewired 80
Velocity of Light 22
Vibration and Taste 191
Volcano-Lake 45

Volcanoes and the Telephone 273
Vultures and Telephone Wires 113

Watching the Circulation of Blood 140
Water-Carrying Tortoise 101
Waterbuck, The First Born in Captivity
  123
Waterproof Paper 241
Way to Montreal 252
Wearing Newspapers 229
Weeding with Salt 231
White Darkroom 217
White Rainbow 258
Wind Flower 77
Witchcraft Disease 188
Wool from the Sea 103
World's Oldest Trumpet 130

Yucca Arch 86

Zebras in Harnesses 122

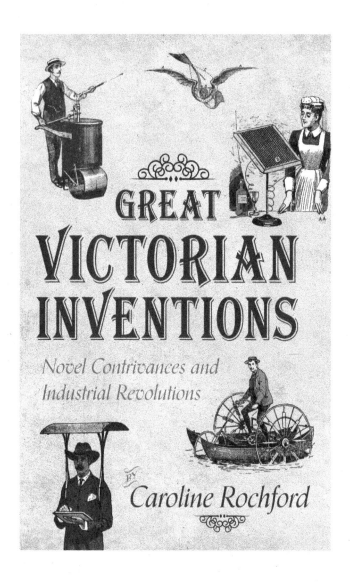